NEITHER JEW NOR GENTILE

NEITHER JEW NOR GENTILE

Exploring Issues of Racial Diversity on
Protestant College Campuses

Georg Yancey

OXFORD
UNIVERSITY PRESS

2010

OXFORD
UNIVERSITY PRESS

Oxford University Press, Inc., publishes works that further
Oxford University's objective of excellence
in research, scholarship, and education.

Oxford   New York
Auckland   Cape Town   Dar es Salaam   Hong Kong   Karachi
Kuala Lumpur   Madrid   Melbourne   Mexico City   Nairobi
New Delhi   Shanghai   Taipei   Toronto

With offices in
Argentina   Austria   Brazil   Chile   Czech Republic   France   Greece
Guatemala   Hungary   Italy   Japan   Poland   Portugal   Singapore
South Korea   Switzerland   Thailand   Turkey   Ukraine   Vietnam

Copyright © 2010 by Oxford University Press, Inc.

Published by Oxford University Press, Inc.
198 Madison Avenue, New York, New York 10016

www.oup.com

Oxford is a registered trademark of Oxford University Press

Yancey, George A., 1962–
Neither Jew nor gentile : exploring issues of racial diversity
on Protestant college campuses / George Allan Yancey.
p. cm.
Includes bibliographical references.
ISBN 978-0-19-973543-3
1. Church colleges—United States. 2. Protestant churches—
Education—United States. 3. Minorities—Education—
United States. 4. Race awareness—United States. I. Title.
LC531.Y36   2010
378'.071—dc22   2009041112
9 8 7 6 5 4 3 2 1

Printed in the United States of America
on acid-free paper

Acknowledgments

Soon after my book *One Body, One Spirit* was published, I began to get requests from churches to help them become more racially diverse. One of my most common recommendations was for them to find racially diverse leadership. However, the colleges and universities from where they hired their leaders were anything but diverse. The dilemma of advising leaders of churches to seek out racial diversity from institutions that were not diverse fueled my desire to study Protestant campuses. My thanks to the churches and individuals, who will remain unnamed to protect their privacy, who prompted me to pursue this fruitful research path.

Whenever I write about issues of racial diversity, I have to acknowledge my good friend and colleague Michael Emerson, who has supported my work in this area as much as possible. While none of this work is based on the original grant we obtained together, this current project definitely builds from my work in that grant. Furthermore, my conversations with him as I told him the results of my work yielded invaluable insight, which I hope comes out in my writing. Along those lines I also am thankful for Curtiss DeYoung, as my interaction with him and what he is doing at Bethel has also been influential in encouraging me to examine Protestant campuses.

Of course, doing research like this always occurs with the support of those who help in collecting and analyzing the data. At different points of the project, Nicole Dash, Kevin Yoder, Natalie Johnson, and Cynthia Cready helped with either advice or the processing of the data. I thank them for their support. This work was also made possible by the professors and instructors who agreed to encourage their students to fill out the qualitative survey. I once again will not provide their names to protect their privacy and that of their students, but I am grateful for their help. I also thank the many different individuals that I interacted with at the various colleges and universities included in this research. I would attempt to name them, but I know I will leave someone out. Regardless, I thank you for taking time out of your busy day to fill out a survey or give me insight into the racial atmosphere at your campus.

Finally, I want to give a shout out to the people I work with at Mosaix, an organization dedicated to promoting multiracial congregations. The main leaders of that organization are Mark DeyMaz, Jim Spoonts, and Willie Peterson. Their commitment to finding ways for Christians to overcome racial barriers is inspiring and helped to motivate me on those days when I was tired of writing or analyzing data.

Contents

NEITHER JEW NOR GENTILE

1

Introduction

In 1954, *Brown v. Board of Education* made it illegal for public schools to forbid the entrance of students of color. There is evidence that this resulted in an exodus of white Christian students to private schools that ensured that they would not have to deal with their parents' fears of integration (Crespino 2007). Christian education among majority group members had already been a racially segregated experience, and this court decision exacerbated that segregation. Yet this segregation was merely in keeping with the rest of the culture in the United States. This exodus started a process that would, over time, make Protestant educational institutions even more racially segregated than the rest of the society.

The process in the opening paragraph generally describes Protestant education in primary and secondary schools. However, this has also probably affected the higher educational system of Protestant institutions. Clearly, those who had sent their children to predominantly white, or all-white, lower educational institutions would also want to send them to predominantly white, or all-white, higher educational institutions. This possibility would explain the low percentage of students of color who attend Protestant colleges relative to other institutions of higher education ("Nation's Best Bible College" 2001). While there is no empirical evidence that white Christians are intentionally keeping their children in predominantly white educational institutions, the reality is that Protestant schools and colleges are more likely to be racially homogeneous than other colleges and universities.

The low racial heterogeneity within Protestant colleges has potentially important effects for Protestants. First, there is research suggesting that a lack of interracial contact hampers the ability of majority group members to understand the challenges people of color face (Oliver & Wong 2003, Troop & Pettigrew 2005, Woods & Sonleitner 1996, Yancey 1999). Majority group members who attend overwhelmingly white colleges and universities may be less willing to deal with the contemporary forms of racism plaguing the United States.[1] Majority group Protestants may be more likely to accept the notions of color blindness and modern racism that help perpetuate the racial status quo. Furthermore, American Protestantism is clearly an institution shaped by a preponderance of racially homogeneous churches and organizations. This homogeneity occurs in spite of the shrinking percentages of European Americans in the United States and the emerging racial diversity that accompanies that shrinkage. Protestant organizations have a need to become more racially diverse to match this new racial reality. However, it is unlikely that overwhelmingly white Protestant institutions of higher education are in a position to provide those churches and organizations with the necessary leadership to deal with higher levels of racial diversity. Finally, the relative lack of students of color within these institutions of higher education indicates that these institutions are potentially sites that are not welcoming to those students. If this type of de facto rejection is an accurate reality for these students of color, then they may have fewer educational choices than majority group students. Those who desire a Protestant educational experience in an atmosphere where they perceive racial acceptance have to find a racially diverse Protestant institution, which is relatively difficult. These potential effects are made all the more important because more than 800,000 students in the United States attend Protestant colleges of one type or another.[2] While they make up only about 4.5 percent of all college students,[3] it is not a minor number of college students influenced by possible effects of racial educational homogeneity on Protestant campuses.

Understanding the dynamics of racial attitudes on Protestant campuses is also important for scholars in general. The degree of variability of diversity efforts is probably much greater within Protestant campuses than within other campuses since a significant number of such campuses may be willing to adopt a color-blind conservative approach to racial issues. This suggests that such campuses can be an ideal setting for testing the possible effects of diversity initiatives in creating educational racial diversity. Furthermore, an examination of these campuses can also inform us about the possible effects of religious environments on racial dynamics. If these campuses can be envisioned as proxies for religious settings in general, then the results generated by studying them can inform us about how racialization plays itself out in religious environments. Rich empirical and theoretical information can be gained by a study of racial dynamics on Protestant campuses.

Recent academic literature indicates that the nature of racist attitudes has changed in recent years (Bobo, Kluegel, & Smith 1997, Bonilla-Silva 2003, Kluegel 1990a, Virtanen & Huddy 1998). Even among those who are racist, exhibitions of overt racism are no longer socially desirable. As such, contemporary majority group individuals are unlikely to conceptualize a desire to avoid people of color as their reason for wanting their children to attend Protestant institutions of higher education. Furthermore, none of the major Protestant denominations endorses overt racism (Roberts 2003, p. 257). Indeed, researchers have found that many Protestant educators indicate a desire to increase the racial diversity on their campuses (Cross & Slater 2004, Saggio 2004, Young & Redmond-Brown 1999). To the degree that there has been a historical incentive for Protestant colleges and universities to maintain their racially homogeneous nature to attract majority group students, there is little reason to believe that such an incentive is still powerful. The relative lack of students of color on Protestant campuses comes in spite of, not because of, the wishes of administrators and professors on those campuses.

The purpose of this current research is to explore the racial climate of Protestant colleges and universities with an intention of finding ways to increase racial diversity. I will attempt to understand why some of these institutions fail to attract students of color and why students of color who do attend these institutions sometimes do not stay at them. Understanding the modern barriers that students of color may face on Protestant campuses is an important academic project for several different audiences. First, it obviously has important implications for leaders of Protestant institutions of higher education who want to increase the racial diversity on their campuses. The research in this book will help them achieve that goal. Second, this project will also provide insight for those scholars who study issues of education, as it explains why some educational institutions have an easier time becoming more racially diverse than others. Since Protestant campuses are less likely to be racially diverse, understanding factors that can help them overcome their tendency toward racial homogeneity will tell education scholars how other educational institutions can become more racially diverse. Third, this research can inform those who study religion about the intersection of race and religion in American institutions. Recently, those who study religion have paid more attention to the importance of race and ethnicity in the religious experience. This work is in keeping with this recent pattern. Fourth, recent growth in the number of students at Protestant educational institutions indicates that these campuses are more influential than many believe. More than 800,000 students attend such institutions, and their influence on our larger society is consequential.

Given how influential such organizations are, it is important to assess the sort of racial atmosphere that predominate on these campuses so that we may understand what is shaping the racial perspective of the many students who have attended or will soon attend them. Fifth, this research is helpful for those who investigate racial division in the United States. Because education is a popular pathway for economic success, understanding how to create advantageous situations for people of color to gain educational success should be of interest to such academics.

At the end of this book, we will discover that there is hope for Protestant colleges and universities that are willing to invest in altering their educational curriculum, hiring faculty of color, and supporting student-led multicultural organizations. I will argue that this curriculum and the instructors who deliver it hold more promise of effectively altering the racial atmosphere of Protestant campuses than other diversity institutional initiatives. I will show the process by which minority professors and diversity courses can produce such alteration, in the hopes that this success may be replicated in other areas of educational diversity reform. However, multicultural student organizations also prove to be a mechanism that can promote racial diversity.

Racial Diversity on College Campuses

In recent years, racial diversity has become a valued goal on university campuses (Aleman & Salkever 2003, Bagnall 1994, Mayhew, Grunwald, & Dey 2005, Smith & Lusthaus 1995, Turner 2000). Several researchers have argued that racial diversity provides important benefits for students (Antonio et al. 2004, Chang 2001, Gurin, Nagda, & Lopez 2004, Johnson & Lollar 2002, Laird 2005, Terenzini et al. 2001). These benefits will undoubtedly become more important as racial diversity becomes more prominent. Therefore, institutions of higher education have attempted to use a variety of programs to increase racial diversity (Cross & Slater 2002, Townsend 1994).

The civil rights movement of the 1960s occurred in the context of the New Left movements that originated on progressive college campuses. Thus, ideals of racial diversity have gone hand in hand with modern progressive social movements. Until that time, many college campuses either limited or outright banned the inclusion of certain nonwhite racial groups. But it soon became clear that inclusion of racial minorities would be a mark of progressiveness and tolerance. As racial equality became a prominent feature of the New Left, many colleges and universities sought to become havens of racial progressiveness. They did not want to resemble traditionalists from the southern parts of the United States who resisted racial integration.

However, promotion of racial integration was often easier said than done. In theory, educational institutions are a meritocracy in which only the best students are given space to participate. But many minority racial groups had lingered on the margins of society, and historically most members of these groups were ill suited for competing for a place on a college campus. Many educators began to question how much they should compromise their academic standards in an effort to produce racial inclusion. Furthermore, many racial groups, most notably African Americans, had reacted to white racism by generating a parallel set of educational institutions for their communities. African Americans had historically black colleges and universities where they could feel comfortable and protected from the potential humiliation and violence they might experience on white campuses. Merely because formerly segregated campuses were now open to them did not mean that students of color were eager to take advantage of these new educational opportunities. Predominantly white colleges and universities in the late 1960s and early 1970s found that to create the diversity dictated by their emerging progressive values, they would have to become proactive in their attempts to recruit potential students of color.

Consequently, an upsurge in programs designed to promote racial diversity emerged from the modern civil rights movement. During the 1960s, unprecedented numbers of African American, Latino, Asian American, and Native American people gained entrance to this country's universities and colleges. These students found the environment of academia to be hostile to their presence, and canonical teachings often bore explicit and implicit assertions supporting the dominance of whites and degradation of minorities. Hence, they demanded changes at multiple levels of the academy. As Ramon Gutierrez, director of the Ethnic Studies Department at the University of California, San Diego, recounts, "Minority students demanded that the curriculum reflect their presence and that safe havens exist for them in what they rightly perceived as alien and hostile environs"(Gutierrez 1995, p. 158) They fought for separate space on college campuses where students and scholars from marginalized communities could assemble and articulate their interests in achieving cultural and political autonomy within the United States. As a result, a number of Black studies and Chicano studies programs were established—103 and 100 programs, respectively, by 1980.

Ethnic studies departments developed in an attempt to introduce non-European perspectives into the academic curriculum. However, we also saw the emergence of multicultural programs in a variety of educational institutions during the 1960s and 1970s. While some of these programs also attempted to create more diversity within the academic curriculum (Garcia 1993, Kirp 1991), others were designed to create an atmosphere of acceptance for students of color. Many of these programs focused on ways to support cultures of color. This often meant sponsoring Black, Hispanic, Native American, or Asian Pacific American history months or cultural events such as Kwanzaa, Cinco de Mayo, or Chinese New Year on these campuses. Such efforts provided a cultural space for students of color. Another way such cultural spaces can be provided is through the development of student-led multicultural organizations. Before the civil rights movement, there were relatively few students of color on campuses to populate such organizations. However, as more students of color entered institutions of higher education, they sought to provide support for each other. Indeed, previous research has indicated that student organizations are one of the more effective ways to provide support for students of color (DeSousa & Kuh 1996, Guiffrida 2003, Murguia, Padilla, & Pavel 1991).

Furthermore, to deal with racial diversity, some educational institutions attempted to provide economic and academic support for incoming students of color. Programs of financial aid that targeted students of color became more popular during the last half of the twentieth century (St. John & Noell 1989, Stampen & Fenske 1988). Programs to provide financial and academic support had not been new for educational institutions; however, the idea of tying such support to membership in a racial category did prove to be a relatively common progressive innovation. The general idea behind such programs was to aid these students so that they could overcome the economic and scholarly disadvantages of structural racism in the United States.

Finally, the 1960s and 1970s saw the popularization of diversity training programs as a way to create diversity within secondary organizations. For example, by 1996 about 75 percent of the 500 largest companies in the United States had some type of diversity management program (Caudron 1998). Such desires also led to the development of diversity programs on campuses, which provided tools for administrators, professors, staff, and other employees at educational institutions. Today, many have evolved into antiracism programs, which take a very proactive approach to eliminating racial bias at educational institutions. In many ways, these programs were set up to confront the notion among social and political conservatives that we have rid ourselves of racial bias and can ignore contemporary racial issues. These antiracism programs allowed educators to challenge this disregard for our continuing racial struggles and helped them promote notions of social and racial justice.

Yet it is unclear which, if any, of the programs are most effective in attracting and retaining students of color. There is no systematic research on whether race-based programs are correlated with more attendance of racial minorities at a given college or university or whether that college or university retains those minority group students long enough for them to graduate.[4] Understanding how educational institutions are able to attract and retain students of color is important if we are going to learn how to make organizational changes that support racial diversity in our colleges and universities.

Racially Based Religious Segregation in American Protestantism

Protestant colleges and universities offer a unique opportunity for researchers to understand the power of given educational programs to shape the racial diversity of institutions of higher education. Some of these educational institutions have resisted the implementation of overt efforts to encourage racial diversity (Cross & Slater 2004, Saggio 2004).[5] Other Protestant educational institutions have incorporated most, if not all, of the measures found at most nonsectarian campuses. This allows researchers to compare colleges and universities with few institutional efforts toward diversity with similar colleges that have made a great many efforts toward diversity. This range of responses is much greater than that found at most non-Protestant campuses and makes research into the potential racial diversity on Protestant campuses particularly fruitful for those desiring to understand the dynamics of racial diversity in educational institutions.

Racial diversity is not equally likely to occur in all possible social situations. For example, several scholars have noted the existence of what is termed a white racial identity (Dyer 1997, Hartigen 1999). This identity includes characteristics such as individualism, color blindness, and Eurocentrism (Dalton 2002, Lipsitz 1998, Twine 1997). Majority group members with such an identity are unlikely to create a social atmosphere that welcomes individuals of color. Social conditions that encourage majority group members to accept a white racial identity are also likely to be conditions that do not encourage racial diversity. It is likely that such conditions encourage majority group members to ignore institutional and structural racism to protect a racial status quo that has served them well. Within a social atmosphere dominated by white racial identity, racial diversity is unlikely to flourish.

American Protestantism is an institution highly segregated by race (Emerson & Smith 2000). Less than 5 percent of all evangelical congregations and about 2 percent of all mainline congregations are racially diverse (Chaves 1999).[6] As noted earlier in this chapter, there is little reason to assert that Protestant college campuses are any more racially mixed than the churches that support them. Emerson and Smith (2000) argue that this racial segregation is connected to the enforcement of a relational and individualistic ideology that inhibits the ability of majority group members to understand the social structures that perpetrate modern forms of racism. Thus majority group Christians are more likely than non-Christians to accept elements of a white racial identity that perpetuate racialized social structures.

It is plausible that such racial divisions also enhance the ability of Protestant college campuses to perpetuate a racial social atmosphere conducive to majority group members but not necessarily to people of color. The historical lack of students of color allows norms that dismiss the cultural needs of racial minorities to flourish on these campuses. Such norms also enforce perceptions that neglect the political and racial concerns of students of color. Thus, Protestant colleges may merely reinforce the general propensity of majority group Protestant institutions to maintain an ideology that works to their benefit. People of color would find such institutions a bad fit for their own cultural, social, and political needs. Institutions of higher education possess natural challenges in creating a social atmosphere of racial diversity. But Protestant colleges and universities may have an additional challenge as they emerge from a social atmosphere not conducive to such diversity.

Divisions in American Protestantism

American Protestants are not a monolithic group. They show a significant level of ideological and theological diversity. Understanding this diversity is critical for comprehending how the social atmosphere in Protestant institutions is influenced by racial elements. The key division within American Protestantism is between evangelical and mainline Protestants. While both groups adhere to the basic tenets within Protestantism, there are critical differences between them that help to shape their ability to attract minority group members.

In the early part of the twentieth century, American Protestantism was engaged in a conflict between those who advocated rejection of the encroaching modernity they feared would corrupt their faith and those who sought to incorporate the lessons provided by the new modern philosophies into their faith. The former group emphasized a return to biblical fundamentals and became known as fundamentalists. They would eventually give rise to evangelicals, Pentecostals, and other versions of conservative Protestantism. The latter group emphasized the social gospel, a Christian call to meeting the material and social needs of the marginalized. They sought to put more energy toward the promotion of government and economic programs for the marginalized rather than promoting the distinctiveness of their Christian faith. As a result of this disagreement, a split developed within Protestantism that separated into evangelical and fundamentalist on the one hand and mainline Protestants on the other. This split led to two distinct religious cultures. They are linked by some basic theological agreements, but each promotes distinctive understandings of the social reality in the United States.

Evangelicals and fundamentalist Protestants[7] tend to have a more conservative theological perspective than mainline Protestants. This perspective influences such individuals to be more likely to accept a color-blind, individualistic approach to issues of race and ethnicity. Emerson and Smith (2000) document how conservative Protestants envision the solution to racial conflict by ignoring structural racism and developing cross-racial friendships. This is in contrast to black Protestants who have a structuralist approach to racial issues that emphasizes the importance of institutional racism. Since institutional racism hampers the lives of people of color, such a perspective reflects the social reality they face. As such, people of color often perceive attitudes that promulgate a color-blind, individualist perspective as unable to meet their social needs to confront racialized social structures.

Emerson and Smith go on to argue that the racially homogeneous nature of Protestant churches prohibits the development of productive cross-racial relationships among Christians. Furthermore, the unwillingness of white evangelicals to explore the institutional and structural elements of racial inequality inhibits their ability to understand the perspectives of people of color. Because white conservative Protestants attend churches that are predominantly white, they are not exposed to Protestants of color who have a more structuralist perspective on racial issues. This lack of exposure reinforces the individualist, color-blind ideology promulgated within their churches, since there are few voices of color to challenge this ideology. Conservative Protestants often are unable to attract people of color into their religious institutions because they promote a racial vision people of color cannot relate to. There is little reason to believe that the inability of conservative Protestants to develop a racial philosophy that attracts people of color is limited to just churches. Conservative Protestant colleges and universities are also likely to promote an individualistic, color-blind ideology that discourages the attendance of students of color.

Mainline Protestants have a more progressive theological and political underpinning than evangelical and fundamentalist Protestants. Their overall progressiveness also reflects mainliners' attitudes on racial issues. It is not an accident that mainline Protestants are more likely to have progressive racial attitudes than conservative Protestants (Kirkpatrick 1993, Laythe, Finkel, & Kirkpatrick 1997). Mainline Protestants are more likely to share similar racial attitudes as Protestants of color. Yet white mainline Protestant congregations have an even more difficult time attracting nonwhite congregants than white conservative Protestant congregations. These congregations have a traditional and liturgical approach to worship. Mainline Protestant congregations tend to be inflexible in the alteration of their worship services, unlike conservative Protestants, who are willing to adjust their approach to worship in an effort to attract novel populations. This approach inhibits mainline Protestant congregations from creating a cultural atmosphere within their church services that is comfortable for people of color. As a result, people of color are less likely to identify with mainline Protestantism than they are with conservative Protestantism.

A further complication also makes it difficult for mainline Protestant congregations to draw congregants of color. While mainline Protestants often advocate a progressive brand of politics, the theology of nonwhite Protestants tends to be very conservative. The overall progressive theology of mainline Protestants enables them to fashion a racial ideology conducive to attracting people of color, but it is also often incompatible with the theological conservatism of nonwhite Protestants. Protestants of color and white mainline Protestants have deep disagreements on theological issues such as biblical inerrancy and social issues such as homosexuality. These disagreements can create further barriers between the two groups and prevent them from worshiping in the same congregation.

This pattern within congregations probably reflects the ability of white mainline Protestant colleges to attract students of color. Traditional worship styles may indicate the promotion of a cultural atmosphere that inhibits the social innovation needed to attract students of color. Mainline Protestant campuses may also have a traditional Eurocentric atmosphere that does not allow for the development of the type of social innovation that attracts students of color. Furthermore, there are elements in the progressive theology of mainline Protestants that may be a bad fit for Protestants of color. For example, while white mainline Protestant campuses may be more open to multicultural and antiracism programs that are intended to meet the social and political needs of students of color, such colleges and universities may also promote gay and lesbian programs offensive to the conservative theology of minority group Protestant students.

In sum, conservative Protestant educational institutions may not attract students of color because of their relative insensitively to the racial issues such students face; mainline Protestant educational institutions may not attract such students because of their incompatibility with such students on nonracial issues. For different reasons, white conservative and mainline Protestant educational institutions may be less able to attract students of color than non-Protestant educational institutions. Neither provides the racially progressive, yet theologically conservative, social atmosphere that can be attractive to Protestants of color. In a sense, they are both a bad fit for minority Protestants. To understand the struggles of Protestant educational institutions to become more racially diverse, it is vital to account for the different challenges that mainline and evangelical and fundamentalist educational institutions have.

Why Study Protestants?

In this book, I will examine important dynamics that will help us understand the racial atmosphere that dominates Protestant colleges and universities in the United States. It would be valuable to include non-Christian educational institutions; however, the numbers of Christian educational institutions, in comparison to all other colleges and universities, make it easier to collect sufficient data for this analysis.[8] Therefore, I find it more feasible, given limited resources, to concentrate on one particular group of colleges and universities rather than attempt to study all of them.

I have alluded to some additional reasons for what we can gain by examining Protestant campuses. There are reasons to believe that the range of efforts at diversity is greater on Protestant campuses than at any other subset of colleges and universities. This range makes it more useful to assess the possible effects of diversity initiatives. I will have the ability to compare campuses with almost no diversity initiatives to those that make a tremendous institutional effort to diversity, and I can include all levels of effort between these extremes. This will help me to assess if diversity efforts truly make a difference in the ability of a campus to attract and retain students of color. While it would be ideal to have a large subset that included all types of educational institutions, a second best option is to explore a subset of colleges and universities that represent all of the different levels of diversity initiatives that are theoretically possible. This can be achieved through an examination of Protestant campuses.

There has been an increase in recent academic literature that explores the intersections of race and religion in the United States. This work clearly fits into that trend. Some have suggested that religion lessens racial hostility if it is intrinsic (Allport 1958, Gorsuch & Aleshire 1974, Kirkpatrick 1993); others suggest that even intrinsic religion contributes to racial intolerance (Griffin, Gorsuch, & David 1987). But none of this work assesses whether majority group members of faith, even those who may be intrinsically less racist than others, create an atmosphere accommodating to people of color. There is work on multiracial churches that explores some of the dynamics that occur in these congregations to encourage racial diversity (Deymaz 2007, Emerson 2006, Yancey 2003a), but such congregations are a relatively small part of Christendom (Emerson 2006) and thus may be more of an anomaly then a true representation of the effects religion has on creating hospitable racial atmospheres.

This research allows me to assess how religion in general, and Protestantism in particular, may react to the racialized nature of American society. These results are generated on educational campuses and thus may not be totally generalized to other types of religious organizations, but these results will still provide some understanding of how religion and race interact.

Of course, Protestants are not the only Christians who have an opportunity to deal with issues of race and racism. Ideally, I would also include analysis of Catholic educational institutions. I did not do so for two reasons. The first is quite practical. I had limited resources to conduct this analysis and found it not feasible to collect all of the information needed to confidently make assertions. To include Catholic institutions would have meant accounting for another important theological predictor of the potential findings of this research. While some of the conclusions drawn from this work undoubtedly apply to Catholic educational institutions as well, it would take a much larger sample than I could afford to collect to confirm which findings are applicable across the Protestant-Catholic divide. Second, Catholicism has only recently left its status as a minority religion in the United States. Thus, it does not have the same majority-minority racial history that has impacted racial dynamics on Protestant campuses. While racism among Catholics is a part of our history, many times Catholics were also active in attempting to fend off prejudice from the majority religious group themselves. Historically, white Catholics would have been less able than white Protestants to utilize majority group power over racial minority groups. To gain a full sense of how the majority group status has affected racial dynamics in an educational setting, it is more useful to limit the study to Protestants.

Outline of the Book

The organization of this book is as follows. In the next chapter, I explore sociological theories as they concern racial diversity on college campuses in general and how such theories may predict racial diversity in Protestant educational institutions. To do this, I look at the development of Protestant institutions of higher education thatwhich will provide insight into the type of barriers that these colleges and universities may have as they attempt to become more racially diverse. I will also explore some of the recent efforts these campuses have made toward diversity.

To accomplish the stated objectives of this book, I utilize data collected from a couple of outside sources and from my own personal research. To be specific, I have surveyed Protestant campuses throughout the United States with an internet tool and also used that tool to administer an in-depth questionnaire to students from several of those campuses. I also used data collected from the Integrated Postsecondary Data System found in the 2006 National Center for Educational Statistics (NCES) and the *Princeton Review's Complete Book of Colleges* to provide further light on these colleges and universities. In chapter 3, I introduce the reader to these data and the general methods utilized to collect that data. I then explore what the data state about why students of color are more or less likely to attend certain Protestant educational institutions. I want to see what programs tend to attract and retain students of color. I found that institutional diversity programs are not as effective as faculty issues, curriculum reforms, and student-led multicultural groups in promoting racial diversity on Protestant campuses. A diverse, trained faculty, educational courses, and student-led groups that deal with racial issues are more highly correlated to a diverse student body than multicultural, antiracism, community, or non-European cultural programs.

It is also important to investigate the attitudes of students attending Protestant campuses. Chapter 4 utilizes data collected from my Internet survey of white students at Protestant colleges and universities to investigate their reaction toward diversity initiatives. I found that the reaction majority group students have toward professors of color and diversity courses helps to explain why such courses have more potential for shaping a more positive racial atmosphere than other diversity initiatives. Majority group students are relatively quite receptive to altering their attitudes with such professors and courses. In fact, diversity programs tend to be either ignored or rejected as unnecessary by white students. On the other hand, the most effective positive predictor of racial diversity is the use of minority professors and diversity courses. I speculate that because such courses and professors fit within the generally accepted purpose of the college or university, they may be in a better position to shape racial perspectives than other diversity initiatives. However, it is also clear that whether these students take a personal liking to a professor is also a key to why these courses and professors are influential. So how a professor teaches or a course is organized plays an important role in influencing the racial attitudes of majority group students.

Chapter 5 explores the attitudes of minority students of color who attend Protestant campuses. I once again use the internet survey to explore the attitudes of minority students of color who attend Protestant campuses. A significant percentage of such students have racial attitudes similar to majority group students. However, minority students who have not adopted such attitudes struggle with the racial atmosphere on Protestant campuses. I term the first group of students of color "assimilated" racial minorities and the second group "racialized" racial minorities. Neither assimilated nor racialized students of color have a powerful belief in the general diversity programs, but their unbelief occurs for different reasons. Assimilated students of color find such programs ineffective because they may be offensive to majority group students; racialized students of color perceive the unwillingness of majority group students to acknowledge their racial struggles as the reason that such programs fail to work. Furthermore, like majority group students, students of color are more likely to perceive professors of color, diversity courses, and student-led multicultural organizations to be more helpful than general diversity programs; however, they are not as likely to tie this perception to the personality of a professor or to affection for a particular professor.

Since it was so critical to shaping the campus racial atmosphere, in chapter 6 I look at what students say about professors of color and diversity courses. I argue that there is a process by which these professors and courses can shape the racial atmosphere of Protestant colleges and universities. Such professors and courses allow open, honest discussions among students, which lead to more awareness of cultural differences and acknowledgment of the lingering effects of racism. However, when such professors and courses are seen as sources of hostility toward majority group students, they can create more racial tension instead of productive dialogue. Professors, courses, and other diversity initiatives that can create such dialogue and awareness should also be able to create such a positive effect.

Finally, in chapter 7, I present practical advice for faculty and administrators of Protestant educational institutions who want to create a more diverse atmosphere. This advice is not built on my own biases or desires but rather on the results of this research. Given the results of this work, I suggest that Protestant colleges and universities seek to establish a curriculum that deals with issues of racial diversity and find opportunities to create productive dialogue. Such educational institutions have to prepare to deal with professors who are not committed to addressing issues of diversity because they can build resistance among students against such a dialogue. Finally, I speculate that while the importance of personal relationships among white students may not easily generalize into non-Protestant settings, the importance of diversity courses and professors of color probably is important in those settings. Future work can examine whether interracial dialogue is as important on non-Protestant campuses as it is on Protestant ones.

NOTES

1. Furthermore, Emerson and Sikkink (2008) suggest that, contrary to the expectations of most scholars, educational attainment leads to even more social distance because the highly educated are more likely to live a racially segregated lifestyle. This tendency would only be exacerbated by a predominance of colleges and universities that are predominantly white, as is the case with many Protestant schools.

2. This is according to information found in the 2006 data from National Center for Education Statistics (see http://nces.ed.gov/).

3. According to the Statistical Abstract of the United States (2007), there are roughly 17.6 million college students in the United States.

4. Bowen and Bok (1998) did investigate the effects of racial awareness in the college selection process at selective universities and attendance of African Americans. However, their work focuses on only twenty-eight elite universities and is not a systematic approach to all colleges and universities. Furthermore, it does not take into account a variety of ways educational institutions encourage racial diversity, and the latest data were collected twenty years ago.

5. Thus it is not surprising that Protestant colleges and universities have higher percentages of white students than other colleges and universities. Eliminating colleges and universities known for having a minority student body such as historically black colleges and universities, I found that white students made up 77.8 percent of all students at mainline educational institutions and 76.9 percent of all students at conservative educational institutions, but whites make up only 68.4 percent of the students at non-Protestant campuses. The difference is significant at the .001 level.

6. For the purposes of such research, a racially diverse congregation is defined as having no more than 80 percent of any single racial group.

7. One mistake many individuals make is to automatically equate evangelicals and fundamentalists. Smith et al. (1998) point out critical differences between the two groups. For example, they observed that evangelicals tend to engage with society while fundamentalists attempt to separate themselves from the society. This difference helps to explain many of the contrasting views that these two groups hold. Regardless of these contrasts, both groups have tended to accept a similar conservative perspective on racial issues, and it is reasonable to group them together for the purpose of this discussion.

8. It could be argued that the same could be said about studying non-Christian educational institutions (Jewish, Muslim) as well. However, here the number of institutions is generally too few in the United States to allow for the type of quantitative analysis performed in chapter 3. Furthermore, because it has been the dominant religion in our society, the history of Christianity and racism is likely to play an important role in shaping the effects of religion on dealing with racial issues in ways that would not be captured in the examination of other faith traditions. Thus, I did not want to confound my analysis by adding educational institutions from other faith traditions.

2

Race and the Protestant College Campus

Encouraging more racial diversity is a common problem for most institutions of higher education in the United States. With notable exceptions, colleges and universities generally seek to bring more students of color to their campuses. They are often stymied by the relatively low numbers of students of color who apply to their institutions and troubled by the lower likelihood of students of color to graduate. These factors make it difficult for institutions of higher education to maintain the racial diversity they often seek.

Protestant educational institutions are not exceptions to this trend. Although it is not clear that all such institutions value racial diversity as much as other colleges and universities, many of them still desire racially integrated campuses. While they face many of the same problems as other educational institutions, Protestant campuses have unique challenges, and perhaps opportunities, for achieving racial diversity. Thus it is vital to explore the basic issues that confront colleges and universities in general concerning issues of racial diversity and then look at the unique racial situation created by the desire of Protestant educational institutions to create a religious experience for their students.

Theories about Racial Diversity

Previous researchers have documented the value of racial diversity in college classrooms. Such diversity is linked to higher levels of students' community involvement (Johnson & Lollar 2002, Laird 2005), academic self-confidence

(Chang 2001, Laird 2005), problem-solving skills (Laird 2005, Terenzini et al. 2001), cultural awareness (Johnson & Lollar 2002), and satisfaction with their educational experience (Chang 2001). Furthermore, racial diversity on campuses is connected to development of more racially diverse social networks among students (Fischer 2008), which may lead to more positive race relations.

Given the racial history of the United States, there is value in finding out why people of color are likely to join certain social institutions. Obviously, people of color participate in certain institutions for utilitarian reasons. For example, having an occupation is generally necessary to gain the funds for the material goods we use to sustain our lives. One should expect that people of color will desire jobs that pay them well for their efforts. However, people of color are less likely to obtain higher paying jobs than majority group members (Cose 1995, Torrecilha, Cantu, & Nguyen 1999, Woo 1999). Research has indicated that institutional barriers often prevent individuals of color from gaining the occupations they desire (Cross et al. 1990, Kirschenman & Neckerman 1991, Takaki 1989). So although racial minorities, like majority group members, desire highly prestigious occupational settings, they generally have fewer resources to help them obtain entry.

Likewise, obtaining an education has tremendous financial value. Individuals with bachelor's degrees possess greater earning power than those who are merely high school graduates. People of color have an incentive to attend institutions of higher education to gain social and economic assets. Like occupations where people of color are underrepresented because of institutional barriers, however, research has shown a plethora of institutional barriers limiting the ability of students of color to obtain a college education (Carter 1970, Frankenberg, Lee, & Orfield 2003, Kozol 1991, Tyson, Darity, & Castellino 2005). Educational institutions that have lower barriers for students of color may attract and retain more such students.

However, it is important to go beyond institutional barriers in our effort to understand why people of color favor certain educational institutions. A potential college student who has decided to attend college then has volitional options as to where to attend. Understanding why potential students decide to attend a certain educational institution is critical to developing colleges and universities that are fertile settings for racial diversity.

It is fair to consider why attention should be given to assessing the social atmosphere for students of color. Ideally, the same social dynamics that make colleges and universities attractive in general will also make them attractive to students of color. Yet this may not be the case. Students of color have challenges that make their experience different from majority group students. For example, students of color are more likely than white students to come from a family that has no one with a college degree (Terenzini et al. 1996, Zalaquett 1999). This means that they are less likely to have access to individuals who can prepare them for their collegiate experience. Furthermore, these students are also less likely to see racial in-group professors once they come on campus. Since individuals tend to gravitate toward members of their own social group for mentors (Hinch 1993, Leon, Dougherty, & Maitland 1997, Tillman 2001), mentorship may be a more difficult commodity to find for students of color than it is for white students. In addition, there may be social-psychological pressure that students of color have to face that majority group students do not have to undergo. Because they are underrepresented on college campuses (Stoops 2004),[1] it is plausible that they are often seen as representatives of their racial group. This can create additional pressure on them since failure may be seen as letting down their race, not merely themselves. The more communal and less individualistic social culture of some groups of color (Emerson & Smith 2000, Lewis 1966, Tsai 1986) may intensify this social pressure.

There is also the greater possibility that students of color will encounter racism than majority group students. It is tempting to perceive institutions of higher education as bastions of racial tolerance, yet there is evidence that these institutions are not as tolerant as we may tend to believe. Unfortunately, racist incidents are not uncommon on college campuses (Schaefer 1996), and there is evidence that the perceived ability of these institutions to promote tolerant racial attitudes is overstated (Schaefer 1996, Sikkink & Emerson 2008). Given these dynamics, students of color are likely to encounter some forms of racism during their time at educational institutions. This racism may be subtle or overt; however, dealing with racism is generally something that majority group students do not worry about. Thus students of color often carry a burden white students can avoid.

Given these additional challenges, there is little wonder why educational institutions have a more difficult time attracting and retaining students of color. Yet, by definition, without students of color it is impossible for colleges and universities to maintain a high level of racial diversity. Such institutions have to discover ways to help students of color scale the higher barriers they face. This has meant developing initiatives that create a racial atmosphere that students of color find comfortable. Such an atmosphere can make it easier for students of color to graduate and help a college or university gain a reputation as an acceptable place for students of color to attend.

Using Institutional Indicatives to Develop Racial Diversity in Educational Institutions

Students of color should be more willing to attend, and graduate from, educational institutions that create a more comfortable racial atmosphere for them. How to create a more comfortable atmosphere is a question with no clear answer. For example, some have argued that students of color suffer in educational settings that do not address academic issues that pertain to them (Banks 1993, McLaren 1995, Sogunro 2001). These scholars argue that our educational system is built on notions of Eurocentrism and that people of color are not recognized by such a system. These pedagogical barriers hamper the efforts of students of color at educational obtainment.

There may also be social barriers that people of color must deal with. If colleges and universities have not paid enough attention to the social and cultural needs of students of color, then these students will not easily find support on college campuses for cultural aspects that they normally find within their own communities. Majority group students can attend a college or university confident in the knowledge that elements of their culture will be celebrated in social gatherings, holidays, or cultural events. Students of color often do not have such assurances. Without these assurances, they may question their social position on a particular campus and be less likely to assimilate into the social world at their educational institution. This would put them at a distinct disadvantage relative to majority group students.

The disadvantaged position of people of color may also account for some of the difficulty minority students have in attending and graduating from institutions of higher education. For example, it is likely that the lower average socioeconomic status of students of color hinders their ability to attend and/or graduate from institutions of higher education. While there are poor whites who also face financial barriers, they may not face racial stereotypes connected to their poverty. Furthermore, the institutional challenges that people of color encounter probably give them a different social and political reality than majority group members (Ogbu 1978, Portes & Zhou 1993). Students of color may be quite aware of their need to overcome these institutional challenges and can seek out a social environment that is amenable to their political concerns. Educational institutions that attempt to address these needs may create an atmosphere conducive to students of color.

These ideas have led to several different types of programs educational institutions utilize in their efforts to increase racial diversity.[2] Educational institutions can make their intentions clear with a declarative statement of racial diversity. They can also incorporate offices of diversity to aid them in attracting and retaining students of color. Some endeavors emerging from these offices include multicultural programs that emphasize respect of non-European cultures, antiracism programs that challenge a passive attitude toward confronting racism, and community programs that bring students into communities of color. Such offices also can promote cultural celebrations of people of color such as Hispanic heritage month, student-led diversity committees, and multicultural student groups, although these programs can emerge even without an office of diversity. Finally, financial aid targeted toward students of color is another important institutional measure that colleges and universities have attempted to use to attract and retain racial minorities.

Institutional diversity programs may not be, by themselves, very effective in creating a welcoming racial atmosphere for students of color. There is also value in shaping the academic curriculum. As noted earlier, much of the traditional curriculum has focused on the concerns of majority group members. As a result of this focus, students of color may feel alienated by the lack of attention to racial and cultural issues they find important. Programs of ethnic and racial studies and courses that focus on issues of concern for people of color may help to shape a positive academic experience for nonwhite students. Many colleges and universities have implemented academic ethnic studies programs, which allow them to introduce scholarly material that will interest students of color. While often they may use a general ethnic studies program, it is also common to utilize studies programs of specific racial groups. Some programs often produce courses that focus on issues of race and ethnicity. Related to the lack of scholarly concern that may be reflected in academia is the relatively low number of professors of color within academic circles (Trower & Chait 2002). The shortage of professors of color probably contributes to the neglect of scholarly issues that pertain to students of color, but it also means that there are fewer role models and mentors for students of color. As a result, such students may receive less personal and social encouragement than majority group students for attending and graduating from institutions of higher education.

Yet, there is no systematic work documenting the relative success of efforts to obtain racial diversity for college campuses. There is literature documenting some of the efforts certain colleges and universities are making toward improving diversity on their campuses (Clayton-Pedersen et al. 2007, Cross & Slater 2002, Hasseler 1998, Townsend 1994). There are also case studies of certain universities that have implemented a given program (Melnick & Zeichner 1998, Velcoff & Ferrari 2006). But this work does not assess whether particular programs initiated by colleges or universities have any effect on the attraction or retention of students of color. If we are uncertain about why colleges and universities in general are able to attract and retain such students, then it is difficult to assess the properties of Protestant educational institutions that do a superior job of attracting and retaining students of color.

Who Graduates and Why?

It is well established that students of color who begin a program of higher education are less likely than majority group students to complete it (Alon & Tienda 2005, Kroc et al. 1995, Rosenbaum, Deil-Amen, & Person 2006). Previous research indicates that important predictors of graduation rates tend to be the family characteristics (Goldin 1992, Tinto 1975), the economic backgrounds of students (Kroc et al. 1995, Muraskin & Lee 2004, Scott, Bailey, & Kienzi 2006, Vartanian & Gleason 2002), and the academic abilities (Astin & Oseguera 2002, Light & Strayer 2000, Mortenson 1997, Schnell, Louis, & Doetkett 2003) of the students entering the programs. Disadvantaged students of color may fail to graduate at the same rates as majority group students because they possess different family structures and levels of economic status and educational training than majority group members. But this research focuses on the personal characteristics of the students rather than on understanding how institutional factors within a given college or university may affect the ability of disadvantaged students of color to graduate. The little work that has assessed possible institutional factors (Bowen & Bok 1998, Kroc et al. 1995, Rosenbaum et al. 2006) has not utilized a national sample diverse enough to make strong generalizable assertions.

Tinto (1975) developed an early model of student retention that concentrates on the normative and structural integration of students. According to his model, the more commitment a student has to the goal of degree completion and the more integrated that student is into the educational institution, the lower the chance that this student will leave that educational institution. Thus commitment to institutional goals and integration into the social and institutional system of the educational institution are positively related to the retention of a college student. Bean (1980, 1983) builds on this work in his assertion that the degree to which students are satisfied with the organizational mechanisms of a college or university is directly correlated to their willingness to persist in their educational pursuits at a particular campus. Braxton, Hirschy, and McClendon (2003) updated this theory with their argument that Tinto's conclusion may not be as relevant for residential, community, and two-year colleges. They contend that issues of the institution's commitment to the student's welfare and the student's ability to pay are important in less prestigious institutions. Because students of color are more likely to attend residential, community, and two-year colleges, Tinto's model may have less general ability to explain their retention (Braxton et al. 2003). For my purposes, however, the Braxton et al. critique may have less relevance because I am concentrating on Protestant institutions that are usually not residential, community, or two-year schools.

Correlates of Why Students of Color Attend and Graduate from Educational Institutions

Pollard (2004) points out the need for solid research to build diversity programs. But while there is substantial work on individual-level (Astin & Oseguera 2002, Light & Strayer 2000, Mortenson 1997) and institutional factors (Kroc et al. 1995, Pascarella & Terenzini 2005, Scott, Bailey, & Kienzi 2006,

Velez 1985) that predict attendance and graduation at colleges and universities, this work does not focus on the factors concerning students of color. There is work on the actual decision of students of color to attend college (Freeman 1997, Hurtado et al. 1997, Jackson 1990) but little on which colleges or universities they choose to attend. Several researchers have documented that certain programs (Gordon 2004, Stewart 2004, Turner 2004) or characteristics (Moody 2004, Williams 2004) at a particular college creates a more hospitable racial atmosphere. However, this work does not tend to be systematic in its approach due to the case study methodology generally used. Some researchers have offered advice based on their observations from several different academic institutions and reading of previous research (Hurtado et al. 1999, Jones 2001, Moore 2001) on how to increase racial diversity in a student body. Yet such advice is not necessarily based on a systematic study easily generalized outside the author's experience and insight. There is some generalizable work that documents perceptions of prejudice related to the retention of students of color (Cabrera et al. 1999) but little, if any, on the characteristics of the educational institutions that produce such perceptions.

Because of the dearth of systematic empirical work on why students of color are more likely to attend and to graduate from certain educational institutions, I embarked on a research project to address these issues. Utilizing information collected from the 2006 National Center for Education Statistics and the 2006 *Princeton Review Complete Book of Colleges*, I was able to determine the most important factors that predict attraction of students of color for all colleges and universities in the United States.

Based on this research, I found that educational institutions located near communities of color and those with a comparatively high number of minority faculty enroll higher numbers of students of color than other educational institutions (Yancey 2007b). Colleges and universities located in a racially diverse community or able to attract a relatively high number of faculty of color are clearly more able to attract students of color than other educational institutions. Other institutional characteristics explain relatively less variation in the racial diversity of entering undergraduate students.[3] Furthermore, it has been documented that the graduation rate of students of color is highly predicted by the graduation rate of majority group members (Small & Winship 2007), indicating that the same factors influence the graduation rates of both groups.

Despite the evidence that similar forces shape majority and minority group graduation, there are still reasons to believe that students of color understand educational challenges differently than majority group students. The social atmosphere of colleges and universities that welcomes majority group students may not be hospitable for students of color. For this reason, there is value in speculating about what sort of educational atmosphere is most likely to be attractive to students of color.

A Welcoming Racial Atmosphere for Students of Color

Students of all different races share certain similar concerns (grades, social relationships, separating from their parents), but it is a mistake to assume that the experiences of majority group students are identical to those of students of color. Because of overt and subtle racism students of color have experienced, they will have distinctive interpretations of their social reality and different challenges than majority group students. Understanding these contrasting interpretations and challenges is important if we are to theorize about what sort of educational culture would be most welcoming to students of color.

As I noted in the first chapter, Emerson and Smith (2000) found that African American evangelicals are more likely to have structuralist attitudes on racial issues than other African Americans, and European American evangelicals are more likely to adhere to individualism than other European Americans. This difference illustrates a key area in which students of color may be uncomfortable at educational institutions. The social values of individualism may dominate the culture at Protestant colleges and universities. These values emphasize the accomplishments of individuals over the group. Since there is evidence that people of color are more likely to possess communal values (Sastry & Ross 1998, Weaver 1997, Wilson 1989), which prioritize one's group more than the individual, students of color may not find as much affirmation of their cultural values as majority group students find. This particular cultural difference represents the fact that most colleges and universities are based in Eurocentric values. Colleges and universities that are more flexible in accepting non-European cultural values should have an environment that is more welcoming to students of color.

The presence of individualism among majority group Christians also represents an important political difference between majority and minority group students. Individualism is one of the characteristics of white racial identity (Bonilla-Silva & Lewis 1999, Twine 1997). This identity favors maintaining the status quo. It is not an accident that a key element of this identity is color blindness (Bonilla-Silva 2001, Bonilla-Silva & Lewis 1999), which is the idea that the best way to deal with racial issues is to ignore race. Such a perspective condemns both overt racism against people of color and attempts by those people of color to call attention to institutional racism. These types of attitudes lead to political solutions that downplay the presence of institutional racism in our societies. Since students of color are more likely than majority group students to experience the effects of this racism, they are likely to be more willing to seek out proactive solutions for the racial struggles they face. Educational institutions that attempt to downplay individual and institutional racism instead of confronting them are less likely to create an atmosphere in which students of color feel safe and/or respected. Such discomfort should create a less welcoming atmosphere to students of color.

Even some of the challenges majority group students face may be intensified for students of color. Since people of color generally have lower financial resources than majority group members (McKinnon 2003, Ogunwole 2006, Ramirez & de la Cruz 2003), it is fair to assume that students of color have lower financial resources than majority group students. Lack of financial resources may create more pressure for students of color and make it less likely for them to enjoy academic success. Campuses that do not provide opportunities for students of color to overcome their financial disadvantages may be campuses that do not have a social atmosphere conducive to their success.

This speculation suggests that colleges and universities that want to help students of color socially integrate have to concern themselves with creating a welcoming social atmosphere for such students. The same should also be true for Protestant educational institutions, reflecting the reality that they face many of the same problems as other colleges and universities concerning issues of racial diversity. Yet, Protestant colleges and universities intend to provide a unique religious environment for their students, and in doing so, additional factors may come into play in their ability to recruit and maintain racial diversity on their campuses.

The Origin of the Protestant College in the United States

Christian education did not start in the United States. Much of the traditional classical Western education contained teaching based on biblical texts. The Roman Catholic Church created educational auxiliaries that helped establish the development of the university (Patterson 2001). This Christian influence on education can be seen in the early universities that were established in the United States. Prominent universities such as Harvard and Yale started out as overtly Christian educational institutions. These universities were not seminaries or Bible colleges, but they did possess theological studies that promoted a Christian ideology. Much of the religious influence was wielded by Protestants who hoped to escape the dominance of the Church of England or the Roman Catholic Church. By and large, these studies promoted a Protestant understanding of Christian theology. The domination of Protestantism within the early colleges and universities in the United States reflected the superior status of this religious tradition in the culture of the United States.

Even state-sponsored educational institutions promoted a Protestant perspective and generally required their students to attend chapel.

In the latter half of the nineteenth century, the hegemony of Protestant Christianity began to experience challenges from other social forces in the United States (Marsden 1996, Patterson 2001). Catholicism gained more power, although it did not rival Protestantism. New elite universities such as Stanford and Cornell developed without religious backing but rather were beholden to capitalist interests. The Enlightenment movement that had spread throughout Europe also had a powerful influence on intellectual thought in the United States. Among intellectuals, this led to a desire to foster the separation of church and state, and more educational institutions sought to avoid religious entanglements in order to maintain good standing with the government. This desire first influenced the state school that had previously accepted a Protestant orientation.

The reaction of many mainline Protestant universities was adjustment to the changing times. Patterson (2001) argues that many of them accepted the prevailing modernist ideologies. As a result of that acceptance, they de-emphasized their denominational ties and promoted generalized moral values (Marsden 1996). Many of their actions were in response to the challenges mainline denominations encountered from fundamentalists.[4] Allegiance to science became a rationale for reducing some of the overt religious presence on their campuses. A type of liberal Protestantism became the operating social framework that shaped the way these educational institutions perceived the role of religion (Marsden 1996). In this framework, religion and morality were valued, but there was a relativist approach to what sort of religion one wanted to adopt. Science, rather than religion, was seen as the source of ultimate truth.

Some of these educational institutions continued down a path toward a modernism that eventually led to a level of secularization that made them almost identical to nonsectarian schools (Ringenberg 1984). Many of the same arguments mainline Protestants used to reduce the influence of fundamentalists (need for science, value of relativity) were later used to reduce the influence of mainline Protestants. As such, it can be argued that many of those educational institutions became quite similar to the nonreligious colleges and universities developing around them. This is not to argue that mainline Protestant educational institutions are indistinguishable from nonsectarian campuses; however, there is little, if any, research that clearly differentiates the two types of colleges and universities.

In response to these changes, a movement toward the establishment of Bible colleges began toward the end of the nineteenth century (Patterson 2001, Ringenberg 1984). Many of them developed in response to the modernist criticisms and liberal theology that developed in state and mainline educational institutions. Thus these colleges moved toward accepting a conservative Protestantism that reinforced the authority of scripture and challenged the relativism they feared was influencing Christian students. This effort mirrored the larger movement within conservative Protestantism to resist modern versions of theologies that emphasized the social gospel. These Protestants feared that Christians would be swept away by modern values and lose the distinctiveness of their faith. Many conservative Protestant colleges began to act as fortresses to protect the next generation from the secular values they feared. This fortress mentality served the purposes of many of them, as they were relatively unaffected by the social upheaval faced by other educational institutions in the 1960s (Ringenberg 1984).

After World War II, some conservative Protestant theologians, such as Carl F. H. Henry, began to challenge their peers to come out of their fortress mentality and engage with the rest of society. Although their call was not answered by all conservative Protestant schools, some of them attempted to continue to protect their students from the influences of modernism, even as they also sought to engage with the larger society. This lead to the development of a version of conservative Protestantism that was an evangelicalism that worked toward altering society while they maintained their religious values (Smith et al. 1998). Conservative Protestant educational institutions reacted to these changes by attempting to generate distinctive Christian perspectives on education and academic pursuits. Many of these institutions began to affiliate as they pursued common goals. Organizations such as Council for Christian Colleges and Universities and the Association of Theological Schools helped link these Christian institutions of higher education.

Why Protestant Colleges and Universities May Have Less Racial Diversity

Christian universities continue to lag behind nonreligious schools in racial diversity on their campuses (Wolfe 2006). Because they fail to produce an atmosphere of racial diversity, students who attend these colleges often do not gain the advantages of racial diversity, and these colleges may be failing to provide the best education possible. Information from the previous section indicates why Protestant colleges and universities may have more difficulty obtaining racial diversity than other educational institutions. Mainline Protestant educational institutions may not be highly differentiated from nonsectarian campuses. Yet they developed out of a religious tradition that had not been racially diverse. Many of the mainline denominations tend to be very racially homogeneous, even though they endorse a racially progressive ideology. This has clearly affected the institutions these religious organizations have developed. For example, work on multiracial congregations has shown that mainline congregations are more likely to be racially homogeneous than non-Christian, Catholic, and even conservative Protestant congregations (Emerson 2006).

Likewise mainline colleges and universities were, until recently, generally bastions for majority group students. These educational institutions often do not have the social traditions or interpersonal ties that can help them draw in students of color. Students who choose to attend a religious educational institution may do so because it supports the family faith. Yet the racially homogeneous nature of mainline denominations indicates that there will be few students of color who will come to their college because of a loyalty to a family faith. Furthermore, mainline denominations are less likely to engage in proselytizing than other Protestants (Boys 2000, Kelley 1972). These denominations may attract fewer individuals of color because there is less effort given to converting them. This also limits the potential pool of minority students who perceive an attachment to colleges and universities sponsored by mainline denominations. Overall, mainline Protestant educational institutions often lack the social and relational ties needed to attract potential students of color. Even today, these campuses tend to struggle to attract non-white students.

The lack of cultural influences for cultures of color can make it exceptionally difficult for mainline Protestant colleges and universities to adequately serve students of color. Since historically they have not had many people of color in their congregations, they do not have cultural traditions to draw on as they attempt to attract and graduate students of color. This may create a catch-22 situation, as they do not have the cultural traditions to develop racial diversity, their relative nondiversity means that they do not have the individuals to teach them nonwhite traditions, they maintain Eurocentric traditions that reinforce their lack of diversity and so on.

However, different challenges exist for conservative Protestant colleges and universities. Because of desegregation efforts, some whites found their children bused to schools to encourage racial integration. Thus, many white Christians sought to prevent their children's exposure to black children by sending them to all-white, or mostly white, secondary Christian schools (Crespino 2007, De la Torre 2006). Given this reality, there is little doubt that many whites also sent their children to conservative Protestant educational institutions in an effort to limit their children's exposure to those of different races. The relatively late elimination of prohibition of blacks from some of the conservative Protestant colleges and universities[5] supports this thesis, as such organizations obviously realized their value to such parents as bastions of whiteness. Because of this process, it is plausible that subtle and overt racism still inhibits these campuses' ability to attract students of color.[6] Such racism may contribute to an inhospitable social environment on these campuses for students of color.[7]

Furthermore, racial minorities are quite aware of the history of racism that plagues conservative Protestant denominations. It is no secret that many members of these denominations acted to resist efforts that people of color made at obtaining civil rights. Although such overt racism is today uncommon, many conservative Protestant leaders still work against the progressive political agenda that many Protestants of color support. As a result of this history and the contemporary political schism, there is likely to be a great deal of mistrust between people of color (even if they are Protestant themselves) and institutions established by conservative Protestant denominations.[8] This mistrust can play itself out in whether students of color are willing to attend educational institutions sponsored by conservative Protestant denominations. Attendance at such institutions may threaten the racial identity of students of color in that they may believe themselves to be gaining their educational training from those who work against their own racial interest. Even if they share similar theological beliefs, conservative Protestant colleges and universities may be at an extreme disadvantage in attracting students of color on account of the historical mistrust they face from such students.

Contemporary racial struggles are more likely to be driven by notions of color blindness than by attempts at overt white superiority (Bonilla-Silva 2003, Carr 1997). Such color blindness flows naturally from the political conservatism that has been linked to conservative Protestants. The reality that students of color may not be comfortable on a campus that emphasizes elements of white racial identity can help to explain an additional barrier conservative Protestant campuses may face. In their efforts to reject a progressive political agenda, they may perpetuate a Eurocentric idea about racial identity that students of color find hard to accept. Thus these colleges and universities may offer powerful support for politically conservative constructs such as color blindness and individualism, which do not well serve the interests of the students of color they wish to attract. This creates a level of political Eurocentrism that inhibits such institutions of higher education from successfully recruiting and/or retaining students of color.

These barriers do not mean that it is impossible for Protestant colleges and universities to attract and retain students of color. But it does mean that for such educational institutions to become more racially diverse, they may have to make a greater effort than other educational institutions. Mechanisms that enable certain Protestant colleges and universities to experience success are likely to be successful for non-Protestant campuses as well. To this end, it is useful to explore what these efforts are and assess the degree to which they have been and will be effective.

What Efforts Are Being Made by Protestant Colleges to Address Issues of Racial Diversity?

It can be expected that many of the same attempts Protestant colleges and universities utilize to increase the degree of racial diversity would be similar to the initiatives used by non-Protestant colleges and universities. It is possible that their religious beliefs would allow different ways to implement such programs, but there is little reason to believe that diversity initiatives utilized by Protestant educational institutions should significantly differ from those on other campuses. However, it is not clear the degree to which Protestant colleges and universities use these initiatives to encourage racial diversity. Knowing which educational institutions utilize certain types of diversity initiatives allows a researcher to determine which types of programs are linked with successful efforts to recruit and retain students of color.

I obtained information from a survey sent to Protestant colleges and universities. Of course, many colleges and universities have Protestant roots but no longer recognize their religious origin. However, I am interested in campuses that currently recognize a religious identity. I utilized *The Princeton Review Complete Book of Colleges* to locate colleges and universities in the United States that currently maintain a Protestant affiliation or that actively promote a Protestant religious identity.[9] This book indicates whether a particular college or university is affiliated with a Protestant denomination. I also identified some of the "Bible schools" through the Coalition for Christian Colleges and Universities Web site. This allows me to gain nearly all of the names of Protestant colleges and universities in the United States.[10]

A sample of selected questions from the original survey can be seen in figure 2.1. The survey was sent to the 406 Protestant colleges and universities in the United States. I used the Web pages of these institutions to determine to whom I should send the survey. Generally I targeted, when I could find them, the directors of multicultural programs. When such a director could not be easily found, I looked for the director or dean of student affairs. The vast majority were sent out by e-mail with the use of the Web site Survey Monkey. However, the e-mail addresses of forty-five of the appropriate targets could not be found. Those individuals were sent hard copies of the surveys by postal mail. A reminder was delivered about a month after the first mailing to increase the number of respondents. With 161 colleges and universities returning the survey, the overall response rate of the mailing was 39.66 percent. For the e-mail mailing, this rate was 37.95 percent; the response rate of the postal mailing was higher at 53.33 percent.[11]

As a result of this survey, I can assess which Protestant colleges and universities use many of the initiatives designed to increase racial diversity at a

Does this University have a department/office that deals with issues of race and ethnicity? (RACE/ETHNICITY DEPT)

Yes   No

Over the past school year, about how many times have issues of race and ethnicity been addressed by the main speaker in a chapel service? (RACE-CHAPEL)

0   1–2   3–4   5–6   7–8   9–10   More than 10

Does your college have an official statement that supports efforts at racial diversity, racial reconciliation, and/or multiculturalism? (RACE STATEMENT)

Yes   No

Does your college have an Ethnic Studies program? (ETHNIC STUDIES)

Yes   No

Does your college have an African American Studies program? (BLACK STUDIES)

Yes   No

Does your college have a Hispanic American Studies program? (HISPANIC STUDIES)

Yes   No

Does your college have an Asian American Studies program? (ASIAN STUDIES)

Yes   No

Does your college have a Native American Studies program? (INDIAN STUDIES)

Yes   No

How many antiracism programs or events does your college support each year? For the purposes of this survey, antiracism can be defined as attempts to end racism by the promotion of racial and/or social justice. (ANTI-RACISM)

0   1   2   3   4   5   More than 5

How many multicultural programs or events does your college support each year? For the purposes of this survey, multicultural can be defined as attempts to celebrate nonwhite cultures. (MULTICULTURAL)

0   1   2   3   4   5   More than 5

How many programs or events that serve communities of color does your college support each year? For the purposes of this survey, this indicates ministries that provide material resources or personal attention for the practical needs of people of color. This does not include programs that *only* intend to evangelize people of color. (COMMUNITY)

0   1   2   3   4   5   More than 5

About how many times a year does the college sponsor cultural events focused on non–European American groups? (e.g., Cinco de Mayo, Indian Powwows) (CULTURAL EVENTS)

0   1   2   3   4   5   6   7   8   9   10   More than 10

FIGURE 2.1. Selected Questions from Survey of Protestant Colleges

Does your college celebrate African American History month? (BLACK MONTH)

Yes   No

Does your college celebrate Hispanic Heritage History month? (HISPANIC MONTH)

Yes   No

Does your college celebrate Native American History month? (INDIAN MONTH)

Yes   No

Does your college celebrate Asian American History month? (ASIAN MONTH)

Yes   No

Does your college have programs for recruiting potential students of color? (RECRUIT MINORTY STUDENTS)

Yes   No

Does your college have programs to recruit faculty of color? (RECRUIT MINORITY FACULTY)

Yes   No

Does your college sponsor any scholarships or financial aid programs that are directed at only certain racial groups of color? (SCHOLARSHIP)

Yes   No

If so, then which racial groups are recipients of these scholarships or financial aid programs? (circle all that apply) (BLACK SCHOLARSHIP, HISPANIC SCHOLARSHIP, INDIAN SCHOLARSHIP, ASIAN SCHOLARSHIP)

African Americans   Hispanic Americans   Native Americans   Asian Americans   Other

Does your college have programs to train faculty for dealing with racial issues? (TRAIN FACULTY)

Yes   No

Does your college have a student committee dedicated to dealing with issues of racial diversity? (STUDENT COMMITTEE)

Yes   No

About how many multicultural student-led organizations are in your college? Please exclude organizations that concentrate on international students instead of racial groups based on those born in the United States. (# of MULTICULTURAL STUDENT ORGANIZATIONS)
Provide Number_____

FIGURE 2.1. (*continued*) Selected Questions from Survey of Protestant Colleges university. In table 2.1, I document the extent to which Protestant educational institutions utilize diversity initiatives. Unfortunately, I do not have a sample of non-Protestant colleges to compare these results with, and so I am not in a position to make empirical claims about the degree to which Protestant educational institutions utilize programs that may provide a more racially accepting atmosphere on their campuses. However, most individuals who have been exposed to issues of educational diversity will quickly perceive that many of the mechanisms I measured are quite commonplace. Thus the fact that only 61.4 percent of the conservative Protestant campuses and 64.4 percent of the mainline Protestant campuses have an office or department to address multicultural issues is quite enlightening; in my own limited experience, I have yet to find a nonsectarian school without such an office.[12] I am sure that such nonsectarian schools exist, but I believe that they are relatively rare, in comparison with the relative commonness of Protestant schools without such offices or departments.[13]

There is further evidence of the relative unwillingness of Protestant schools to adopt programs of racial diversity. For example, a little more than a third of all conservative Protestant schools (38.6%) and a little under half of the mainline Protestant schools (45.3%) offer scholarships that target African Americans. This is against the general trend within higher education to use financial incentives to attract students of color (Cross 2000, Ethridge 1997, Howard-Hamilton, Phelps, & Torres 1998). Furthermore, the mean number of multicultural student organizations on conservative Protestant campuses is only 2.524, and on mainline campuses, 3.386. This seems to be a low number of student organizations for an educational institution.[14] Although the formation of student organizations that address racial issues is not directly under the control of college and university administrators, clearly the racial atmosphere on a particular campus can either facilitate or inhibit the development of such organizations. It is fair to state that Protestant educational institutions do not create particularly fertile ground for such organizations.

I broke down the analysis into conservative and mainline Protestant schools. Despite some similarities between the two groups, when there was a significant difference between the two groups, mainline Protestant campuses were more likely to adopt diversity initiatives. For example, mainline campuses were more likely to offer Ethnic Studies degrees, antiracism and multicultural programs, non-European cultural events, and African American and Hispanic American history[15] month celebrations than were conservative campuses. This probably reflects the more progressive political and theological philosophies within these denominations.[16] Mainline Protestant denominations are more likely to assign a high value to racial tolerance and multiculturalism than are conservative Protestant denominations. This progressive ideology has clearly

TABLE 2.1   Means of Selected Variables from Survey of Protestant Colleges

	Conservative Protestants	Mainline Protestants
Race/Ethnicity Dept	61.4% (88)	64.4% (73)
Race Statement	76.2% (84)	73.6% (72)
Ethnic Studies	11.4% (88)	22.2%* (72)
Black Studies	10.2% (88)	16.9% (71)
Hispanic Studies	8% (87)	7% (71)
Asian Studies	8.1% (86)	5.6% (72)
Indian Studies	3.4% (87)	2.8% (72)
Antiracism	2.233 (86)	3.145[a] (69)
Multicultural	3.893 (84)	4.609[a] (69)
Community	3.143 (84)	3.246 (65)
Cultural events	3.048 (83)	4.456[b] (68)
Black month	73.3% (86)	84.5%[a] (71)
Hispanic month	31.8% (85)	53.5%[b] (71)
Indian month	17.4% (86)	25.4% (71)
Asian month	21.2% (85)	26.8% (71)
Black scholarship	38.6% (70)	45.3% (64)
Hispanic scholarship	34.3% (70)	34.4% (64)
Indian scholarship	27.1% (70)	29.7% (64)
Asian scholarship	22.9% (70)	31.3% (64)
Student committee	37.8% (82)	45.7% (70)
# of multicultural student organizations	2.524 (82)	3.386 (70)

* = significantly different at .1 level; a = significantly different at .05 level;
b = significantly different at .01 level.

created a programmatic difference between conservative and mainline Protestant campuses. However, it remains to be seen whether this more progressive ideology results in a more hospitable racial atmosphere for students of color.

The relatively low percentage of Protestant colleges and universities utilizing many of these common diversity initiatives supports a common perception about Protestant educational institutions—that they generally are not making as much of an effort to deal with issues of racial diversity on their campuses as other colleges and universities. In chapters 4 and 5, I look at some qualitative evidence about the effects of these efforts at these educational institutions, but for now it seems unlikely that Protestant colleges and universities put forth the same degree of effort as non-Protestant educational institutions. This is not to disparage those that have put forth a tremendous amount of effort to diversify their campuses, nor does it mean that these schools have no concern about the lack of racial diversity on their campuses. But if, as I suspect, there are fewer diversity initiatives on Protestant, especially conservative Protestant, campuses than at other educational institutions, then one can rightly claim that racial diversity has been given a lower priority on these campuses than on other campuses. That may provide some insight as to why some of these educational institutions have struggled to become racially diverse.

Conclusion

The challenge of creating racial diversity at colleges and universities is one that is common across many different educational institutions. This diversity can be very beneficial to students who attend these colleges and universities. Such racial inclusion can also help colleges and universities to fulfill their commitment to improve our larger society by serving populations that have been ignored and marginalized throughout our history. Yet achieving this diversity may be especially difficult for Protestant institutions of higher education. A history of racial homogeneity in mainline Protestant denominations and of racial discrimination in conservative Protestant denominations probably reduces these educational institutions' ability to attract a high number of students of color. In both cases, these Protestant colleges and universities may develop a social atmosphere on their campuses that discourages racial diversity. Students of color may quickly learn to avoid attending certain Protestant campuses, or they may find it more difficult to graduate from these campuses because of cultural Eurocentrism or racial insensitivity. Learning how some Protestant colleges and universities have developed racial diversity in spite of these barriers is valuable for comprehending how colleges and universities can deal with the challenges of establishing a racially diverse campus.

To this end, some Protestant institutions of higher education have adopted many of the diversity initiatives of their non-Protestant counterparts. The rationale for such programs is clear, given the types of racial hurdles they must leap to develop a more racially diverse campus. However, how successful such initiatives are in developing and sustaining racial diversity on their respective campuses is unclear. Furthermore, if they are successful, it is not certain why they succeed. Because of the additional barriers that Protestant campuses may face, diversity initiatives that are fruitful in these educational settings should be more likely to support racial diversity on other campuses. Careful research can also provide us insight into the process by which diversity initiatives can facilitate a more positive and accepting racial atmosphere.

I have outlined some of the difficulties that await Protestant colleges and universities that are attempting to become more racially diverse. The next step in this process is to conduct research that addresses the result of these attempts. To this end, I have conducted a quantitative study in which I examine the correlation between diversity initiatives and curriculum alterations and the level of racial diversity in Protestant colleges and universities. In the next chapter, I begin to report my findings from this effort. While the generalization of these findings must be done carefully, these results will provide us insight into what sorts of educational reforms are likely to succeed in creating a social atmosphere where racial diversity can thrive. This insight will help answer the question of which reforms are more likely to succeed, which will then allow me to concentrate, in future chapters, on why they may be successful.

NOTES

1. The key exception to this trend is Asian Americans. It is well documented that even though they are a minority group, Asian Americans are more likely to attend and graduate from an institution of higher education than majority group members (Hirschman & Wong 1986, Mau & Bikos 2000).

2. This is not to state that the only reason educational institutions have engaged in such programs is the attraction and retention of students of color. There are other pedagogical values in many of these efforts, regardless of their potential success in creating racial diversity on campuses. However, at least part of the reason for these diversity programs is to create a welcoming atmosphere for students of color.

3. For example, I (2007b) found that those two factors accounted for .441 of the variation of the number of African American students at a college campus. Adding all other institutional variables only explains .121 more variation beyond these two variables. For Hispanic Americans, these factors account for .651 of the variation. Adding all other institutional variables explains only .022 more variation beyond these two variables.

4. At this time in history, the schism between fundamentalists and mainline denominations dominated much of the religiously charged atmosphere of these colleges and universities. Fundamentalist institutions brought with them a powerful anti-intellectual culture (Noll 1994) that created distrust they directed toward educational institutions. This hostility served to further remove certain types of Christian influence from colleges and universities and eventually led to the establishment of fundamentalist educational institutions promoting a more sectarian social vision.

5. For example, Bob Jones University is well known for its ban, until recently, on interracial dating. But this college also did not allow African American admissions until the 1980s.

6. It also may be that such efforts were not motivated by racism. Part of the progressive theology that comprised the social gospel was linked to support of the modern civil rights movement. Attempts to reject that theology can naturally lead to rejection of the civil rights movement as well, although this rejection would be on theological, instead of racist, grounds. Yet, even if racism did not motivate the rejection of civil rights efforts, the results still led these educational institutions to lag behind others on issues of racial diversity.

7. This argument is supported by research suggesting that a conservative Protestant philosophy is correlated to less racial tolerance (Griffin, Gorsuch, & David 1987, Kirkpatrick 1993, Roof & McKinney 1987).

8. Anecdotally, I have encountered people of color who share the same theological beliefs as evangelicals, yet refuse to allow themselves to be labeled as evangelicals. Often this hesitation is based on their understanding of evangelicalism as a white and politically conservative religion. Thus, theological agreement is not a powerful enough motivator for Protestants of color to accept the evangelical label.

9. There are Protestant campuses that specifically cater to students of color. To be specific, some historically black colleges and universities have a religious emphasis and some African American students can have their need for a religious education met through them. Since I want to assess how efforts at predominantly white educational institutions help or hinder the ability of that institution to attract students of color, I eliminated these colleges and universities, and a predominantly Indian college, from the sample studied in this book.

10. To decide if a campus promoted a mainline or conservative Protestant orientation, I looked at the denomination affiliated with the campus. To determine how to categorize a denomination, I used Kellstedt et al.'s (1997) conservative and mainline breakdown of different Protestant denominations. Furthermore, by examining their Web sites, I found that the "Bible schools" in my sample tended to have a conservative religious orientation, and so I classified them as conservative Protestant schools.

11. I compared the universities that returned a survey with those that did not. I found that both groups were alike except that those who returned the survey instrument were younger and more likely to be conservative Protestants. It is possible that the age of the educational institutions may affect the racial atmosphere on those campuses, but controls for age do not affect the recruitment and retention of minority students. Much of my further analysis separates conservative Protestants from mainline Protestants, and thus the bias toward the conservative Protestants is unlikely to bias my findings.

12. This number may be somewhat inflated since I counted anyone who held an office that focused on multicultural issues on these campuses. In fact, 26 percent of the schools have a non-tenure-track director, and precisely 25 percent of these schools have a staff person in the position. Only 12 percent of these colleges assigned someone as high as a vice president to be in charge of multicultural affairs, and another 21 percent had a dean-level individual in charge of multicultural issues. Once again, I do not have information on non-Protestant educational institutions, but my experience at state universities is that generally individuals in charge of multicultural affairs have at least the authority of a dean.

13. The lack of programs actually makes it easier to do research into the correlates of racial diversity on college campuses. The degree of variability within these educational institutions allows for a viable test of whether the presence or absence of such programs is correlated with the percentage of racial minorities who attend and graduate from a given educational institution. If upward of 90 percent of all colleges and universities have certain diversity programs, such as celebrating black history month, then tests for the effects of these programs are much harder, if not impossible, to conduct.

14. I located six private schools (Rice University, Bowdoin College, Keystone College, Oglethorpe University, Tiffin University, and Swarthmore College) of comparable size

to Protestant campuses and looked up how many multicultural student organizations they had. They averaged a little more than five such organizations on their campuses. While this is not a probability sample, it does suggest that non-Protestant campuses are more likely to have such organizations than Protestant campuses.

15. The celebration of such months is referred to heritage, rather than history, months for nonblack racial minority groups. In the body of the text, I use heritage when appropriate, but in the tables I refer to these events as history months in order to keep things simple.

16. The difference is not connected to the possibility that mainline institutions are larger than conservative institutions and thus have more resources for multicultural student groups and initiatives, as the size of mainline colleges and universities (m = 2,139.4) is not significantly greater than conservative colleges and universities (m = 2,048.1).

3

Minority Students on Protestant Campuses

Protestant campuses have unique challenges and opportunities for attracting students of color. The challenges arise in the possibility that highly religious Protestants may be more likely to exhibit racial prejudice than non-Protestants (Wilmore 1972, Yancey, Hubbard, & Smith 2007). Furthermore, there is evidence that white Protestants, especially conservative Protestants, are less willing to confront issues of institutional racial discrimination than other whites (Emerson & Smith 2000, Kirkpatrick 1993). This can create a higher barrier for Protestant colleges, relative to other educational institutions, in attracting students of color. On the other hand, research also indicates that some racial minority groups possess a higher level of religiosity than majority group members (Chatters, Taylor, & Lincoln 1999, Gallup & Lindsay 1999, Jacobson, Heaton, & Dennis 1990, Yancey 2005). If such work is accurate, then people of color should desire a religious-based education more than majority group members. This desire may aid Protestant campuses in attracting students of color.

In the previous chapter, I described using an online survey to assess the number and types of diversity programs Protestant colleges are using to address issues of racial diversity. In this chapter, I explore the propensity of Protestant colleges and universities to attract and graduate students of color with information from that survey. Doing so provides insight into what diversity initiatives are useful in creating and sustaining racial diversity.

Why Students of Color May Attend Certain Colleges and Universities

Previous efforts at enhancing racial diversity at institutions of higher education are connected to ideas about creating a more comfortable racial atmosphere for students of color. These ideas can, for simplicity's sake, be categorized as institutional, educational, financial, interpersonal, and political dimensions of why students of color are attracted to and/or able to graduate from institutions of higher education. The various dimensions may predict racial diversity at colleges and universities.

For example, the environment at educational institutions tends to be dominated by Eurocentric concerns (Asante 1991, Gorski & Clark 2002, Hudson 2003, Hunn 2004). This majority group focus may discourage people of color from attending and remaining at educational institutions. Colleges and universities able to use institutional programs to de-emphasize this Eurocentric culture may produce an attractive social atmosphere for students of color and allow them to succeed once they start to attend their college or university. Campuses may attempt to address their lack of diversity with institutional programs that recognize the historical months of people of color, sponsor cultural events for such students, develop multicultural programs, provide programs in antiracism, and community programs. If these institutional efforts cater to the needs and concerns of students of color, then colleges and universities with such programs should have an easier time attracting and retaining minority students.

However, educational concerns may be the key to creating an atmosphere for racial diversity. It is quite plausible that educational institutions that craft their pedagogy to address concerns of people of color do a better job of attracting and retaining them. A program of ethnic studies or the studies of specific racial groups is one of the ways such pedagogical concerns may be addressed. Specific courses that deal with issues of race and ethnicity can also attempt to engage students of color in issues pertaining to them. These efforts may create a more comfortable academic atmosphere that allows students of color to follow scholarly pursuits that are of interest to them and teaches majority group students about the concerns of people of color.

Financial constraints may also hinder the educational attainment of students of color. These financial issues can be compounded by the unique challenges connected to racial status. For example, it has been documented that African Americans possess lower levels of self-efficacy than majority group members (Hughes & Demo 1989). This lower self-efficacy is not merely due to lower economic resources but can also reflect the low confidence African Americans have that they operate in a system that is fair to them. It is plausible that financial aid helps them overcome such beliefs and produces more benefits for poor African Americans than for poor majority group members who do not lack self-efficacy. Hispanic and Native Americans may also face financial barriers that inhibit their attendance at institutions of higher education. General programs of financial aid may not necessarily increase racial diversity, but scholarships that specifically target students of color may be more effective in producing diversity.

There also may be efforts to address the potential interpersonal barriers that inhibit diversity. The degree to which students of color experience support may depend on the type of peer relationships they develop. Previous research (Steinberg 1997, Steinberg, Dornbusch, & Brown 1999) suggests that for all different racial groups, peers are a critical part of why students succeed or not in high schools. Peers may also either motivate students or deter them from attending or remaining at a college or university. Student-headed organizations can also play an important factor in promoting racial diversity in that they can provide the sort of interpersonal support students of color need. Such organizations can allow students to gain support from peers who understand their social and spiritual needs better than administrators and professors. They also may empower minority group students and provide them with a sense of control on a campus where they lack institutional power. Finally, these organizations may promote the interpersonal relations between majority and minority group students that buttress a healthy racial atmosphere. If these arguments are accurate, then the degree to which Protestant colleges and universities promote student-led organizations may shape their ability to become racially diverse.

It may also be vital to address the potential political concerns students of color bring to campus. Campuses that fail to allow them to express their political concerns or that even sanction activism may discourage such students. However, campuses that actively seek to address racial issues may be attractive to students of color and produce a level of acceptance that makes obtaining a degree easier. Colleges that seek to meet such needs can do so through chapel services that address concerns of students of color and/or offices of race or ethnicity that express the concerns of students of color.

Some of the variables collected from this survey do not easily fit into any one of these dimensions. For example, I measured whether there are programs to recruit students and/or faculty of color. Such programs may attempt to recruit such individuals by addressing their educational, financial, and/or political concerns. These questions do not identify what sort of programs these colleges or universities are using. The questionnaire also asks whether faculty on campus are trained to deal with issues of racial diversity, but it does not ask what sort of training has been conducted for them. Thus, once again I am unsure which of these dimensions are buttressed by the training faculty members may receive. But questions about faculty training and other hard-to-classify aspects of diversity will be included in the analysis as a way to investigate other, possibly unknown, dimensions by which students of color are drawn to and stay at particular Protestant colleges and universities.

Findings

In table 3.1, I compare the racial diversity of Protestant colleges and universities with the different diversity initiatives they may use to create a welcoming atmosphere for students of color. The initiatives I measured include whether they had a race or ethnicity office, discussion of race in chapel, a statement on diversity, a general ethnic studies program, a program for a given racial minority group, antiracism programs, multicultural programs, community programs, non-European cultural events, celebration of history months (such as black history month), efforts to recruit minority students and/or minority faculty, minority scholarships, efforts to train faculty for diversity, student committees dedicated to diversity issues, multicultural student organizations, and race-based academic courses. I compare the percentages of minority racial groups in educational institutions that have these initiatives with those that did not have them.

One thing to note about interpreting these tables: To keep the table short, I did not want to list all four racial groups when describing initiatives of ethnic studies, history months, scholarships, and race courses. For example, I did not want four rows of African American ethnic studies, Hispanic American ethnic studies, Native American ethnic studies and Asian American ethnic studies when each program applies to only one minority group. So in the table I use the term "specific racial group studies" to denote that for black students I am looking at the effects of African American studies, for Hispanic students I am looking at Hispanic American studies, and so on. Similar adjustments were made for the variable exploring history months, scholarships, and race courses.

Deciding how to separate the two groups to compare is an important task for this analysis. With some of the measures, it was clear how to create the divisions between the two groups. For example, either the college or university has scholarships for Native American students, or it does not. Either the institution possesses a statement on race, or it does not. But I also asked the informants questions such as how many community service programs or how many courses that deal with race or ethnicity are at the college or university. For such questions, I strove to determine a relative midpoint so that I had roughly equal groups to assess the impact of having more of a given diversity initiative at an institution. For example, 61 of the institutions indicated no

TABLE **3.1** Percentages of Black, Hispanic, Indian, and Asian Students by Diversity Initiatives[1]

	Percent	Percent	Percent	Percent
	Black	Hispanic	Indian	Asian
Race/ethnicity office	6.1%[b] (89)	3%[a] (89)	0.5% (89)	2.2% (89)
No race/ethnicity office	11.3% (49)	5.1% (49)	0.7% (49)	2.1% (49)
2 or fewer chapel talks	8.3% (72)	3.8% (72)	0.7% (72)	1.7%* (72)
More than 2 chapel talks	8.1% (53)	3.7% (53)	0.6% (53)	2.5% (53)
Race statement	7%* (97)	4% (97)	0.6% (97)	2.3%* (97)
No race statement	10.4% (35)	3% (35)	0.7% (35)	1.4% (35)
General ethnic studies	7.9% (19)	3.2% (19)	0.6% (19)	2.1% (19)
No general ethnic studies	7.9% (112)	3.8% (112)	0.6% (112)	2.1% (112)
Specific racial[2] group studies	6.6% (13)	6.6%* (9)	1.5% (4)	3.6%* (10)
No specific racial group studies	8.1% (123)	3.6% (126)	0.6% (132)	2% (125)
0 or 1 antiracism programs	7.1% (47)	3.4% (47)	0.8% (47)	1.7% (47)
More than 1 antiracism program	8.7% (83)	3.9% (83)	0.5% (83)	2.3% (83)
5 or less multicultural programs	11.4% (61)	3.7% (61)	0.8% (61)	1.7% (61)
More than 5 multicultural programs	5.4% (69)	3.8% (69)	0.5% (69)	2.4% (69)
2 or fewer community programs	8% (56)	3.5% (56)	0.7% (56)	1.6%* (56)
More than 2 community programs	8.5% (70)	4.0% (70)	0.6% (70)	2.4% (70)
2 or fewer cultural events	8.1% (56)	3.4% (56)	0.7% (56)	1.4%* (56)
More than 2 cultural events	8.3% (72)	4.0% (72)	0.6% (72)	2.6% (72)
Month celebration[3]	9.2[a] (101)	4.1% (57)	0.9% (30)	2.6% (33)
No month celebration	4.3% (28)	3.2% (71)	0.6% (99)	1.9% (95)
Recruit minority students	6%[b] (76)	3.4% (76)	0.4%[a] (76)	2.3% (76)
No recruit minority students	10.7% (48)	4.5% (48)	0.9% (48)	2.1% (48)
Recruit minority faculty	9.7% (30)	5.9%[b] (30)	0.6% (30)	3.4%[b] (30)
No recruit minority faculty	7.8% (91)	3.0% (91)	0.6% (91)	1.7% (91)

continued

TABLE **3.1** (*continued*)

	Percent Black	Percent Hispanic	Percent Indian	Percent Asian
Any race scholarship	6.5%[a] (52)	4% (52)	0.6% (52)	2.2% (52)
No race scholarship	10.1% (63)	3.5% (63)	0.7% (63)	2.3% (63)
Specific race[4] scholarship	6.7% (51)	4.8%* (43)	0.5% (36)	2.3 (35)
No specific race scholarship	9.9% (64)	3.1% (72)	0.7% (79)	2.2% (80)
Train faculty	7.4% (27)	5.9%[a] (27)	0.4% (27)	3.4%[b] (27)
No train faculty	8% (95)	3.2% (95)	0.7% (95)	1.8% (95)
Student committee	7.3% (52)	4.3% (52)	0.6% (52)	2.8%[a] (52)
No student committee	8.2% (74)	3.4% (74)	.6% (74)	1.8% (74)
2 or fewer multicultural student organizations	5.9% [a] (50)	4.2% (50)	0.4% (50)	2.8% [a] (50)
More than 2 multicultural student organizations	9.1% (76)	3.5% (76)	0.8% (76)	1.8% (76)
Ethnic courses	8.2% (89)	3.8% (89)	0.4%[b] (89)	2.1% (89)
No ethnic courses	7.5% (46)	3.7% (46)	1% (46)	2.1% (46)
Specific race[5] courses	8.7% (76)	5.7% [a] (21)	0.4% (37)	10.7% [c] (4)
No specific race courses	7.1% (59)	3.4% (114)	0.7% (98)	1.9% (131)
1 or 0 total race courses	7.9% (48)	2.7%* (48)	1%[b](48)	1.7%* (48)
More than 1 total race courses	8% (87)	4.3% (87)	0.4% (87)	2.4% (87)

1. * = significantly different at .1 level; a = significantly different at .05 level; b = significantly different at .01 level.

2. Each racial group is tested by whether the college or university has a program for it. Thus when measuring the percentage of African Americans in an educational institution, I looked at programs of African American studies. For Hispanic Americans, I looked at Hispanic American studies, and so forth. To keep the table reasonably short, all four groups are included on this line of the table.

3. I contrasted the percentage of each group with celebration of the relevant group. For example, Asian Americans students were compared with Asian Pacific Islander heritage month. This was done for all four minority racial groups.

4. This variable sought the effect of scholarships targeting a particular group. Thus the percentage of Native American students was explored if the school provided scholarships for Native Americans. This was done for all four minority racial groups.

5. Thus I compared the percentage of African Americans to whether there were courses about African Americans, the percentage of Hispanic Americans to whether there were courses about Hispanic Americans, the percentage of Native Americans to whether there were courses about Native Americans, and the percentage of Asian Americans to whether there were courses about Asian Americans.

more than 5 multicultural programs, and 69 of them indicated more than 5 such programs. This leaves two groups of roughly equal size for comparison. However, it was not always possible to get groups of equal size.

The results of table 3–1 provide important insight into the presence of these initiatives and the racial diversity on these campuses. For African Americans, the only initiatives significantly positively correlated with a higher percentage of African American students are the celebration of black history month and the presence of multicultural student organizations.[1] For example, colleges and universities that celebrated black history month are 9.2 percent black, and those that did not are only 4.3 percent black. Those that had more than two multicultural student organizations were 9.1 percent black, and those with no more than two multicultural student organizations were only 5.9 percent black. Interestingly, statements on race, a diversity office, and a minority scholarship were significantly negatively related to the percentage of blacks at a college or university. Most of the diversity initiatives are simply not related to a higher percentage of African Americans.

There is a similar outcome for Native American students. The only diversity initiative positively and significantly related to a higher percentage of Native American students is the total number of diversity courses of instruction that a college or university offered. None of the other initiatives is significantly tied to a higher percentage of Native-American students, and some initiatives, such as efforts to recruit minority students, even have a negatively significant relationship with the percentage of Native American students.

There is more evidence that diversity initiatives are related to the relative number of Hispanic and Asian American students on a given Protestant campus. Protestant colleges and universities with Hispanic studies programs, attempts to recruit minority faculty, scholarships aimed at Hispanics, diversity training for faculty, courses that deal with Hispanic American issues, and courses that in general deal with racial issues have higher percentages of Hispanic American students than other Protestant colleges and universities. Likewise, those institutions that offered more than two chapel talks on racial issues, a statement on race or ethnicity, Asian American studies programs, community programs, non-European cultural events, minority faculty recruitment, diversity training for faculty, a student committee for diversity issues, courses that deal with Asian American issues, and courses that in general deal with racial issues have higher percentages of Asian American students than other institutions. Although diversity initiatives are generally not related to higher percentages of African American and Native American students, they do appear to be related to increased numbers of Hispanic and Asian American students.

It is worthwhile to ask what Hispanic Americans and Asian Americans have in common. These two racial groups have largely come to the United States as immigrants. This is different from the experiences of Native Americans, who faced an invasion from European Americans, and from African Americans, who were forced into the United States. It is possible that this historical immigrant experience has an effect on why these groups are more likely to be influenced by diversity initiatives. These experiences may have contributed to a perception of these groups as foreigners or outsiders to the American mainstream (Pyke & Dang 2003, Tuan 1998, Wu 2003). They may seek signals that they will be welcomed by majority group members. Efforts to exhibit inclusiveness may be more attractive to these racial groups than to African Americans and Native Americans, for whom there is evidence of a powerful sense of alienation (McGary 1998, Yancey 2003b) and a strong oppositional nature (Ogbu 1978, 1990). Students from these groups may not have a strong desire to become integrated into mainstream society. Thus the same institutional efforts that may have some success in attracting Hispanic Americans and Asian Americans can be less potent with African Americans and Native Americans. The former groups may be more open toward assimilative efforts than the latter groups.

Finally, it is vital to ask what sorts of diversity initiatives are effectively related to these higher numbers of Hispanic American and Asian American students. For both groups, training faculty and recruiting minority faculty are positively related to higher percentages of these minority students. This clearly indicates that faculty issues are related to attracting these immigrant minority students. It suggests a new dimension not discussed in my previous speculations. It is possible that there is a faculty dimension in that the faculty has an important impact on the atmosphere of diversity present at a Protestant campus.[2] Furthermore, these students are attracted to campuses that offer courses about their particular racial group and courses in race and ethnicity in general. Thus curriculum issues have to also be considered in assessing how to attract individuals of color. Finally, sponsored events such as multicultural or community programs appear to be related to an increase in Asian Americans, but such programs appear to have little effect on Hispanic Americans. The educational dimension is a more important dimension in explaining minority student retention.

It is also important to assess the ability of Protestant colleges and universities to retain the students of color they are able to attract. In table 3.2, I show the graduation rates of each of the minority groups, separated by whether the educational institution utilizes a given diversity initiative. Thus Protestant campuses with race and ethnicity offices graduate 38.7 percent of their African American students, and those without such offices graduate only 30.5 percent of their African American students. This difference is significant at the .1 level. When I combine this with the fact that in all four racial minority groups there are significantly higher percentages of students graduating from schools with race and ethnicity

TABLE **3.2** Percentages of Graduate Rates of Black, Hispanic, Indian, and Asian American Students by Diversity Initiatives

	Black	Hispanic	Indian	Asian
Race/ethnicity office	38.7%* (86)	49.7%* (87)	48.8% (52)	56.7% (80)
No race/ethnicity office	30.5% (51)	38.8% (48)	32% (32)	41.6% (37)
2 or fewer chapel talks	30.7% (71)	43.9% (67)	39.9% (42)	47.3%* (56)
More than 2 chapel talks	40.3% (71)	42.9% (67)	39.9% (42)	47.3% (56)
Race statement	36.3%* (97)	47.2% (95)	40.4% (61)	53.1% (84)
No race statement	31.1% (35)	42.2% (34)	48.4% (20)	44.1% (29)
General ethnic studies	29.9% (22)	45.9% (20)	26.6% (14)	55.3% (18)
No general ethnic studies	36.4% (114)	45.5% (114)	45% (69)	51.2% (98)
Specific racial group studies	46.1% (14)	54.6%* (11)	0%* (3)	62.2% (10)
No specific racial group studies	34.7% (121)	45.9% (121)	43% (79)	50.2% (105)
0 or 1 antiracism programs	34.5% (45)	44.9% (44)	31.7%*(29)	44.4%* (32)
More than 1 antiracism program	36.3% (85)	46.2% (83)	48.3% (52)	56.9% (78)
5 or fewer multi-cultural programs	32.2% (63)	40.4%* (60)	36.5% (38)	49.7% (50)
More than 5 multicultural programs	39% (67)	50.5% (67)	47.6% (43)	56.2% (60)
2 or fewer community programs	32.6% (57)	45.7% (54)	41.5% (34)	52.8% (45)
More than 2 community programs	36.6% (70)	46.3% (69)	40.2% (44)	52.1% (62)
2 or fewer cultural events	29.5%[a] (55)	48.9% (50)	44.6% (34)	53.5%* (40)
More than 2 cultural events	40.3% (74)	45.3% (74)	41.5% (47)	52.5% (69)
Month celebration	37.8% (103)	48.9% (58)	53.3% (20)	58.4% (32)

continued

TABLE **3.2** (*continued*)

	Black	Hispanic	Indian	Asian
No month celebration	35.5% (27)	44.9% (67)	39.8% (62)	50.4% (77)
Recruit minority students	39% (79)	49.7% (77)	40% (52)	53.6% (71)
No recruit minority students	32.1% (46)	43.9% (45)	47.7% (26)	51% (36)
Recruit minority faculty	38.8% (31)	47.1%[b] (29)	41.6% (20)	56.9% (29)
No recruit minority faculty	35.7% (91)	47.8% (89)	42.4% (56)	51.5% (75)
Any race scholarship	37% (53)	45.1% (53)	42.1% (41)	51.5% (48)
No race scholarship	36.6% (62)	47.2% (56)	50.9% (32)	57.9% (50)
Specific race scholarship	37.6% (51)	47.2%[*] (42)	50.9% (27)	57.9% (30)
No specific race scholarship	36.1% (64)	45.5% (67)	36.6% (46)	51.3% (68)
Train faculty	33% (30)	48.6% (29)	50% (17)	55.3% (26)
No train faculty	36.7% (93)	46.3% (92)	39.9% (58)	50.5% (79)
Student committee	40.9%[*] (54)	48.3% (54)	44.3% (33)	55.1% (48)
No student committee	33% (73)	45.9% (70)	40.4% (46)	50.8% (60)
2 or fewer multicultural student organizations	30.9%[b] (77)	43.1%[*] (75)	31.2%[b] (46)	47.9%[*] (81)
More than 2 multicultural student organizations	44.7% (50)	52.9% (49)	57.2% (33)	58.9% (47)
Ethnic courses	38.1% (92)	46.6% (85)	40.7% (57)	51.6% (81)
No ethnic courses	30.2% (59)	45.1% (47)	42.8% (26)	53.5% (34)
Specific race courses	38.3% (76)	46.5% (22)	38.3% (27)	38.2% (4)
No specific race courses	32.1% (59)	46% (110)	42.8% (56)	52.6% (111)
1 or 0 total race courses	27.2%[b] (46)	45.2% (49)	44% (26)	53.2% (37)
More than 1 total race courses	39.9% (89)	46.6% (83)	40.1% (57)	51.6% (78)

[*] = significantly different at .1 level; a = significantly different at .05 level;
b = significantly different at .01 level.

offices than from those without such offices, I have some confidence that these offices are creating an atmosphere that helps retain students of color.

What else is important to the retention of minority students? Students in all four minority groups were more likely to graduate if they attended schools with more than two multicultural student organizations. Thus the more powerful predictors of graduation of minority students across the different racial groups were if the college or university sponsored an office that dealt with the issues of minority students and if it had student-led organizations that focused on multicultural issues. It is not unreasonable to think that such offices probably lead to the development of these organizations and that these two factors work together.[3] Later in the chapter, I speculate about the implications of a possible linkage.

There are other significant variables as well. For example, having a statement on racial diversity, more than two non-European cultural events, a student-led committee on diversity, and more than two courses on race are positively connected to higher graduation rates for African American students. Having a Hispanic American studies program and more than five multicultural programs is linked to a higher graduation rate for Hispanic American students. Having more than one antiracism program is connected to higher graduation rates for Native Americans and Asian-Americans. But these effects are sporadic when we look across racial groups, and thus the most powerful predictors of minority student graduation rates remain the existence of a race or ethnicity office and student multicultural groups.

As I noted earlier, the potential differences between mainline and evangelical Protestants have to also be taken into account. For this reason, I decided to analyze mainline and conservative schools separately. To simplify my analysis, I looked at one minority racial group at a time. Thus table 3.3 explores diversity measures in relation to African Americans, table 3.4 explores diversity measures in relation to Hispanic Americans, table 3.5 explores diversity measures in relation to Native Americans, and table 3.6 explores diversity measures in relation to Asian Americans. To keep from utilizing tables with so much data that it would be difficult to go through them, I also decided to include only variables where there was a positive significant relationship either in attracting members of that racial minority group or in a higher graduation rate of that group.[4]

In table 3.3, we gain reconfirmation that diversity efforts are generally not related to a higher percentage of African Americans on campus. Only the celebration of black history month is positively related to a higher percentage of African Americans students. Furthermore, this was significant only on conservative Protestant campuses. Those campuses that celebrated black history month are 10.9 percent black; those that did not are only 4.7 percent black. On conservative campuses, several diversity initiatives are correlated with a higher graduation rate for African Americans: campuses with more than two

TABLE **3.3** Percentages and Graduation Rates of African Americans, by
Selected Diversity Initiatives and Type of College or University

	% in School		Graduation Rate	
	Conservative Protestant	Mainline Protestant	Conservative Protestant	Mainline Protestant
2 or fewer chapel talks			25.9%[a] (35)	35.3% (36)
More than 2 chapel talks			42% (32)	37.9% (22)
2 or fewer cultural events			30% (33)	28.6%[a] (22)
More than 2 cultural events			36% (33)	43.8% (41)
Month celebration	10.9[a] (49)	7.7% (52)		
No month celebration	4% (17)	4.7% (11)		
Student committee			45.5%[b] (25)	36.9% (29)
No student committee			26.4% (40)	41% (33)
2 or fewer multicultural student organizations			28.8%[a] (45)	34% (30)
More than 2 multicultural student organizations			44.9% (20)	44.5% (32)
Ethnic courses			38.9%[*] (42)	37.5% (50)
No ethnic courses			27.7% (29)	35.4% (14)
Specific race courses			41.9%[b] (47)	41.9%[a] (42)
No specific race courses			23.5 (17)	27.6% (22)

* = significantly different at .1 level; a = significantly different at .05 level;
b = significantly different at .01 level.

chapel talks on racial issues, a student committee on diversity, more than two
multicultural student groups, ethnic courses, and courses that dealt with African Americans. Among mainline schools only having more than two cultural
events and having courses that deal with African Americans are linked to a
higher graduation rate.

TABLE 3.4   Percentages and Graduation Rates of Hispanic Americans, by
Selected Diversity Initiatives and Type of College or University

	% in School		Graduation Rate	
	Conservative Protestant	Mainline Protestant	Conservative Protestant	Mainline Protestant
Race/ethnicity office			50.1% (43)	49.3%* (44)
No race/ethnicity office			42.3% (26)	34.6% (22)
5 or fewer multicultural programs			43.8% (35)	35.6%ª (25)
More than 5 multicultural programs			48.7% (30)	52% (37)
Month celebration	5.6% (22)	3.2%* (35)		
No month celebration	4.1% (43)	1.7% (28)		
Recruit minority faculty	7.8%ª (15)	3.9%* (15)		
No recruit minority faculty	4% (46)	2.2% (45)		
Specific race scholarship	5.4% (22)	4.2%ᵇ (21)		
No specific race scholarship	4.3% (35)	1.9% (37)		
Train faculty	7.1%* (17)	3.7% (10)		
No train faculty	4% (45)	2.4% (50)		
2 or fewer multicultural student organizations			47.2% (43)	37.5%ª (32)
More than 2 multicultural student organizations			48.0% (20)	55.7% (29)
Specific race courses	5.9% (11)	5.4%ᶜ (10)		
No specific race courses	4.7% (59)	2% (55)		
1 or 0 total race courses	3.3%* (30)	1.8% (18)		
More than 1 total race course	6% (40)	2.8% (47)		

* = significantly different at .1 level; a = significantly different at .05 level;
b = significantly different at .01 level.

These findings suggest that there is little either conservative or mainline Protestant campuses can do to attract African Americans. However, academic courses and students' participation in multicultural student organizations on conservative Protestant campuses may contribute to a higher graduation rate for African Americans. Diversity initiatives are less effective on mainline Protestant campuses.

Diversity initiatives are more likely to encourage attendance of Hispanic students (table 3.4). Conservative Protestant campuses that overtly attempt to recruit minority faculty, train current faculty, and have more than a single course that deals with racial issues have significantly higher percentages of Hispanic students. Mainline Protestant campuses that celebrate Hispanic heritage month, seek to recruit minority faculty, offer scholarships aimed at Hispanics, and have courses specifically aimed at Hispanics have significantly higher percentages of Hispanic students. None of the diversity initiatives is significantly positive in predicting the graduation rate of Hispanic students at conservative Protestant educational institutions. But for mainline Protestant campuses, an office that deals with racial issues, more than five multicultural programs, and more than two multicultural student organizations are correlated with higher graduation rates for Hispanic students.

The results for Hispanic American students differ from the results of African American students in two key ways. First, more of the initiatives help explain the attendance of Hispanic students relative to black students, but fewer initiatives help explain their graduation rate relative to black students. Second, for African Americans, diversity initiatives are more predictive on conservative Protestant campuses than on mainline campuses, but the reverse is true for Hispanic students.

The reality of Native American students is similar to that of African American students. On table 3–5, we once again see that only celebration of Native American heritage month is predictive of Native American students' attendance and then only on conservative Protestant campuses. But none of the diversity initiatives is positively significantly predictive of higher graduation rates for Native American students on conservative Protestant campuses. Mainline Protestant campuses with an office devoted to dealing with racial issues, Native American scholarships, and more than two multicultural student organizations have higher graduation rates of their Native American students. Thus few diversity initiatives are correlated with a more conducive atmosphere for Native American students.

The reverse is true for Asian American students. A wide variety of diversity initiatives are positively correlated to an atmosphere that welcomes and keeps Asian American students (table 3.6). Conservative Protestant campuses with more than two cultural events, minority faculty recruitment, faculty training, a

TABLE **3.5** Percentages and Graduation Rates of Native-Americans, by
Selected Diversity Initiatives and Type of College or University[1]

	% in School		Graduation Rate	
	Conservative Protestant	Mainline Protestant	Conservative Protestant	Mainline Protestant
Race/ethnicity office			43.7% (26)	54%[b] (26)
No race/ethnicity office			40.5% (17)	20.2% (15)
Month celebration	1.2[b] (12)	0.6% (18)		
No month celebration	0.5% (54)	0.7% (45)		
Specific race scholarship			41.9% (11)	57%[a] (16)
No specific race scholarship			41.9% (25)	30.8% (21)
2 or fewer multicultural student organizations			34.5% (26)	59%[b] (19)
More than 2 multicultural student organizations			54.8% (14)	26.8% (20)

1. * = significantly different at .1 level; a = significantly different at .05 level;
b = significantly different at .01 level.

student-led diversity committee, more than two multicultural student organizations, Asian American courses, and more than one course that deals with race have higher percentages of Asian Americans. Mainline Protestant campuses with an office that deals with racial issues, more than one antiracism program, more than five multicultural programs, more than two community programs, celebration of Asian Pacific American heritage month, recruitment of minority students, scholarships based on race, and more than two multicultural student organizations have higher percentages of Asian American students. While for both types of campuses a fairly wide variety of initiatives were significant, for conservative Protestant campuses, overt efforts to recruit minority faculty and students and the inclusion of diversity academic courses typified what appears to attract Asian American students. For mainline Protestant campuses, the use of institutional diversity programs is relevant to the attendance of Asian American students.

Diversity initiatives are less relevant to the graduation rate of Asian American students. On conservative Protestant campuses, there are not any variables significant to the .1 level, but having more than two multicultural student organizations is almost significant ($p = .102$). On mainline campuses, having an office that deals with race and ethnicity and having more than two chapel talks

TABLE **3.6** Percentages and Graduation Rates of Asian Americans, by Selected Diversity Initiatives and Type of College or University[1]

	% in School		Graduation Rate	
	Conservative Protestant	Mainline Protestant	Conservative Protestant	Mainline Protestant
Race/ethnicity office	2.6% (44)	1.7%[a] (45)	60.5% (41)	52.6%* (39)
No race/ethnicity office	2.9% (27)	1.1% (22)	47.6% (21)	33.7% (16)
2 or less chapel talks			55.5% (31)	58.7%* (19)
More than 2 chapel talks			54.1% (28)	40.4% (28)
0 or 1 antiracism program	2% (30)	1.1%* (17)		
more than 1 antiracism program	3.1% (37)	1.7% (46)		
5 or fewer multicultural programs	2.2% (36)	1%[b] (25)		
More than 5 multicultural programs	3.1% (31)	1.8% (38)		
2 or fewer community programs	2.2% (29)	1.1%[b] (27)		
More than 2 community programs	2.9% (38)	1.8% (32)		
2 or fewer cultural events	1.8%[a] (34)	.9% (22)		
More than 2 cultural events	3.5% (31)	1.9% (41)		
Month celebration	3.1% (15)	2.2%[c] (18)		
No month celebration	2.5% (50)	1.2% (45)		
Recruit minority students	3% (36)	1.8%[a] (40)		
No recruit minority students	2.9% (26)	1.1% (22)		
Recruit minority faculty	4.6%[a] (15)	2.1% (15)		
No recruit minority faculty	2.2% (46)	1.3% (45)		

continued

TABLE **3.6** (*continued*)

	% in School		Graduation Rate	
	Conservative Protestant	Mainline Protestant	Conservative Protestant	Mainline Protestant
Any race scholarship	2.5% (25)	1.9%[a] (27)		
No race scholarship	3.2% (32)	1.3% (31)		
Train faculty	4.2%[a] (17)	2.1% (10)		
No train faculty	2.2% (45)	1.4% (50)		
Student committee	4.2%[a] (23)	1.7% (29)		
No student committee	2.1% (41)	1.4% (33)		
2 or less multicultural student organizations	2.3%[a] (44)	1.1%[b] (32)	50.4%^{2} (37)	44.2% (24)
More than 2 multicultural student organizations	4.1% (29)	2% (30)	65.1% (19)	54.7% (28)
Specific race courses	10.7%[c] (4)	---		
No specific race courses	2.2% (66)			
1 or 0 total race courses	1.9%* (30)	1.2% (18)		
More than 1 total race courses	3.3% (40)	1.6% (47)		

1. * = significantly different at .1 level; a = significantly different at .05 level;
b = significantly different at .01 level.
2. $P = .102$

on diversity are also significant regarding a higher graduation rate of Asian American students. Thus while diversity initiatives may play a role in attracting Asian American students to Protestant campuses, they appear to be less predictive of whether such students stay until degree completion.

Looking across the racial groups provides further insight into which diversity programs create an atmosphere conducive to racial diversity. For example, in all four racial groups, having more than two multicultural student organizations is, or nearly is, significantly correlated with higher graduation rates of the minority group. For African American and Asian American students, this effect is seen at conservative schools; for Hispanic and Native American students, it is present at mainline institutions. These student organizations may create a social atmosphere that makes it easier for minority students to complete their degrees. The presence of an office of race and ethnicity is also correlated to higher graduation rates at mainline institutions for all groups except African Americans. Concerning the actual diversity of the school, celebrating the month of each group is linked to higher percentages of each minority racial group. Somehow Protestant colleges and universities engaging in such celebrations are able to do a better job of attracting students of color. Perhaps this celebration reduces internal interracial conflict on campus by providing enlightenment or creates a more hospitable social atmosphere for people of color, or it may simply be that colleges and universities that engaged in such celebrations are located in areas with more racial diversity and thus have more opportunities to recruit students of color.[5]

There were variables that rose in importance when both percentage of minority students and minority student graduation rates were considered. For example, offering courses in the specific racial tradition of each group had varying effects. African American courses were positively related to the graduation rates of black students at both conservative and mainline Protestant campuses. Hispanic American and Asian American courses were positively related to the percentages of Hispanic American students in conservative institutions and Asian American students in mainline institutions, respectively. Furthermore, the total number of courses offered concerning race and ethnicity is related to the percentages of Hispanic American and Asian American students in conservative institutions. This indicates that the educational dimension is quite important for explaining racial diversity.

At the other end of the spectrum, what did not show up as important is noteworthy. Generally speaking, if we exclude the effect of history months on the attendance of African American and Native American students and the effects of multicultural programs on the graduation rate of African American and Hispanic students on mainline campuses, institutional diversity programs had little relationship to racial diversity on Protestant campuses. The only other exception was in predicting the percentages of Asian American students on mainline campuses. Even among Asian Americans, the only such programs to be effective on conservative campuses were non-European cultural events. These tables suggest that institutional diversity programs are likely to be effective only in the recruitment of Asian American students, and then only for mainline Protestant campuses. These are definitely less robust findings than what was observed with diversity courses, which seem to have effects across the different minority student groups and on both conservative and mainline Protestant campuses.

Because people of color generally have more modest financial resources than majority group students, efforts to meet their financial concerns should make it easier for them to attend and graduate from institutions of higher education. But the results of this research do not provide tremendous support for such an assertion. On table 3.1, we see that only among Hispanic students are scholarships aimed at a racial group positively correlated to a higher percentage of minority students. Offering racial scholarships in general or for a particular minority group was not positively significantly correlated to a higher graduation rate for any of the minority racial groups. There is some evidence that financial aid has limited effectiveness on mainline campuses. On mainline campuses, Hispanics were more likely to attend if offered scholarships specifically for Hispanics, Native American students were more likely to graduate at schools that offered scholarships specifically for Native Americans, and Asian Americans were more likely to attend schools that offered scholarships based on race in general. Financial aid was not shown to be linked to an increase in minority student population or higher graduation rates in any of the measures for conservative Protestant schools. The results concerning the effectiveness of financial aid are overall weak in comparison to the findings concerning the educational and interpersonal dimensions of encouraging diversity. In chapter 5, we will see more evidence that financial concerns are not students' most pressing reason to attend the Protestant college or university where they are.

Valuable general findings can be cultivated from this assessment. First, there seems to be relatively little that Protestant colleges and universities can do institutionally to enhance their ability to attract African Americans and Native Americans. Except for the inclusion of black history month and Native American heritage month, there seems to be little that conservative Protestant colleges can do that may possibly attract, respectively, African American and Native American students. This seems to be a minor change to be recommended to conservative Protestant educational institutions, given the number of other possible diversity initiatives tested. However, as we will see in the next couple of chapters, such celebrations also bring their own particular problems. For mainline Protestant educational institutions, none of the diversity initiatives is related to higher percentages of African Americans or Native Americans on their campuses.

The second assertion involves Hispanic and Asian American students. Multiple diversity initiatives appear to be correlated with the percentage of these students on Protestant campuses. These effects may be shaped by the fact that these groups tend to come from immigrants. Individuals from such groups may appreciate organizational diversity efforts as a way to experience acceptance into the mainstream of society. While a variety of programs attracted immigrant minority groups, issues of faculty and curriculum appear to provide the most consistent effects for drawing such students. Thus the educational dimension appears to be important for attracting Hispanic and Asian American students. Having an office that addresses diversity issues and encouraging multicultural student organizations are clearly the two most important measures that help to create an atmosphere conducive to minority student graduation. These efforts may encourage the type of peer support vital to retain immigrant students of color. This suggests that addressing the interpersonal and political needs of minority students is an important feature in creating an educational environment that supports racial diversity.

The value of multiple diversity initiatives was true for both conservative and mainline campuses as it concerned Hispanic American students but truer on mainline campuses as it concerned Asian American students. Diversity initiatives that are not effective in other contexts could still be effective in attracting Asian American students. For example, only at mainline Protestant campuses and with this population is there a discernible and consistent effect of institutional programs such as antiracism, community events, and multicultural events, as shown in table 3–6. It may be the case that the actual program is less important than the fact that a college or university is making an effort to address issues of diversity. Thus a holistic effort to foster racial diversity can be important for signaling Asian American students about an accepting racial atmosphere. Since Asian Americans are often perceived as outsiders in our society (Pyke & Dang 2003, Tuan 1998), students from this racial group may be worried about facing rejection at their educational institution.

Third, there are differences between conservative and mainline campuses. For example, chapel talks, student committees, multicultural student organizations, ethnic courses, and African American courses are positively significantly related to a higher graduation rate for blacks on conservative campuses. For mainline campuses only, non-European cultural events and African American courses indicate a higher black graduation rate. Thus diversity measures are more effective in retaining African Americans on conservative campuses relative to mainline campuses. However, in other racial minority groups, diversity measures are more effective on mainline, instead of conservative, campuses. For example, none of the diversity variables is linked to higher graduation rates for Hispanic Americans on conservative campuses, but three of the measures (having a race or ethnicity office, having multicultural programs, and having multicultural student groups) are significant in predicting a higher graduation rate on mainline campuses. The same is true for Native Americans in that there were three measures (having a race or ethnicity office, offering a scholarship for Native American students, and having multicultural student groups) that are significantly positively related to the graduation rate of Native Americans on mainline campuses, but none on conservative campuses. For Asian American students, the story is different. A wide variety of measures positively predicted a higher percentage of Asian Americans students on mainline and conservative campuses. Relatively few measures positively predicted the graduation rate of Asian Americans. Generally, diversity initiatives are more effective for predicting the retention of black students on conservative campuses and retention of Hispanics and Native Americans on mainline campuses. Their effectiveness is relatively similar on both conservative and mainline campuses for Asian American students.

These differing levels of effectiveness do not appear to shape the overall ability of conservative and mainline Protestant campuses to attract students of color. There is not much of a difference between conservative and mainline Protestant educational institutions in the percentage of white students who attend them (77.9 percent for mainline campuses versus 76.7 percent for conservative campuses: $p = .195$). However, there are conservative-mainline differences in the percentages of Hispanic and Asian American students on campus. Conservative campuses have a significantly higher percentage of Hispanic American (4.2 percent versus 3.0 percent: $p < .01$) and Asian American students (2.5 percent versus 2.0 percent: $p < .1$). Diversity initiatives at mainline campuses have not enabled them to attract as many Hispanic American students as conservative campuses.

A similar story about the unique effect on black students can be seen in the graduation rates of minority students. The only significant difference in graduation rates is found among African Americans. Black students at mainline campuses are significantly more likely to graduate (42.44 percent versus 35.49 percent: $p < .05$). There is no significant conservative-mainline difference in graduation rates within any of the other minority groups. It is possible that the diversity initiatives on mainline campuses may have helped to create this difference among African Americans, but the insignificant differences found with the other minority racial groups indicates the limits of these diversity initiatives in fostering a conservative-mainline distinction.

In chapter 2, I discussed Tinto's model, which suggested that goal attainment and social integration are key in explaining student retention. If Tinto's model is accurate, then it provides insight into why students of color may be uncomfortable at Protestant educational institutions. Although all educational institutions have a challenge in the promotion of goal attainment and integration of students of color, Protestant educational institutions may face greater barriers. Many of the Protestant educational institutions were started by denominations that focused on majority group concerns. It is reasonable to assert that such institutions are not prepared to motivate nonwhites to complete their degrees. Thus these institutions may struggle to support students of color to highly value educational attainment. Such students would have to find support for their academic endeavors from their peers. This may be why having an office and student organizations to address minority student issues is vital for retaining students of color. Such mechanisms may provide opportunities for students of color to receive support from academic peers.

I earlier suggested that addressing the political and interpersonal needs of students of color may be vital for creating a more supportive atmosphere.

However, it is plausible that linking race or ethnicity offices and multicultural student organizations indicates a greater importance of interpersonal needs over political concerns. Although offices of race and ethnicity can help students of color address political issues, they also can encourage social networks that meet the interpersonal needs of students of color. Multicultural student organizations can be used to address the political needs of students of color, but we will see in later chapters that those focusing on the specific needs of a given racial group are less effective in supporting diversity than those that help to unite students of different races. This suggests that promotion of a political agenda that seems to favor one group over others does not help student-led organizations produce a more accepting racial atmosphere. Thus it is unlikely that these offices' success in retaining students of color is largely based on political activism. It is more likely that the interpersonal, rather than the political, support provided by these offices and by multicultural student organizations accounts for the results picked up in these data.[6]

Because students of color are less likely to obtain their degrees than majority group members regardless of whether they attend a sectarian or nonsectarian institution, it is not clear whether Protestant educational institutions present higher than normal barriers for such students to graduate. It is not my intention to make such an argument. Indeed, it can be argued that since African Americans, and to a lesser extent Hispanic Americans, have a higher degree of religiosity than majority group members, religious campuses may be able to create a more hospitable atmosphere for these groups than state or nonreligious private campuses. I find no evidence in the data I collected that the graduation rates of students of color are dramatically different based on the religious nature of the campus.[7] Thus, it is not immediately clear which findings can be generalized to nonreligious schools. However, these findings are a valuable starting point for gaining more of an understanding of which factors shape the educational outcomes of students of color.

The implication of these findings is that the most important predictors of attendance of minority students are efforts to create a more diverse and diversity-trained faculty and a more diverse curriculum. The data also suggest a faculty dimension that helps to account for diversity and supports the importance of the educational dimension. But these initiatives were effective only for immigrant minority groups. Perhaps there are ways in which such initiatives can be altered to attract African American and Native American students, but the results of this quantitative work do not immediately indicate such possibilities. Efforts to encourage minority group retention should include an office to deal with race and ethnicity issues and promotion of multicultural student organizations. Whether we are considering attracting more students of color into a given educational institution or retaining the students of color who already attend that institution, we are still addressing issues of student diversity. There-fore, all of the initiatives found to be relevant to increasing that diversity must be taken into account for Protestant educators who desire to promote racial diversity on their campuses. Given this reality, this work recommends that such educators should promote changes in the curriculum, address issues of faculty diversity and diversity training, and develop student-led diversity orga-nizations.

By contrast, efforts such as financial aid and institutional diversity pro-grams do not appear to have a consistent effect on either attracting students of color or retaining the students of color who already attend the Protestant cam-pus. The only exception to this trend was with Asian American students, where it seems that the very fact that efforts are made may attract such students. If Asian American students are not the main target of educators on Protestant campuses, then they may not want to emphasize financial aid programs and institutional diversity programs as ways of increasing racial diversity on their campuses.

Conclusion

So far, I have analyzed information gained from a survey of Protestant educa-tional institutions. The information sheds light on the possibilities, and the limitations, of efforts to increase racial diversity at Protestant colleges and uni-versities. These results are incomplete, but we should assess what we know thus far. We know that the best way to attract and retain students of color involves some combination of faculty issues, multicultural student organizations, and curriculum alterations.

As I noted earlier, my previous work has shown that the presence of faculty of color is correlated to student racial diversity within all colleges and univer-sities. The presence of in-group racial minority professors is linked to the attendance of students of color at these Protestant campuses as well.[8] Although I did not directly use the information to test for the possible effects of hiring more faculty of color, the fact that colleges and universities that make efforts to recruit faculty of color are also able to attract Hispanics and Asian Americans indicates that having a more diverse faculty helps to diversify the student body.[9]

These reforms probably work in concert to produce an atmosphere that encourages students of color to come and stay at these Protestant schools. For example, it is plausible that curriculum alterations produce the need to hire faculty of color. At the very least, they create courses where faculty of color are more likely to have expertise. I have already argued that having an office that deals with issues of race and ethnicity is likely to lead to the creation of more student multicultural organizations. It is also plausible that such offices and student multicultural organizations produce more demand for the diversity courses that create the need for minority faculty. They may also advocate for diversity training of current faculty members, especially if there is a racial incident as a precipitating event. If there is a political dimension that promotes racial diversity, it may do so indirectly by promoting the development of diverse curriculum and faculty, rather than directly by promoting political awareness among students of color. The likely interaction between the variables found to be effective in promoting racial diversity is definitely an area that needs further exploration.

But such exploration is better done with qualitative, rather than quantitative, measures. Thus, these findings are tentative until we can obtain a qualitative understanding of what is behind them. The instruments used to generate the findings in this chapter are not the best for establishing powerful causal arguments or for helping us understand the nuances that buttress these results. To further determine the important institutional mechanisms that may be used to recruit and graduate students of color, it is useful to talk to students themselves. Such qualitative work can document how students of color perceive the institutional efforts of their college or university to create racial diversity. This analysis can also help us perceive whether diversity initiatives help majority group students become allies of minority students or whether such efforts are ineffective. In the following chapter, I directly assess the attitudes of students on Protestant campuses in an effort to address some of these questions.

NOTES

1. Because of the relatively small numbers included in the analysis, I measure whether the differences were significant at the .1 level.

2. Further supporting the possibility that this is a tangible dimension is the fact that whether a college or university offers diversity training is significantly positively correlated to whether it also attempts to recruit faculty of color ($r = .231$).

3. In fact, these two variables are significantly positively correlated with each other ($r = .256$).

4. Information on the insignificant and negative relationships is available from the author.

5. Regression analysis indicated that when I controlled for percentage of a given group in the city, the effect of having a celebration month was insignificant except for Asian American students. Thus the percentage of blacks in the city was a better predictor of the percentage of blacks on campus than whether black history month was celebrated, and the effect was powerful enough to neutralize the effect of the celebration month. The same was true for Hispanic and Native American students as well. The

percentage of Asian Americans in the city was a more powerful predictor than whether a college or university celebrated Asian Pacific American history month, but the effect of celebrating that month was still significant after applying the control of city diversity.

6. Another way to investigate whether the interpersonal dimension or the political dimension is the better way to understand these findings is to look at the other variables conceptualized to illustrate these dimensions. For example, chapel talks that deal with racial issues are clearly a way in which the political agenda of students of color can be put forward. Yet such talks are positively related only with higher attendance of Asian American students and a higher graduation rate of African American students on conservative campuses. On the other hand, student committees to deal with diversity can be conceptualized as another way in which interpersonal relations help to create an atmosphere that supports racial diversity. Such committees are significantly related with higher graduation rates of African American students overall and on conservative campuses and with higher percentages of Asian American students overall and on conservative campuses. Although both chapel talks and student committees fail to show the sort of power that offices of race or ethnicity and multicultural student groups have to enhance diversity on Protestant campuses, the explanation more theoretically rooted in the interpersonal dimension (student committees) is more powerful than the one rooted in the political dimension (chapel talks).

7. I tested the graduation rates of the four minority racial groups on Protestant campuses in comparison to the other campuses in the National Center for Education Statistics. African Americans on Protestant campuses were less likely to graduate than on other campuses (42.6 percent versus 39.4 percent: $p < .05$). But comparisons with the other racial groups produced no significant differences.

8. But real evidence of this effect can also be seen by the correlations of faculty racial diversity and student racial diversity. The correlation of number of black professors and percentage of black students on campus is .542. This correlation is .418, .473, and .13 for, respectively, Hispanic, Native American, and Asian American professors and percentage of in-group students.

9. Ah, but we should ask if these efforts are actually correlated to a higher percentage of faculty that is not white. Indeed, efforts to recruit minority faculty are only positively significantly correlated to the percentage of Asian or Asian American faculty ($r = .296$: $p < .01$) and not to the percentage of African or African American professors ($r = .119$: ns), Hispanic or Hispanic American professors ($r = -.009$: ns), or Native American professors ($r = -.079$: ns).

4

The Impact of Diversity Initiatives on White Students—What Do the Students Say?

The work in the previous chapter suggests that institutional diversity programs (antiracism, multicultural, community, non-European cultural) do not appear, relative to the use of diversity faculty and curricula and student-led organizations, to have great power to enhance the ability of Protestant colleges to attract and retain certain racial groups of color. There is still a need to investigate the process by which diversity curricula and faculty may be more effective than institutional diversity programs. Listening to how students react to different diversity initiatives can provide knowledge about their potential effects. Documenting quantitative differences between Protestant campuses in their ability to attract students of color provides only part of the answer to the question of why some educational institutions are better suited for attracting students of color. Exploring how social and interpersonal mechanisms operate to attract and retain these students requires listening to the students' own words. To this end, it is valuable to ask Protestant students questions about their racialized experiences on their campuses and their perceptions about institutional efforts to increase racial diversity.

In addition to the investigation conducted with the survey of Protestant campuses, I examined the attitudes of students on these campuses toward the diversity initiatives. In this chapter, I focus on the attitudes of majority group members. In the next chapter, I come back to this research to explore whether, and how, certain diversity programs shape the lives of students of color. In the following section, I discuss the methods of obtaining Protestant students' perceptions of the diversity measures taken by their college or university.

Obtaining the Attitudes of Protestant Students

Even though I live in the Bible Belt, I work at a state school and do not have a natural outlet by which I can find students on Protestant campuses. The metropolitan area I live in does contain several Protestant schools, yet interviewing students from only those campuses would produce the possibility of a regional bias. I wanted to gather the attitudes of Protestant students from colleges around the United States, yet I did not possess sufficient funding to travel to other schools. To collect these data, I once again used the Web site Survey Monkey to gather responses. The questionnaire can be seen in figure 4.1. Several of the questions are open-ended, which allowed the students to more deeply elaborate their perspectives on the racial atmosphere on campus. The method suffers from the lack of an interviewer to probe some of the answers, and it is likely to be the case that students who are most agitated about racial issues are the ones who are most likely to respond in detail to this questionnaire. Furthermore, I make no claim that this is a random sample. Yet it provides voice to the experiences of majority and minority group members and allows us to see the similar and different ways they interpret the racial atmosphere on their campuses.

To find students to fill out the questionnaire, I contacted ten social science professors throughout the country. Six of the professors taught at a conservative Protestant campus and four of the professors taught at a mainline Protestant campus.[1] Some, but not all, professors encouraged their students' participation by offering extra credit. I collected the names of the students for professors who offered extra credit, but those professors were not allowed to see any data related to their campuses unless it was aggregated. Thus, none of the students can be identified with their particular answers. I collected answers from 460 students from these campuses. Of those students, 324 were white, 45 were black, 31 were Hispanic, 25 were Asian, 23 were multiracial, and 10 labeled themselves as other.[2] This allows enough racial variety to conduct a majority-minority comparison. More than twice as many students from conservative campuses were included in the sample than from mainline campuses (321 to 138). Females in the sample were almost twice as many as males in the sample (293 to 164).[3] These differences will be evident as I provide representative quotes.

Mainline versus Conservative Protestants

One major difference I discovered between mainline and conservative Protestants was that students at mainline Protestant campuses were less likely than students at conservative Protestant campuses to state that their faith has altered

University _____

Name _____

Classification: Freshman   Sophomore   Junior   Senior   Grad Student

Major_____

Sex: Male   Female

Race: White   Black   Hispanic   Asian   Multiracial   Other

1. Why did you choose to attend this particular college? Be sure to list any factors that were relevant to your decision.

2. Has your religious faith influenced your beliefs on racial issues?

   Yes   No

3. If yes then, how do you think your religious faith has influenced your beliefs on racial issues?

4. Do you think there is a positive racial atmosphere on this college campus? Why or why not (Please be specific)?

5. Do you generally feel comfortable on your campus because of your race? Why or why not do you feel this way?

6. Do you think that people on this campus are generally sensitive to the needs of people of your race? Why or why not?

7. Have you ever heard anything preached in a chapel service that you think helped to improve the racial atmosphere on your campus? If so then what is it and why do you think that it helped to improve the atmosphere?

8. Do you think that your college's anti-racism programs have helped improve the racial atmosphere on your campus?

   Yes   No   I do not know if we have such programs

9. If you answered yes or no then why did you answer in that way?

10. Have you participated in any anti-racism programs on your campus?

    Yes   No   I do not know if we have such programs

11. If yes then how did participating in those programs make you more or less comfortable with the racial atmosphere on the campus?

12. Do you think that your college's multicultural programs have helped improve the racial atmosphere on your campus?

    Yes   No   I do not know if we have such programs

FIGURE 4.1. Internet Survey of Students at Protestant Campuses

13. If you answered yes or no then why did you answer in that way?

14. Have you participated in any multicultural programs on your campus?

    Yes   No   I do not know if we have such programs

15. If yes then how did participating in those programs make you more or less comfortable with the racial atmosphere on the campus?

16. Do you think that your college's community programs have helped improve the racial atmosphere on your campus?

    Yes   No   I do not know if we have such programs

17. If you answered yes or no then why did you answer in that way?

18. Have you participated in any community programs on your campus?

    Yes   No   I do not know if we have such programs

19. If yes then how did participating in those programs make you more or less comfortable with the racial atmosphere on the campus?

20. Do you think that non-European cultural programs sponsored by your college (i.e. Cinco de Mayo, Indian Pow-Wows, Kwanzaa) have helped improve the racial atmosphere on your campus?

    Yes   No   I do not know if we have such programs

21. If you answered yes or no then why did you answer in that way?

22. Have you participated in any of these cultural programs?

    Yes   No

23. If yes then how did participating in those programs make you more or less comfortable with the racial atmosphere on the campus?

24. Have you participated in celebrating African-American History Month, Hispanic Heritage Month, Native American History Month or Asian American History Month at your college?

    Yes   No   I do not know if we celebrate these months

25. Do you think that these celebrations have improved or worsen the racial atmosphere at your campus? Why or why not (Please be specific)?

26. Have you taken any classes from faculty members who are racial minorities?

    Yes   No   I do not know if we have such faculty members

27. How has taking such classes influenced the way you think about racial issues?

FIGURE 4.1. (*Continued*)

28. Do you think that these professors of color improve or worsen the racial atmosphere at your campus? Why or why not (Please be specific)?

29. Have you taken classes that focused exclusively on racial issues (i.e. Sociology of Race, African-American Literature, Native-American History)?

Yes   No   I do not know if we have such classes

30. If so then which classes did you take?

31. Did these classes alter how your ideas about racial issues and if so then how did it alter your ideas?

32. Which class was most influential in changing your ideas and why?

33. Do you think that these classes have improved or worsen the racial atmosphere at your campus? Why or why not (Please be specific)?

34. Do you know of any student committee dedicated to dealing with issues of racial diversity on your campus?

Yes   No

35. If so then do you think that this committee has improved or worsen the racial atmosphere at your campus? Why or why not (Please be specific)?

36. Have you participated in any student lead multicultural organizations at your college?

Yes   No   I do not know if we have such organizations

37. Do you think that these organizations have improved or worsen the racial atmosphere at your campus? Why or why not (Please be specific)?

38. How many of your best three friends are individuals at your own race?

0   1   2   3

39. Of all of your friends at the college, what percentage of them are individuals of your own race?

40. What, if anything, do you think your college should do to improve the racial atmosphere on your campus?

their perspective on racial issues. This effect was found for both majority and minority group members and may be due to the fact that mainline institutions focus less than conservative ones on creating religious distinctions. Because of that lack of a "faith" effect, students who attend mainline Protestant colleges and universities may be less likely to differentiate themselves from students who attend nonreligious educational institutions. This is not to claim that students at mainline Protestant campuses are identical to those at non-Protestant campuses, but the difference from non-Protestant campuses may not be as great as it is for conservative Protestants. This is a useful distinction, but since there are not many differences between the two types of campuses, I will not focus too much on the mainline-conservative distinctions in my analysis of the responses of Protestant students. In fact, there will be only one other situation, discussed in chapter 5, where I will elaborate on a possible mainline-conservative effect with this qualitative analysis.

The Racial Atmosphere on Protestant Campuses

Before I assess the racial attitudes of majority group members, it is important to document how these students contributed to the racial climate on their campus. The responses of both majority and minority group members indicate the important role majority group students played in creating a racial atmosphere that discourages students of color. A majority of the students did not talk about racial strife on the campuses, but an important group did indicate that these campuses were not free from the effects of racism. A sampling of responses illustrates this propensity:

> Being Southern Baptist I believe that people should stay in their own race when it comes to relationships and other parts of family life. (Conservative White Junior Male)

> There are a lot of racists on campus. . . . There is little appreciation for diversity. (Conservative White Senior Male)

> The stigma behind our color of skin is of a "dumb Mexican who will settle for less and work for minimum wage." I encountered a couple of people with that stigma and generalization toward us at my school. (Conservative Hispanic Sophomore Male)

> [Chose the school because of] the nondiversity aspect of the school. I went to public school, which was also nondiverse and I did not want such a shock in college. (Mainline White Sophomore Female)

The reaction I get from most whites they seem be scared of me, but when they get to know me they are okay with me. (Conservative Black Senior Male)

I do not support interracial dating or marriage; however, I do think that all people are equal and deserve equal opportunities and equal rights. (Mainline White Sophomore Female)

It's not talked about but generally racial jokes are made all the time, there is more racism here than in public school HS in IL. A common saying is "I don't mind black people but I hate niggers." (Conservative White Junior Male)

I do not think that people on this campus are sensitive to the needs of Korean Americans. First of all, most people do not see the needs eye-to-eye. Since Asians and Caucasians were brought up so differently, it is hard for Caucasians to see the various needs and struggles that Asians go through on campus. Furthermore, I feel like while in class, the "white" people seem to care, in reality, they don't. (Conservative Asian Senior Female)

. . . we went to a poorer area with all white people and they would say comments about the minorities and I am one of them. (Conservative Hispanic Freshman Female)

And then there is this gem. Notice the use of "colored" by this mainline white senior female:

I think the class with the colored professor taught me the most because it forced me to look at situations from a different point of view. It changed my ideas because growing up I assumed everyone had a similar lifestyle as I did but I was dead wrong. This helped broaden my horizons by just having a colored professor, not even taking a class based around racial issues.

I use these examples to document that racial tension on Protestant campuses is quite real and must be dealt with. I do not argue that the racial tensions on Protestant campuses are any worse than at other institutions of higher education. I do not have the data that would allow me to make such an assertion. But it is a mistake to believe that Protestant campuses have been able to overcome racial tensions because of their adherence to religious principles. While I do have not the data from non-Protestant campuses that would enable me to compare the racial atmosphere of Protestant campuses to other colleges, it is fair to argue that Protestant campuses are not likely to have more harmonious racial environments than other campuses.[4]

Majority Group Responses

Majority group students clearly affect the social environment of students of color. They can help such students feel welcomed or ostracized. They can show support for institutional efforts toward diversity, or they can be a very powerful barrier to such efforts. It is one thing if students of color face racial insensitivity from an administration and can turn to their white peers for support. It is quite different if students of color must face both an insensitive administration and a hostile majority group student body. Since a major focus of this book is to explore the racialized lives of students of color, there is great value in exploring the attitudes of majority group students.

I immediately noticed a pattern among the responses of some of the majority group students toward diversity programs. Many majority group students perceived these programs as sources of racial conflict rather than solutions to racial animosity. As a result, majority group students direct a great deal of resentment at these programs. Their opinions are important because these students are the numerical and social majority on these campuses. Their nonsupport of programs that serve students of color make it more difficult for those programs to be effective.

For example, some white students on these campuses perceive the student-led multicultural committees as sources of racial division, with comments such as:

> Everyone I have talked to about it that is unfamiliar with it thinks it is a white bashing group that just needs to have some space to vent anger about race. (Conservative Junior Male)

> It has almost worsened the racial atmosphere because although many blacks and whites are friends, they generally stay to friends of the same race, and these committees enable people of other races to bond with each other, but not with other races. (Mainline Freshman Female)

> They [students on the multicultural committee] are very judgmental and stuck in the past. (Conservative Junior Female)

It is tempting to think that such student-led committees would obtain a high degree of support since they provide a certain degree of student autonomy. Indeed, the findings of the last chapter indicate that these committees can play a role in the retention of students of color. But some white students perceived them as hostile to majority group members. Yet this was not the case for all majority group students; many students did find value in these student organizations. Indeed, many majority group students did recognize that diversity student committees and/or multicultural student organizations were valuable in raising the level of awareness on campus of cultural differences or the existence of racism.

> . . . it [student committee on diversity] has improved the racial atmosphere because it brings attention to our actions and makes people think twice before doing something that could possibly offend someone. (Mainline Freshman Female)

> I know of a Pilipino culture club, which I think has improved the atmosphere because just knowing more about other cultures is helpful to having understanding and grace about some of our differences. (Conservative Senior Female)

> . . . showed us the struggles and oppressions of other cultures. (Mainline Junior Male)

> The only organization that I can think of is the diversity club. . . . I believe that [they] SIC are improving the racial atmosphere on campus. Instead of separating and making the diversity students an exclusive group, this organization does a wonderful job of making students aware of the beautiful differences in our students. (Conservative Sophomore Female)

Thus, majority group members may be able to use these organizations to develop an awareness that facilitates a more positive atmosphere for students of color. This atmosphere may be why students of color are better situated to finish their education at Protestant colleges and universities that have a relatively high number of student-led multicultural organizations.

Of course, student-led multicultural committees were not the only diversity program that attracted the ire of majority group students. All of the diversity programs listed in the survey drew a certain degree of animosity. Roughly speaking, about 5 percent of the students indicated opposition to the various diversity programs listed in the survey. However, there seemed to be a relatively high amount of hostility directed toward the celebration of history months. This is surprising, given the relationship documented in the last chapter between these history months and the presence of African Americans or Native Americans. Yet, approximately an eighth of white students perceived these celebrations as either an encouragement of racial segregation:

> [celebration of history months] is the sort of program that tends to separate out the races on campus and tends to prevent intermixing. (Mainline Senior Female)

> White people are always looked over. Where is white history month? (Conservative Senior Female)

> I do not understand why African Americans get a certain month of the year just for them. Isn't that showing they are better? Why not Chinese? Or Indian? Or American? (Conservative Senior Female)

> [celebration of history months] just separates people even more. (Mainline Freshman Female)

Or as a source of racial conflict:

> I think it makes the white students a little aggravated. Why must we extravagantly celebrate black history month? I find it annoying. I want to know where white history month is! (Conservative Senior Female)

> I believe that they worsen the racial atmosphere as they [history months] tend to point out divisions among people. (Mainline Freshman Male)

> I think that at times, it is made too big of a deal since there is a big minority of the representative African Americans on campus, and it appears that they are whining or trying to find their roots in a public fashion. (Conservative Senior Male)

How can such resentment exist in light of the positive relationship between celebrating black history month and African Americans on campus, as well as between Native American heritage month and Native Americans on campus? Perhaps these celebrations indicate to African Americans and Native Americans that a campus is relatively safe for them to attend. Yet they have a distinctly opposite effect on majority group students. I suspect that a big reason for this resentment is the popular knowledge of these months. Only 8.8 percent of all white students at these campuses did not know if their college celebrates history months. In contrast, 19.9 percent did not know about multicultural student organizations, 76.5 percent did not know about antiracism programs, 34.4 percent did not know about multicultural programs, 49.8 percent did not know about community organizations, and 78.5 percent did not know about non-European cultural programs on their campuses. History months probably garner a great deal more attention than other institutional programs and thus more resentment as well. This attention may attract African Americans and

Native Americans, but it can also remind majority group students of the attention students of color receive. If white students knew as much about other diversity programs as they do about history months, it is plausible that the other programs would also attract animosity.

It is tempting to dismiss these results because of the relatively small number of white students who express a degree of animosity toward these programs. This would be a mistake. First, it is quite possible that a socially desirable effect creates an underestimation of the number of white students who resent such programs. If students perceive resentment of such programs as a measure of racism, then they have an incentive to hide such resentment from a nosy researcher.[5] However, even if these are accurate percentages of students with an overt dislike, the numbers are still high enough to affect the racial atmosphere on these campuses. If one of every twenty (or, in the case of celebration of history months, one of eight) majority group students overtly resist institutional diversity programs, then students of color are certain to run into such students. These percentages indicate a high likelihood that students of color will hear comments from a white student in a class who opposes these programs or will overhear disparaging comments at a social function from such a student. Such an experience may be particularly disheartening for students of color who may be wondering if they are welcome on these campuses. Although these are not overwhelming percentages of resisting white students, they are in sufficient numbers for shaping the social environment students of color are educated in. And the evidence that white students resented the implementation of diversity programs was consistent enough to find numerous examples of negative responses from white students toward different types of diversity programs:

> To be completely honest, I think most colleges today tend to focus almost exclusively on those students that come from an ethnic background. They receive attention and scholarships that others do not, simply because of their heritage and color of their skin. Yes, I am Caucasian; however, I guarantee that some of those students receiving an additional scholarship are better off financially than my family. I think it is almost racist against white people to assign scholarships to every student who is not Caucasian based on skin color. (Mainline Female Senior)

> I think the cultural programs on our campus may be doing more to segregate the different cultures than they are doing to integrate them. (Conservative Female Senior)

> I think that people tend to overlook or even down trodden white people in the present day because of their color. I believe my children will one

day be at a disadvantage compared to minority children, due to their race. (Conservative Male Junior)

So far, they have only raised more tension. They present so many problems to us, blame us whites for them, and then leave us with no solution or no way for us to try to make things right. It's frustrating. (Conservative Female Senior)

I believe that they [multicultural programs] worsen the racial atmosphere as they tend to point out divisions among people. (Mainline Male Freshman)

Personally, I don't think these celebrations help the racial atmosphere at all. My feeling is that whites resent the attention placed on other races, when whites are left out by all such celebrations. (Conservative Female Sophomore)

Perhaps such sentiments would not be important if white students were merely talking among themselves. But this resistance was not expressed only by whites to other whites. Students of color also experienced this resentment. They often picked up on the antipathy that their white counterparts felt. Their perceptions of the anger felt by white students can be seen in statements such as:

I think it of course informs students of why we have these celebrations but at times I feel like they fear having contact with us even more because they may think we are demonstrating anger and hate, but all we are really doing is showing that we are thankful for who we are and that we want others to understand where we come from. (Conservative Hispanic Female Freshman)

More negative attention and hesitation/anger has aroused instead of integration and understanding and love. (Conservative Multiracial Female Junior)

There are always the insensitive comments every year about, "well, I don't understand why we don't have a white history month." Yes, people actually say that. I think there's just a recognition of "oh, it's February, that means we'll have a black speaker at least once this month. Ok. Moving on with life." . . . so far, it's not really 'celebrated.'. It's more like a cursory observance. (Conservative Black Female Sophomore)

To be sure, there were some comments from white students on how these programs improved the atmosphere on the campus. But such comments tended to be short and not very informative, which is indicative of a response that is not well thought out. The white students who did state that these activities improved the racial atmosphere on campus with more than a short statement of a few words generally offered a conditional response. For example, we can see this tendency in the responses to history months, the program that majority group students were most aware of.

> Students came away from them having learned a lot, but also not quite understanding why we don't have a white month. I understand these concerns seeing that I am white, but I don't think that it is important to voice or get angry over. (Conservative Sophomore Female)

> I think it is a good thing for those students of those races. They improve because it gives those of different races a chance for the heroes of their race to be celebrated as much as those of whites, as equals. However, I have heard some white students comment that it is kind of racist to have those months celebrating those races' history and yet we don't have a white history month or an Irish-American history month or anything like that. (Conservative Sophomore Male)

> I think that at times and among mostly white suburban students they increase racial tension. . . . But I don't feel that that because of an increase of tension among white students from a suburban background means that they should not take place, if anything there needs to be more education the injustice that many people of color faced in the past and how it still is present today. (Conservative Junior Female)

Majority group student support for programs like history months is often qualified. They stated what they enjoyed about these months even as they recognized the racial tension accompanying them. Undoubtedly, the resistance white students have toward these programs affects the racial atmosphere of the campus because people of color pick up on that resentment. Instead of creating a more tolerant racial culture, diversity programs possibly produce opportunities for latent, and not so latent, racial anger to emerge. In the last chapter, I noted that some of the diversity programs were adversely related to the propensity of certain groups of people of color to either attend or graduate from Protestant colleges. These findings indicate a possible reason for this negative relationship. While such programs potentially meet some of the needs of students of color, they also can potentially engender hostility directed at them. Assessing these programs and making them more effective is important because if the hostility they generate is greater than the positive alterations they provide for students of color, then such programs can inhibit the recruitment of students of color and discourage retention of them.

How Should Colleges Change (or Should They)?

The final question in the survey asked the students what sort of alterations they felt their college or university needed to make to develop a better racial atmosphere. I coded the responses of the students along fifteen potential categories.[6] To make sure that my coding did not bias the results, a research assistant also coded the answers for 292 of the students. My answers matched the graduate student's answers 76 percent of the time.[7] One of the codes was for students who stated that the school should deal with the racial atmosphere on the campus by ignoring racial concerns. Not surprisingly, it was generally white students who provided such an answer, although one Hispanic student and one multiracial student stated they also believed that their college or university should not deal with race and racism. To get a flavor for this type of attitude, it is instructive to look at a few of these responses:

> ... stop bringing it up and stop making it such a big deal. it's hard to get it out of our heads that we think of black guys as bad when we keep being reminded of it. (Conservative white sophomore female)

> I don't think it is fair if two students are equally eligible except . . . white kid has a 4.0 GPA and . . . minority kid has a 3.5 and gets accepted because my college is trying to get more minority kids into the program. I think that whoever is better qualified to come in whether it is a minority or not should be the one accepted. (Conservative white sophomore female)

> ... if they start admitting students based on race it is going to back fire and the school will end up sacrificing good students for those of different races. (Mainline white freshman female)

I also had codes for those who believed that the school should not do anything to address racial problems and/or that the college or university was fine in its current state. These responses were added to the ones about the desire to ignore racial issues to indicate students who take a color-blind approach to issues of diversity. I did not include in these codes those students who were not sure what the college or university could do to improve the racial atmosphere, as some of these students may recognize that there is a problem but have no idea of how to handle racial problems.

Given the level of racial tension documented earlier in this chapter, it is clear that students of color are likely to want racial issues to be addressed at Protestant universities. A color-blind perspective does not allow a college or university to look for institutional solutions to racial problems. It also tends to dismiss the concerns some of the students of color enunciated in the questionnaire. Interestingly, there is not a great difference between whites and non-whites on the issue of overtly dealing with racism. Among whites who answered the final question, 39.3 percent suggested that the university needed to either ignore racism or do nothing about it, said everything is fine at their school, and/or reduced the problem down to merely spiritual solutions. Yet 32.1 percent of the students of color advocated such solutions as well.[8] The difference is not statistically significant. A surprising high percentage of students of color also do not want their school to address issues of racial diversity. In the next chapter, we will see that there is a certain type of minority student who may be more willing to accept a majority group perspective on racial issues.

However, the one solution that white students were more likely to advocate than students of color was a call for more racial diversity. I found that 27.7 percent of all white students who answered the final questions address the issue of how to improve the racial atmosphere at their college or university by stating that the campus should gain more racial diversity. Only 15.4 percent of the students of color answered similarly. For both majority and minority group members, these students were more likely to be freshmen or sophomores. Some of the responses that the white students gave were:

I think it's very unfortunate that the student body lacks so much diversity. Getting more racially diverse students here would be a great step. (Conservative Freshman Female)

Try and make the student body as a whole more diverse by admitting more into the school. (Mainline Freshman Female)

Accept more multi-cultural students. (Conservative Junior Female)

Definitely I would love to see a more diverse student body. (Mainline Freshman Male)

I think that they way to do that best would be to somehow encourage racial diversity. I am not sure how that could be possible. (Conservative Sophomore Female)

Accept more students of different races. (Mainline Sophomore Male)

It is interesting to note the passive nature of many of these responses. It is as if the students are hoping that racial diversity will occur without any effort on their part to create the opportunity for diversity. This passivity indicates they have not thought deeply about the subject of racial diversity but have some interest in increasing the level of diversity at their school. In this way, I have located a real distinction between white and nonwhite students. Majority group students are almost as likely as students of color to recognize racial problems on their campuses. However, they are less likely than students of color to seriously consider how to address the issues. Such a finding is to be expected if students of color are more likely than majority group students to suffer the consequences of a segregated campus. Such an assertion comports well with the fact that freshmen and sophomores were more likely to offer limited suggestions, since such students are also less likely than juniors and seniors to think through racial issues. This interpretation suggests that students of color will find inconsistent and weak allies among most majority group students, especially those who are in their first or second year, to work with them to advocate for institutional changes at their place of learning.

Participation of Majority Group Members in Diversity Programs

Further evidence of majority group students' lack of desire to deal with the racial atmosphere on college campuses comes from their lack of participation in the institutional diversity programs offered at these Protestant campuses. For example, I have already established that the program best known by majority group members is the celebration of history months. I suspect that this knowledge has led to the extra resentment that majority group students have toward these celebrations. Less than a third, 31.1 percent, of the majority group students on these campuses have participated in one of these celebrations compared with 45.4 percent of the students of color. Only 18.5 percent of the white students have participated in student-led multicultural organizations compared with 31.9 percent of students of color. Overall, 46.2 percent of all white students did not participate in any of the institutional diversity programs (history month celebrations, antiracism programs, multicultural programs, community programs, or non-European cultural events), whereas only 33.3 percent of nonwhites failed to participate in any programs.

The differences between white and nonwhite students do illustrate less overall interest among majority group students in institutional diversity programs than among students of color. As a result of this lack of participation, majority group students are likely to hear myths and rumors about these programs but have no direct knowledge of them. Whether majority group members actively avoid these programs or merely do not consider them because they do not have to be concerned about racial issues, the result of this lack of participation is the same. Majority group students are not likely to learn about issues of diversity from such programs because they are unlikely to participate in them.

Scholars have argued that efforts to ignore race, or color blindness, create a social atmosphere that inhibits people of color (Bonilla-Silva 2003, Carr 1997, Frankenberg 1993, Lewis 2001). I found evidence that white students who have not participated in any of the diversity initiatives were not very willing to recognize the racial problems on their campus. Such students were more likely than other white students (15.6 percent to 7.4 percent: $p = .03$) to state that their college and university should do nothing to correct racial problems. Given the attitudes of some of the students documented here, it is clear that this ignorance does not aid students of color in their efforts to create a more hospitable environment. The lack of participation of the majority group students has an important effect on students of color as this nonparticipation is connected to white students' unwillingness to address issues of race.

Furthermore, white students—and students of color, for that matter—indicated a lack of awareness of structural racism. When they did note the existence of racism, it was generally linked to expressions of overt racism. Yet few of them discussed structural racism as something that they learned from their minority professors, in their diversity classes, or at diversity programs or events. Rather, when majority group students did attribute a more positive racial environment to these diversity efforts, it was generally due to either more awareness of racial differences or intergroup conflicts:

I think these have improved the racial atmosphere because it made students and staff more aware of these differences and more sensitive to them. (Conservative Female Freshman)

I think they have improved our atmosphere because it helps remind the community of the different cultures found on our campus and the importance of celebrating other racial events. (Mainline Female Sophomore)

They make people more aware of who these people of other cultures really are, which makes dehumanization and racism less possible. (Mainline Male Junior)

. . . it gives students the opportunity to learn about different cultures, which I believe, improves the racial atmosphere. (Conservative Female Sophomore)

Or improvement was seen as happening because more information was being disseminated. Although this information did not generally deal with structural racism, it provided general knowledge to majority group students about racial issues. Thus some majority group students commented positively about a diversity program by stating that it:

> . . . gets information out all throughout campus. (Mainline Male Junior)

> Informs others of different racial issues. (Conservative Female Senior)

> . . . helps other students learn about other culture and creates interest in other types of people. (Conservative Female Freshman)

It is unclear whether this finding is unique to Protestant campuses. However, the failure of students to learn about structural racism may be a key to why many majority group students resented efforts at diversity. They focus on individual efforts to fight and/or perpetuate racism, and thus they are unable to perceive the institutional ways race plays itself out on their college campuses.

Few of the students in this sample illustrated an awareness of structural racism in the questionnaire. It is fair to contend that few of the efforts utilized by Protestant colleges and universities were effective in informing the students about institutional racial issues. Institutional diversity programs did little to alter the attitudes of majority group students except for producing some awareness and general information. Fortunately, such institutional diversity programs were not the only tools Protestant colleges and universities have for altering the racial atmosphere on their campuses. There were also important pedagogical instruments that Protestant colleges and universities could use to shape the racial atmosphere of their campuses.

The Classroom

Diversity programs were not the only measures these colleges and universities used to deal with issues of racial diversity. I found fairly consistent evidence that whites taught in diversity classes or taught by a professor of color were able to rethink some of their previously held ideas about racism. These white students were more likely to develop progressive ideas about racial issues and to become more sympathetic toward the plight of people of color. Some of the experiences these white students shared follow:

It [being taught by a professor of color] has opened my mind to the struggles that blacks and other minorities face, and has initiated many conversations, both in and out of the classroom, that I think have changed my views about race relations in the U.S. (Conservative Female Senior)

I realize that it's hard for them to adjust. One of them struggled with the English language grammar rules and I realized how hard it is. I applied this to other races because it must be hard to face discrimination and everything. His stories helped realize the amount of anger that can arise from being a minority. . . . They have good points of view that I would not get if it wasn't for them because I myself have never went through some of their situations. (Mainline Female Senior)

I took a leadership class lead by an African American, and it was one of the most influential classes I took. He looks at everyone as an equal . . . I have come to realize that although I am not racist, I place judgments on others based off of looks and that is the same as being racist. (Conservative Female Senior)

There were times when majority group students were positively influenced by institutional diversity programs, but these times were not nearly as common as statements about diversity courses and professors of color. The comments students made about what they learned from professors of color and diversity courses tended to be more in-depth than comments they made about learning from institutional diversity programs. Curriculum diversity efforts offer more potential for the alteration of racial attitudes than diversity programs.

Interestingly, the perception of the students toward the instructor was also very important. Whether the majority group student liked a particular professor was linked to whether the student thought these professors brought improvement to the racial atmosphere at the college or university. This was especially the case for professors of color, regardless of whether they were teaching a diversity course. If students had a good impression of the professor, then they were more open to altering previous racial perceptions.

They [professors of color] definitely improve the racial atmosphere because after the students get to know the professor and open up to them, it is usually the first person of a different race they have had to deal with on a day to day basis and they end up more accepting of people of that race by the end of the semester. (Mainline Female Junior)

> I think that certain professors of color have improved the racial atmosphere because they are very popular professors and most students really enjoy being with these professors in class as well as outside of class. (Conservative Female Senior)

> Improve [the racial atmosphere], because they [minority professors] are all outgoing and personable. (Mainline Male Freshman)

> Well it was empowering to be taught by an African American woman and I had great respect and interest in her personal climb/path to where she is now. . . . I now see race as definitely a human made construct, a cultural construct, developing ideas about differences between people; to model for reality by a group. (Conservative Female Senior)

Notice how the personality of the professor is so important for these majority group students. The relationships the professors have with the students were important for helping those professors influence the students. If the students liked who the professor is as a person, then the student was open to the new information the professor had to offer. Unfortunately, the reverse was true as well. When the students did not like the professor or did not feel the professor of color was competent, then their resentment toward that instructor became more evident:

> My teacher was African American and I had her for a New South class and even presently for a US History class. After taking her first class my view changed greatly. Many people that speak out that my race is racist against the African American race tend to be racist themselves against the white race. Instead of leaving in the past I learn. She would mention things and still does that can be seen as hypocritical because the racist issue goes back and forth. (Conservative Female Freshman)

> The class definitely opened my eyes to the hurt and discrimination that colored people in America have felt through out history, however the class was not a history class that was supposed to examine those issues. It was a rhetoric class that the instructor made explicitly about racial issues in America. I learned a lot, but I was definitely annoyed that all we talked about was racial issues. (Mainline Female Sophomore)

> I think that professors of color worsen the racial atmosphere of my campus because they are, generally speaking, two of the worst teachers. I am glad we are accepting of professors of different colors here, but I am unhappy that they are not better teachers. (Conservative Female Freshman)

These students found their professors of color distasteful for one reason or another. As a result of this distaste, their respect for efforts at diversity greatly diminished. In addition to these quotes, several students did not like their professors because they had a hard time understanding their English. This reason is not directly connected to racial differences but to the fact that such professors did not have English as their first language. Regardless, such incidents also produced a certain amount of resentment by majority group students as they connected the professors' racial background to their limited language abilities. Thus, professors of color can improve the racial atmosphere of Protestant colleges and universities but only if they are personally liked by majority group students. Helping these professors become better instructors is vital to aiding the racial culture on Protestant campuses. This may be an unfortunate amount of pressure to place on such professors, but the results of this research suggest that there is an importance to their work that should not be underestimated.

Even though the need for a personal connection may place an unfair burden on professors of color, it is important not to miss an important distinction between resistance toward those professors and resistance toward institutional diversity programs. None of the students questioned the place of these professors on campus, unlike some majority group students who complained about why institutional diversity programs are needed. Professors of color are seen as having a legitimate position on Protestant campuses. Thus, they do not have to justify themselves and are free to fully discuss racial issues in ways that can produce cultural and racial awareness. As long as they are seen as competent and likable, then professors of color can have a powerful influence on Protestant campuses.

Professors of color can also have an impact on the curriculum by bringing out issues normally not covered in traditional college classes. Courses that focus on issues of racial diversity offer this same promise. Majority group students looked toward diversity courses in general for racial insight. Regardless of the race of the professor, majority group students generally found them useful in generating knowledge and awareness about racial issues for them. Majority group students perceived that information and awareness to be important for improving the racial atmosphere on their campus.

> they [diversity courses] allow students to learn about different cultures in great detail. This helps diminish stereotypes, because ultimately, these stereotypes are only based on lack of knowledge about other groups. (Mainline Male Freshman)

> One big main idea that I learned from taking these classes is the idea that we don't want to be a colorblind society, but that we want to be

equal in the fact that we are all human beings, but to encourage different races and to know that there is beauty in all different races. (Conservative Female Junior)

. . . I took a trip to the south to see several civil rights museums and events which broadened my knowledge. (Mainline Male Junior)

I believe I have seen that there are a lot more disadvantages for minorities than I was originally aware of, and I have learned to be more culturally aware and sensitive. (Conservative Female Junior)

I did not ask about the racial background of the professors in these courses, so it is unclear whether such an effect is tied to the race of the professor. However, these comments indicate that the information provided in these courses is a key to influencing these students. Majority group students look for useful information in these classes, and when they get that information, then it is possible for them to gain a new awareness about our racialized society.

Although these classes and professors still did not produce many comments on the importance of social structures, it is clear that the classroom is a setting that offers significant potential for altering the attitudes of majority group members. While some students changed their ideas because of the diversity programs, most of those who indicated alterations in their racial perspectives only discussed an increase in general awareness of the problems that people of color may face. The alterations that happened due to interaction with professors of color or because of diversity courses were more likely to include specific issues about which students altered their opinions. There was also less of a perception that such instruction, relative to the perception of well-known institutional diversity programs such as the celebration of history months, provoked racial conflict. The only exception is when students believed the professor to be either incompetent or unable to communicate in English. Otherwise, learning in a classroom setting seems to produce more racial understanding with less racial resentment than other diversity initiatives.

It is worth speculating why the classroom is a better potential mechanism for attitudinal alteration than institutional diversity programs. Students do expect to be influenced by classes and professors. Educational instruction is one of the reasons, if not always the main reason, they are attending the Protestant school in the first place. Thus majority group students may come into a class setting with more openness to altering previously held ideas than they do when they attend institutional diversity programs or community programs. When attending such programs, the student has an opportunity to dismiss them as extracurricular or as unnecessary baggage the college may be forcing on them. But classroom instruction is likely to be seen as central to the student experience and not easily dismissed as irrelevant.

If minority professors are seen as competent and the instruction in diversity courses is sound, then it appears that the classroom is the most efficient way to alter the racial attitudes of majority group students. This is in keeping with previous research by Chang (2002) on diversity courses and Umbach (2006) on faculty of color. Chang finds that students have more positive attitudes toward African Americans after completing their diversity course requirement than when they first started the course. Umbach discovers that faculty of color provide a broader range of pedagogical techniques and are more likely to interact with students than their white counterparts. This current research effort supports these results because such courses and professors are generally more effective than other diversity initiatives. This additional effectiveness appears to be because majority group students accept their legitimacy more than programs that can be seen as unnecessary. Everyone acknowledges the necessity of courses and professors on college campuses. Diversity courses and professors of color enable educational institutions to send socially acceptable messages of racial inclusiveness. Why they are successful in doing so, beyond the legitimacy they have on a college campus relative to diversity programs, is explored in chapter 6.

Conclusion

The information in this chapter further shows how problematic the idea is that institutional diversity programs, such as history months and multiculturalism, antiracism, community, and cultural programs, are effective in altering the attitudes of majority group students. Either such programs fail to convert majority group students who value color blindness into ones who are sensitive to the racial concerns of minority group members, or majority group students fail to seek out such programs. In many cases, students did not know of these programs or did know of them but felt that they worsen race relations. To the degree that Protestant colleges and universities rely on such programs to alter the racial perspectives of majority group students, these programs are not fulfilling their desired objectives. Some data indicate that student-led organizations may produce awareness among majority group students. Yet some majority group members see such organizations with a degree of suspicion and feel that these organizations do more harm than good.

There are indications that the curriculum and minority professors provided by Protestant colleges and universities can have an impact on the perspectives of majority group students. Majority group students appear to be more open to learning about racial ideals from professors in their classrooms than from speakers in chapels, celebrations of minority cultures, or non-classroom-related programs of diversity. This is not an argument that diversity classes and minority professors automatically produce positive racial alterations within majority group members. When such professors are seen as incompetent or unlikable and courses are seen as being conducted in an ineffective manner, then they may do more harm than good. But these courses and professors offer the possibility that Protestant colleges and universities can help shape the attitudes of majority group members.

It is as yet unclear whether these findings can be generalized to non-Protestant campuses. It is possible that institutional diversity programs on non-Protestant campuses are more effective in altering the racial attitudes of majority group members than the programs on Protestant campuses. The relatively conservative attitude of Protestant majority group students may numb them to the possible effects of such programs. Furthermore, professors and diversity programs may have more authority on Protestant campuses than they do on non-Protestant campuses. Perhaps the religious beliefs of students on Protestant campuses heighten their respect for their professors, allowing those professors to have more influence than faculty on non-Protestant campuses. Ideally, future work will investigate the relative power of diversity programs versus minority professors and diversity classes on shaping the attitudes of whites on non-Protestant campuses.

It is important to examine the possible effects of diversity efforts on majority group students, who are a major factor in the establishment of the racial atmosphere on college campuses. However, the main focus of this book is to evaluate the social world of students of color who attend Protestant colleges and universities. To this end, it is vital to look at the perspectives of student of color on the racial atmosphere of their schools and the potential effects of the diversity programs.

NOTES

1. The campuses used are four from Texas, two from Minnesota, one from California, one from Ohio, one from Pennsylvania, and one from Georgia. These campuses were selected by my efforts to locate professors through my social networks. This explains the overrepresentation of Texas campuses. It is clearly not a random sample, but it still will provide us with qualitative insight into the perspectives of students on Protestant campuses.

2. Two students skipped this question altogether.

3. Three students skipped this question altogether.

4. Indeed, Emerson and Smith (2000) indicate that in critical ways white and black Christians have more divergent racialized attitudes than whites and blacks in general.

5. This possibility is increased by the fact that I was forced to ask for the names of the students to grant them credit for the participating in the survey. While I assured the students that their identities would not be disclosed, it is reasonable to believe that some of them intentionally provided answers that would portray them in a racially tolerant manner.

6. Actually, two variables were created to capture those who gave more than one answer. Rarely did a student provide more than two potential answers, but when one did, I strove to list the answers the student emphasized more or discussed first. When it came time to analyze the data, I included all students who provided an appropriate response in either of the two variables.

7. When there was a disagreement between us, I went with my own assessment.

8. My coding of the color-blind variable matched that of the research assistant 92.12 percent of the time.

5

The Impact of Diversity Initiatives on Students of Color—What Do the Students Say?

In chapter 3, I examined whether diversity initiatives and programs are factors in why students of color are attracted to and likely to graduate from certain Protestant educational institutions. The results indicated doubt as to whether institutional diversity efforts such as antiracism, multiculturalism, and community programs are effective in improving racial diversity on Protestant campuses. Rather, academic courses and programs in race and ethnicity were connected to increased racial diversity. Protestant colleges and universities able to develop such programs and hire professors of color are theoretically more likely to be successful at attracting and retaining students of color. The development of student-led multicultural groups may also buttress racial diversity on these campuses. We saw as well how important the faculty is toward the creation of a campus environment that supports racial diversity. Thus schools with a diverse, trained professoriat and an educational curriculum that supports diversity are in a better position to influence majority group students than those with institutional diversity programs. If the only thing these courses and professors do is prepare majority group members so that these schools can create an accepting environment for students of color, then we would have enough information to assert the power of such courses to encourage racial diversity. Yet these courses and professors probably also influence students of color, and it is also vital to investigate the potential of diversity initiatives to affect the experiences of students of color.

My online survey of students allowed me to conduct such an investigation. It is important to see if there are different patterns among students of color than among majority group students. I was also able to examine how students of color perceive the effects of diversity initiatives. Such perceptions will not provide a final answer on the usefulness of these initiatives in supporting racial diversity on Protestant campuses, but they will help us see the process by which they can play an important role in promoting such diversity. We can hear from the mouths of the students of color who are dealing with issues of diversity and learn from their observations.

Different Types of Minority Students

One of the first clear observations emerging from this work is that there are two different types of minority students attracted to these schools. The first type of student can be described as a racial minority student who has racial attitudes similar to those of majority group students. These students, when asked how their Christian faith shapes their racial attitudes, provide answers like majority group students provide. They generally stated that their racial perspectives were based on notions of color blindness and dismissal of the importance of race. A little more than half of the minority students who provided enough information to determine their orientation toward racial issues fell into this classification.[1] For simplicity's sake, I labeled such students "assimilated" minority students.

A few key characteristics of these students are worth noting. For example, some students often want to downplay racial differences on the campus.

> I don't want anyone to be sensitive to my race, I just want to be treated as a student. (Conservative Black Male Junior)

> I don't particularly feel that my race has specific needs that need to be met on campus. A person's a person and even though I encourage looking at the differences, I feel no need to get special treatment because of my race. (Conservative Hispanic Female Senior)

> Everyone in the campus, I believe, does not care nor even "see" our race, we see each other as one. (Mainline Hispanic Female Senior)

> . . . everyone here is so great and doesn't judge you by the color of your skin that you tend to forget the matter race and focus on who they are in the inside. (Conservative Black Female Sophomore)

These examples indicate that these students are not willing to address the social and racial differences that emerge from the racialized environment on

Protestant campuses. They want their race to be seen as no different from the majority group and to be given no special attention. In this manner, they are adopting the color-blind perspective common among majority group members, which may allow them to have the sensation of assimilating into the dominant group.

Another key characteristic is that assimilated minority students are often sympathetic to the effect of diversity programs on majority group students. Such students did not only look at diversity programs as efforts to create a positive racial atmosphere but also saw such programs as an attack on majority group students. They often sympathized with these students to the degree that their concern for majority group students outweighed their perception of the need for programs to deal with issues of racial justice.

> If anything, one of the African-American speakers we had might have actually caused some tension by what he said. If I remember correctly, he actually stated some ideas that many Christians would disagree with. (Conservative Multiracial Male Sophomore)

> Generally there is not [a positive racial atmosphere]. I attribute this to the fact that programs attempting to solve the problem alienate those who do not agree. (Conservative Hispanic Female Senior)

> I know compared to other institutions, almost everyone here gets along well. However, some groups are so bent on "reconciling" that they point out differences in race or sex in an effort to be better understood when really it just creates a bigger rift. In a way, the parties who claim to be victims of prejudice are instead themselves prejudiced. (Conservative Multiracial Male Sophomore)

> I think that it is important to focus on racial reconciliation on campus because it issue that is easy and comfortable to overlook. However, I sometimes feel that this particular group [student-led diversity committee] comes across as more angry and divisive than its original goal to unify races on campus. (Conservative Hispanic Female Senior)

Thus rather than perceiving diversity initiatives as desirable, they see these programs as problematic. Such programs may have good intentions, but these students perceived them as just making matters worse. The solution for them is merely to ignore racial issues, much as many of their majority group peers would like to do.

I don't think anything needs to be done [about racial diversity]. If there is no problem don't try and fix it. (Conservative Multiracial Female Sophomore)

I believe the college is doing enough already. (Mainline Other Female Sophomore)

I think the university is doing just fine dealing with this situation. (Conservative Other Male Senior)

Thus they take on the color blindness ideas of so many of their majority group peers. These students probably fit easily into the social atmosphere of the Protestant campus. They are unlikely to generate hostility from majority group students, and thus there is little tension to drive such students off. I did not investigate the social background of such students; however, previous research suggests that individuals of color who develop integrated social networks early in their lives continue to have racially diverse friends later in their lives (Emerson, Kimbro, & Yancey 2002). It is reasonable to assert that such students are likely to come from a social atmosphere with more majority group members than other students of color. If that is accurate, then attending a predominantly white Protestant educational institution is merely a natural extension of the culturally Eurocentric life they already live.

However, in these Protestant colleges and universities, there is a contrasting type of minority student with a racial identity shaped by experience in an oppressed group. These students do not perceive racial identity in a similar manner as majority group students, but rather they were more willing to question the racial policies of Protestant educational institutions. As such, they are more likely to take on an oppositional culture than other racial minorities. For simplicity's sake, I labeled such students "racialized" minority students.[2]

Racialized minority students are not as trusting of their majority group peers as assimilated minority students. In fact, they tend to be rather pessimistic about the willingness of majority group students to deal with issues of diversity on their campuses. Like the assimilated minority students, these students have noted the resistance of majority group students to efforts at facilitating racial diversity. However, unlike the assimilated minority students, the racialized minority students do not blame the programs but instead assert that problems among majority group students create the tension.

I feel that the only time student of color gets any spot light is during black history month because event are being offered as well as convocation and its promoted all over camps. Once this month is over it's back to the norm. If I'm the only black student in that class and I can sometimes feel intimidated or scared to speak up if I have a question. This is not in all classes but some. (Mainline Black Female Sophomore)

Most students lack the understanding and care for race. I have seen over the two years I have been at my college that although the faculty, staff and students proclaim and sign a covenant that promotes reconciliation, multi-cultural and multi-ethic awareness they're still ignorant and insensitive to race. My college has taken affirmative action since 5 years ago when racist graffiti was polluting our learning community; for that I am grateful but we shouldn't and mustn't stop to improve our community. (Conservative Asian Female Sophomore)

Staff and Faculty personnel should show equal support to all races on special holidays. [For] example Martin Luther King Day—everyone just seems not interested by white, Asian, Indian personnel. But on Chinese Holidays—individuals of white, Indian, are all excited and bonded India Holidays—individual are dressed up and received lots of attention. But on Black History Holidays the atmosphere is just the same everyone goes as if it does not exist. (Mainline Black Male Freshman)

The majority group does not understand the need for people of color to celebrate their culture . . . so therefore they become angry and want to end the program. (Conservative Black Female Senior)

It's always make this kind of ethnic food at the Cafe or some kind of black, Hispanic or Asian thing going on. It's almost like rubbing it in my face. Somewhat like, "hey you're Hispanic and your parents are from El Salvador, come eat a pupusa." I don't even like pupusas. If it's not that it's the fact that everyone assumes all Hispanics are Mexican. . . . I'm not Mexican . . . I'm Salvadorian, get it right already. (Conservative Hispanic Female Junior)

Racialized students have little faith in their majority group peers' willingness to learn about minority group students and their culture. These perceptions undoubtedly come out of their racialized experiences on the campus. They have confronted racism and are discouraged that majority group students and professors are not serious about ending it. These students freely shared some of the experiences that led to such conclusions.

As for diversity, I think that this campus is very diverse, however sometimes I get an impression that usually the main events on campus, ex.

dances or voting king, queen . . . etc, favored the white community. I think this way because whenever I walked pass a certain information table to Student Union, the White people on the table never stop me to inform me their events, but they stop white students who are behind me or in front of me. (Mainline Asian Female)[3]

At times I get uncomfortable looks and body language speaks big. I do have white friends but all are only the "hi, how are you" type and that's it. Even I have had dinner with them the second offer never comes by. (Conservative Hispanic Female Freshman)

. . . other races don't even want to get to know you or look at you because they think you are a thug or they automatically think you are in a gang because that's the first thing they ask me when they are trying to get to know me. (Mainline Black Male Freshman)

I am the first Latina people here have known on a personal, relational level, they assume things about me like I speak Spanish or I am catholic, and I feel like I am continually teaching people that I am not a stereotype. (Conservative Hispanic Female Senior)

I've been called the 'N' word, singled out in classes. Comments like you're the whitest black person I know, et cetera. . . . As a minority member, whites often don't even remotely [understand] my perspective, nor I their's for that matter. (Conservative Black Male Junior)

I do not know whether racialized students have undergone experiences of more pronounced racism than assimilated students or whether they are more likely to perceive similar situations as racialized. But what is clear is that these experiences weigh more heavily on their minds, and their experiences contribute to the lack of trust they have in majority group members.

Racialized students bring attitudes born within their oppositional culture to their campuses. They are not so eager to forgive the racial failings of their educational institutions. They are the ones who push for diversity programs and reforms on Protestant campuses. The tone they took as they answered the questions was distinctly more confrontational than that of assimilated students. They were not satisfied with the status quo and either sought to endure it or were engaged in some level of activism in an attempt to alter the racial atmosphere on the campus.

The social world of the racialized students is probably different from that of the assimilated students.[4] For example, there is some evidence that they are more isolated from people of different races than are assimilated students of color. Among racialized minority students, a little more than half of their friends were of their own race; among assimilated minority students, only about a quarter of their friends were of their own race. The fact that more than half of the friends of racialized minorities are of their own race is quite significant because most of them attend campuses where their racial group is a small percentage of the campus. It is not clear from this type of data whether these friendship patterns emerged before or after the development of their racialized attitudes. Interaction with students of other races may bring some level of satisfaction to assimilated students of color that escapes racialized minority students. On the other hand, it is quite plausible that racialized students are simply less likely to develop friends of other races because they mistrust racial out-groups.

These two types of students suggest that there are different potential pathways by which students of color may find themselves on Protestant campuses. It is quite plausible that the racial challenges of the assimilated students are not that different from the challenges faced by majority group students. Although these students undoubtedly have to deal with episodes of racism, they were unlikely to discuss those episodes in their surveys. If they focused on racial incidents, then they might find themselves having to create a definition of themselves as a minority person who is different from the rest of the campus. Assimilated minority students may choose to downplay or ignore racism in an attempt to create a "normal" college experience for themselves. This provides two possible directions that Protestant colleges and universities can take to deal with assimilated students of color. Either it is important to allow such students to remain in the social world they have developed as a "normal" student, or it is important to help them recognize that living life as a majority group member is not feasible for them. These students either need to be left alone or need to be "taught" about the realities of racism. Since I do not have empirical information determining which route is most productive for such students, I will not assert which direction may be best. Investigating the potential outcomes for assimilated students of color is a task that needs to be accomplished in future work.

The racialized student of color does not need to be taught about racism, nor is it wise to ignore the concerns of such students. They are disturbed by the overt and subtle racism they experience on campus. Indeed, the types of diversity programs I investigated have often been developed with such students in mind.[5] Somehow these students must be encouraged to overcome their discomfort if they are going to fully benefit from their college experience. Finding the best way to provide such encouragement is an important goal of those who support diversity initiatives.

Understanding these different types of minority group students is important for those who deal with issues of diversity at Protestant institutions of higher education. This understanding will help them recognize that not all students of color are going to be supportive of diversity initiatives. Some may even voice many of the same complaints as majority group students. But these initiatives still may be useful in serving racialized students of color. Advocates for racial diversity at Protestant colleges and universities have to operate with an understanding of the two tracks that students of color may travel down as they navigate their minority status in this educational situation.

The Potential Effects of Institutional Diversity Programs

A general comparison between majority group students and students of color did not produce many differences between the two groups' attitudes toward the value of institutional diversity programs. There were majority group students and students of color who asserted that these programs were unnecessary. These students often indicated that such programs make the atmosphere on campus worse because they promoted racial conflict or segregation. Likewise, there were majority group students and students of color who were strong advocates of these programs. These students perceived these programs as ways to improve the racial atmosphere on campus. The percentages of students in each group varied, depending on the program.

Surprisingly, roughly the same percentages of white students as students of color noted that institutional diversity programs made them more comfortable. However, the way majority group students answered that question differed from the approach taken by students of color. Majority group students were more likely to know that they gained comfort from gaining knowledge about different cultures:

> I have been able to grow in my understanding of other cultures. (Conservative Female Sophomore)

> Participating definitely made me feel more comfortable with who I was as a person and it gave me a feeling of the other kinds of people who were on campus. (Mainline Female Sophomore)

> It gave me a taste of what a normal practice of another culture looks like, as much as it can be enacted here. (Mainline Male Junior)

While similar numbers of students of color also found that diversity programs helped them become more comfortable, their reasoning for this comfort differed. Students of color were less likely to discuss learning about other cultures but were quicker to argue that they gained comfort from having their own culture reaffirmed by these programs:

> . . . because I have learned to be comfortable with my skin color and my culture. (Conservative Black Female Junior)

> They made me feel more comfortable because I participated and met new people of a similar background as myself. (Mainline Multiracial Male Freshman)

> It brought me friends who have similar passions and values but separated me from others who looked down on such activities. (Conservative Hispanic Male Junior)

> It was nice to see the Asian community come together to worship God. On my floor in the dorms I was the only Asian. It is easier to relate with people of the same race sometimes and it is nice to see a wider range of Asians around campus since I grew up without that experience. (Conservative Asian Female Sophomore)

Such differences indicate that diversity initiatives have distinct effects on white students and students of color, even if the overall support of these programs does not greatly vary between the two groups. If administrators intend to use such programs to serve majority group members, then they may want to emphasize a knowledge component to the programs. If they intend to use such programs to aid minority group students, then finding ways to culturally reaffirm them is important. Those who desire to aid both majority and minority groups may have to find a balance between these two needs.

In chapter 3, I documented that the celebration of black history month can be positively related to the percentages of African Americans who attend Protestant campuses. You may remember that this effect seemed most pronounced among conservative Protestant colleges and universities. Now I have an opportunity to evaluate the responses of students of color to the questions surrounding history months in general. Similar percentages of blacks and whites supported the history months. However, why they supported the history months was insightful. Generally, when asked if the history months improved the campus, majority group members who responded with affirmative answers were not very specific about how these months improved the campus. Many merely answered that such events improved the campus without giving any reason that they may have done so. It was not uncommon that all I got was a one-word answer to my question. Other answers from majority group students were generally not much more informative:

> We had a lot of fun events for Black History Month. (Conservative Female Senior)

> They were a lot of fun. Everyone danced in chapel. (Conservative Female Freshman)

> I would think improved but not really sure how. (Conservative Female Senior)

It is almost as if the students knew that they are supposed to state that these months improve the campus but they do not know how such improvement was supposed to take place. On the other hand, African American students were more likely to be explicit about how these months improved the atmosphere on the campus.

> I believe these programs work due to the fact that even if we have people who hate minorities, they have to learn about other cultures. So maybe as they learn, they can grow and stop hating a person due to their race. (Conservative Male Junior)

> . . . when it is black history month the school do things to honor it. like have chapel dedicated to MLK. (Conservative Male Freshman)

> . . . if there are no activities or chapel forums specifically for each month than how can other races be informed besides what they see on TV or read about in certain history books? (Conservative Female Junior)

I have limited myself to students from conservative campuses since the results in chapter 3 indicate that the most potent effects of history months reside at those campuses. To be sure, there were a few majority group members with specific answers to how such history months improved the racial atmosphere on their campus, as well as African American students who provided uninformative answers. However, black students were distinctly more likely to provide specific reasons for the usefulness of history months, and white students who supported the months did not know why they supported the months.

Other than the multiple alterations that seemed to be connected to attendance of Asian students on campuses, black history month was the only institutional diversity initiative tested in this survey that was not directly connected to curriculum or instruction that consistently had a positive relationship with racial diversity on Protestant campuses. Thus, it is here that we should theoretically have the most powerful potential effect of such programs on the creation of more racial diversity on campus. These results suggest that diversity initiatives at their best may encourage students of color in very practical ways. At their best, they allow students of color to experience their culture and to see it respected on a campus that is highly Eurocentric. One might think of them as an oasis of minority group culture in a sea of majority group culture.

These history months also seem to provide majority group students with some assurance that something is done to aid the level of diversity at the college campus, which encourages some of them to support diversity initiatives. However, it cannot be forgotten that such programs can also produce hostility among majority group students. Institutional diversity programs that offer powerful theoretical benefits for majority group students and real practical assets for students of color, without provoking images of segregation and conflict for majority group students, appear to provide the best opportunity to support racial diversity on Protestant campuses. However, the reality is that most institutional diversity programs are unable to meet these varied goals, which is probably why most of them fail to support racial diversity. Future planners of diversity initiatives would do well to consider these goals as they design their programs.

Since I have already identified the differences between assimilated and racialized students of color, it is useful to examine whether these students have different perceptions about institutional diversity programs. It should be expected that racialized students of color would be more supportive of diversity initiatives than their assimilated counterparts, but in an interesting twist, racialized and assimilated students of color were about as likely to believe that such programs are useful. For example, some of the racialized students of color responded to the question about whether institutional diversity programs have improved or worsened the racial atmosphere on campus in this way:

> The majority of the people involved are minorities. So that means that the people we want to inform are not getting involved and showing support. (Conservative Hispanic Female Freshman)

> Lol, I think it's a great opportunity if people come; however, it seems as if we are only preaching to our own choir. (Mainline Asian Male Junior)

> . . . the campus (for a day) learns about another culture, but . . . the majority group does not understand the need for people of color to celebrate their culture. So therefore they become angry and want to end the program. (Conservative Black Female Senior)

> Maybe worsen because people are ignorant to what it really stands for and think that it is a place to hate white people. (Conservative Multiracial Male Junior)

> I think people are so use to them [history month celebrations] every year that they don't partake in it or just ignore it. (Conservative Multiracial Female Sophomore)

These students argue that the programs are not effective since majority group students avoid or misunderstand them. Thus for racialized students of color, the problem is majority group students. This is different for assimilated students of color. When assimilated students of color chose to be critical of diversity programs, they took a different approach. For them, it was the program—and not the majority group students—that was responsible for the failure of such efforts.

> It is good to celebrate these things, however, I feel that Caucasian people can't have a White History Month without people screaming racist. (Conservative Hispanic Female Senior)

> I think it might worsen because it is single out the minorities. (Conservative Black Male Senior)

> I think they are both effective and sometimes counterproductive as well. People need to be informed about inequalities, but White students may feel attacked during these messages. (Conservative Hispanic Female Senior)

> It [non-European cultural programs] just unites that certain group. Other groups may find it offensive. (Conservative Hispanic Male Sophomore)

Thus, assimilated students of color are more likely to place the blame on the ineffectiveness of institutional diversity programs on the programs themselves. It seems that they place themselves in the position of majority group students and fear that institutional diversity programs are offensive to these students. Thus the key feature of assimilated students of color, their unwillingness to challenge white racial identity, shapes their reaction to these programs.

It should be acknowledged that many racialized and assimilated students of color had similar concerns about the programs' lack of impact. In this way, many of their answers were similar. But when these answers differed, it was generally due to how they perceived the role of majority group students. Generally, racialized students of color perceived that white students did not care about investing themselves into nonwhite problems, whereas assimilated students of color were concerned that the programs themselves turned off white students. Both types of students are reacting to the majority group students on their campus but in different ways. The interaction of majority and minority group students is a vital aspect of racial diversity that must be taken into account. How to improve this interaction is probably to tied to the type of student of color (assimilated or racialized) that most populates a particular campus.

This difference between assimilated and racialized students of color once again underscores the importance of understanding the attitudes of majority group students as we attempt to appreciate what factors might aid those who seek racial diversity at educational institutions. Diversity initiatives that seek to serve only students of color are destined to be relatively ineffective. The reactions of students of color indicate that they take some of their cues about the effectiveness of these programs from how such programs influence majority group students. The social engagement of majority and minority group students needs to be made easier by diversity initiatives, if they are going to improve the racial atmosphere on a given campus.

Student-Led Diversity Organizations

Apart from these institutional diversity programs, there was evidence in chapter 3 that student-led organizations possess the potential to promote the retention of students of color. In the previous chapter, there was some evidence that majority group students did not always trust such organizations; however, they could produce some degree of awareness among such students. Thus it is important to assess how such organizations may affect the social environment of students of color.

Students of color generally exhibited an appreciation of these student-led groups. While as a group they gave several reasons for this appreciation, two reasons in particular were most commonly enunciated. First, they noted that such organizations promote learning about other cultures.

> It [student committee on diversity] has improved the atmosphere. I am beginning to see a lot of white students wanting to bring a change on the campus and want to learn more about other cultures other than the white culture. (Conservative Black Senior Female)
>
> . . . gives you the opportunity to learn about others and this gives them chance to talk about their cultures. (Mainline Asian Freshman Female)
>
> . . . this department has worked with many students of different ethnic backgrounds to bring awareness of other cultures to the campus. Retreats, chapels, discussion groups, conferences have been

provided to help improve this issue. (Conservative Multiracial Senior Female)

... it [multicultural student organization] improves because it can help students who have different culture know more about each other and become friends. (Conservative Asian Sophomore Female)

Minority group students perceived these organizations as opportunities for them to teach those of other races about their culture. A few students of color indicated disappointment that majority group students did not always take advantage of these opportunities. But generally, students of color were grateful that student-led diversity organizations offered them the chance to teach about their culture.

Second, these organizations were seen as mechanisms that helped to bring people of different races together.

Those organizations [multicultural student organizations] usually help bring people back together. (Mainline Black Junior Female)

The committee helps students of other races find common ground with each other through different social events and worship events. (Conservative Asian Sophomore Female)

Racial relations have been improved, because it [multicultural student organization] brings minority groups together. (Mainline Black Sophomore Male)

Students found these organizations a valuable way to bring students of different races together. In these organizations, the racial barriers that maintain social distance between the students seemed less important. Thus students of color reflected a desire to see these organizations bring people together that was not evident in the answers provided by majority group students.

These responses indicate why student-led multiracial organizations may help students of color become more fully integrated into the campus environment and thus help them graduate from their college or university. The more minority group members believe that majority group members understand their culture, the easier it is for them to believe that they have an accepted social place on campus. Likewise, organizations that allow individuals of different races to come together as social equals can provide comfort for students of color who perceive themselves as isolated on Protestant campuses. Student-led multicultural student organizations can be a valuable way that Protestant colleges and universities can create a more hospitable environment for students of color.

However, this is not to state that all students of color found these organizations useful. While fewer in number, there were students who were dissatisfied with the effects brought by these organizations. For the most part, their complaints were based on the perspective that these organizations tended to separate individuals of different races from each other.

> I think that it is important to focus on racial reconciliation on campus because it issue that is easy and comfortable to overlook. However, I sometimes feel that this particular group comes across as more angry and divisive than its original goal to unify races on campus. (Conservative Hispanic Senior Female)

> . . . some organizations seem to divide the minorities and the rest of the school instead of incorporating them all together. (Mainline Hispanic Freshman Female)

> they have focused too much on the differences in varying cultures that they distance minorities even more. (Conservative Multiracial Sophomore Male)

> The only problem is that it can set us apart from the rest of the campus. It can make us feel different. (Conservative Asian Freshman Male)

These students of color had an opposing view of student-led multicultural groups than those who valued them. Rather than perceiving these organizations as mechanisms that bring individuals of different races together, they envision such organizations as barriers to racial integration. Thus both students of color who value these organizations and those who do not appreciate them desire the same qualities from them—an ability to pull students of different races together. The difference between the two groups of students is their faith in student-led multicultural organizations to accomplish that task. Protestant colleges and universities that are able to support student-led multicultural groups that promote racial integration are more likely to create social atmospheres that support students of color. This supports my earlier assertion that groups that promote a political "us versus them" mentality are not as effective as those that promote personal relationships between racial groups.

The Potential Effects of Diverse Curriculum and Minority Faculty

As I noted in the quantitative analysis, there is evidence that the course curriculum is a relevant factor in the production of racial diversity on Protestant campuses. We have found that whites and nonwhites do not differ in their support for diversity programs but that there are different reasons this support has emerged. Since there may be greater potential for producing a positive racial atmosphere through a diversity curriculum, it is worth our time to investigate white-nonwhite differences in students' attitudes toward academic programs, as well as any differences between racialized and assimilated students.

The responses of the students indicate similar levels of support from whites and nonwhites concerning attitudes toward professors of color and diversity courses. Generally, whites were no more or less willing to support diversity courses or minority professors than students of color. However, the reason for supporting professors of color differs for students of color. As stated in the earlier chapter, if majority group students enjoyed interaction with a given professor, then that student supported the professor. This was less likely to be the case for students of color. Although a few students of color linked their support of a minority professor to personally liking the professor, they were more likely to indicate support of such professors because of the awareness and information that such professors bring:

> They bring a different perspective on issues we face. In addition, students become more exposed to people of minority races and become more comfortable around them. I have definitely felt more comfortable in classes with professors of color—The whole atmosphere of the class is different, and I feel like people aren't as intimidated to speak up, and associate with people of other races. (Conservative Asian Female Sophomore)

> They improve it [the racial atmosphere] because in class discussions they try to make students look at things from a different perspective. (Conservative Hispanic Female Junior)

> . . . there are always things to learn from other cultures. Having minorities around also makes it less likely for there to be stereotypes about that culture. (Conservative Multiracial Male Sophomore)

Notice that these students of color are not commenting on the personality of the professor. This seldom happened, and it did not happen nearly as much as it did for majority group students. For these students of color, personal relationships with the professor were not critical to their perception that the professor was positively affecting the racial atmosphere; rather, the information that the professor could impart was key. The fact that the professor had additional experiences and perspectives due to his or her racial status turns out to be a plus for such students.

This racial effect was more common on conservative Protestant campuses, as the racial minorities on mainline Protestant campuses were unlikely to perceive minority professors as improving the racial atmosphere on the campuses in any way. This allows me to consider a qualitative difference between conservative and mainline campuses. While the quantitative results indicated that recruitment of minority faculty is valuable for both conservative and mainline campuses,[6] the presence of minority faculty may operate in different ways. Their presence may be a more overt indicator of racial tolerance on conservative campuses than on mainline institutions. This can make it easier for students of color on conservative campuses to perceive the value of these professors than for students of color on mainline campuses.

These racial differences are useful to note since they suggest that interactions between students and professors may be more important for majority group students than they are for students of color. Majority group students appear to be more likely than students of color to be impressed with their interaction with their minority professors. This is counter to notions that minority professors serve a vital function as mentors for students of color. Students of color look to their minority professors for information and awareness but not necessarily for personal guidance. What might explain this racial difference? It is possible that the communal nature of some cultures of color de-emphasizes the personal connections with professors. The individual professor has a place and role to play. If that professor plays that role, then the student of color can gain the information and awareness needed to gain a level of comfort on campus, regardless of how the student personally feels about the professor.[7] On the other hand, majority group members may be more likely to hold ideals of individualism and may be more personally impressed with professors of color. This allows majority group members to be more likely to tie their evaluation of minority professors to those professors' unique accomplishments but to ignore the social position of the professor.

Likewise, minority group students were about as likely to support diversity courses as majority group students. The basic reasons for such support were similar for whites and nonwhites. They perceived such courses as important as a way of imparting knowledge and information.

> Those classes really helped me understand other cultures and I expanded my horizon. . . . I think that these classes open people's mind more, because they learn about things they didn't know before. (Mainline Black Female Junior)

> I think they have improved the atmosphere because people, especially at our university where most people are very privileged financially, can better understand how bring change and help those who are

being oppressed in our own country. (Conservative Hispanic Female Senior)

I was just a little bit shocked how a well developed country, like the U.S. still has problems with races and differences in external appearance. . . . I think it has improved the racial atmosphere because they open up the eyes of many students who do not believe in racial problems in this country. Students who take the class will have more of understanding of how students from the minority groups feel in a campus where everything seems to be alright. (Conservative Other Male Senior)

Students of color seem to be a little more likely to talk about how the information and awareness to be gained in such courses influences other students. But many of these students of color pointed out how they themselves benefited from this information and awareness as well. Thus, there is a similar perspective for whites and nonwhites as to the benefit of diversity courses.

It is also useful to assess whether racialized and assimilated students of color have different perspectives. There was a distinct approach of assimilated students of color toward professors of color. They were relatively likely to assert that such minority faculty members did not improve the racial atmosphere of the campus. Although a few of the racialized students of color also did not see improvement, assimilated students of color were more likely to have this perception. They generally utilized a color-blind framework to justify this assertion:

They are just professors. I don't really think that because they are different race it changes anything. (Conservative Multiracial Female Sophomore)

I believe that any teacher who has a passion for teaching will improve the campus atmosphere regardless of their color. Having a professor of color does not make them better than a white professor regardless of their color, it is how much I learn that helps me gauge how the professor is. (Conservative Hispanic Female Senior)

When I walk into a classroom race is never on my mind. I just want to learn, pass my class, and graduate. (Conservative Black Male Junior)

Racialized students of color did not use such color-blind ideas when they perceived professors to not have an effect; rather, they simply asserted, without an elaborate explanation, that these professors had no effect on the racial atmosphere on the campus. Assimilated students of color may have a high likelihood to accept majority group culture so that they can more easily fit into mainstream society. A lack of acceptance of the communal cultural aspects found within racialized students of color should be expected if assimilated students of color are likely to accept majority group culture.

Once again, there is little difference in attitudes concerning diversity courses between racialized and assimilated students of color. There were similar levels of support for such courses, and the reasons for such support are quite similar. Members of both groups generally perceived these courses as sources of awareness and knowledge. Relatively few students of color, whether they are racialized or assimilated, perceived these courses as making the racial situation on their campus worse. In this way, these students of color continue to have perceptions similar to majority group students' perceptions. Thus diversity courses are generally supported at similar levels by the different groups of students who attend Protestant colleges and universities. It is possible that diversity courses are the one measure that has similar effects on students of all races and most racial orientations. The aspects of diversity courses that buttress a positive racial atmosphere may be similar for students in all types of racial groups. If this is true, then such diversity courses may have tremendous potential to alter the racial climate, and if we can discover which aspects of diversity courses are supporting a positive racial atmosphere, then we can have some confidence that these aspects will resonate with a wide range of students.

Racial Differences in the Reason for Attending Protestant Colleges and Universities

Since racial diversity depends on initially attracting students of different races to the campus, it is useful to ask why individuals of different races chose to attend a particular college or university. To this end, one of the questions provided on the survey assesses if there are any cross-racial differences in this decision. Previous research has investigated racial aspects about the decision individuals make to attend an institution of higher education (Emerson et al. 2002, Freeman 1997, Hurtado et al. 1997, McDonough, Antonio, & Trent 1997, Perna 2000). This work discovers that factors such as cultural capital (Freeman 1997, Perna 2000) and athletic opportunities (McDonough et al. 1997) are important for helping students of color decide to attend college. Surprisingly, financial aid is not found to be sufficient for increasing college access (Perna 2000). The question on my survey will help me to extend this work by investigating whether students of color attend Protestant colleges and universities for different reasons than majority group members do.

I coded the responses provided to the question of what students stated as the reason they chose to attend their particular college or university. The responses were coded as the student attending the college for athletic, academic, financial support, spiritual, location, or small classes reasons. The vast majority of students provided one or two of these reasons. For simplicity's sake, I coded only the first two responses of those few students who provided more than two reasons.[8] This allowed me to assess which category, or two, each student falls into for why they are attending their given educational institution. A breakdown of these categories by race can be seen in table 5.1.

Because of the nonprobability and subjective nature of the coding, I am less interested in finding significant differences than I am in discovering larger trends. An important trend that immediately becomes clear is that African Americans generally offer different reasons than students of other races for attending their Protestant college or university. For example, a clear racial difference in the reason African Americans attend Protestant colleges and universities is their higher likelihood to attend because of athletics.[9] As seen in table 5.1, about 37 percent of all black students who attended Protestant colleges and universities did so to participate in athletics.[10] This is at least three times the percentage of students of other races.[10] This sample is not random, and thus I cannot claim that this is an accurate generalizable difference. But this difference is great enough to suggest that athletic teams are a bigger draw for blacks than for others.

However, a desire for spiritual enlightenment was not as compelling a reason for black attendance at Protestant colleges and universities as it was for other racial groups. The desire for spiritual growth is generally powerful among Protestant students at conservative colleges and universities. Such Protestant students provided spiritual reasons such as:

TABLE 5.1 Breakdown of Reasons Individuals of Different Races Chose to Attend Protestant Educational Institutions

	Whites N=324	Blacks N=46	Hispanics N=31	Asian N=24	Multiracial N=21
Athletic	40 (12.3%)	17 (37.0%)	3 (9.7%)	1 (4.2%)	2 (9.5%)
Academic	100 (30.9%)	12 (26.1%)	6 (19.4%)	7 (29.2%)	7 (33.3%)
Financial support	44 (13.6%)	2 (4.3%)	6 (19.4%)	1 (4.2%)	4 (19.0%)
Spiritual	138 (42.6%)	9 (19.6%)	18 (58.1%)	10 (41.7%)	9 (42.9%)
Location	96 (29.6%)	11 (23.9%)	3 (9.7%)	3 (12.5%)	5 (23.8%)
Small classes	33 (10.2%)	6 (13.0%)	2 (6.5%)	4 (16.7%)	1 (4.8%)

Wanted to go to a Christian college and this seemed like the best one I could find. (Conservative White Male Sophomore)

. . . to gain Christian perspectives on learned material. (Conservative White Female Freshman)

Because of the Christian environment and the population of the school. (Conservative Asian Female Freshman)

. . . would be a place where I could grow spiritual and experience a Christian community. (Conservative Hispanic Female Senior)

This is the place that I felt God was calling me to. (Conservative White Male Freshman)

They try to integrate your major with your Christian life, so you can effectively use what you are learning for Christ. (Conservative White Male Junior)

Because it is a Christian University with a warm, welcoming atmosphere. (Conservative White Female Senior)

I wanted to learn science from a Christian perspective rather than a secular one. (Conservative Hispanic Female Freshman)

Fewer than one in five blacks mentions spiritual reasons like these for choosing to attend a Protestant college or university.[11] This is less than half the rate of those of other races. While some African Americans offered spiritual reasons, they are distinctly less likely to provide them than students of other races.[12] By their very nature, conservative Protestant colleges and universities are designed to produce an education that is based in a Christian spirituality. Yet a desire for spiritual growth does not account for why African Americans attend these schools.

Neither does financial aid explain why African Americans attend Protestant institutions of higher education. As indicated in table 5.1, they are about three times less likely than European American students to state that financial support was why they attended Protestant colleges and universities.[13] Since I do not have information that allows me to compare these results to non-Protestant campuses, it is unclear whether this result is due to a general propensity of African American students to not rely on financial aid to attend educational institutions or because Protestant institutions are less likely than other schools to financially support African Americans.[14] However, Perna's finding that financial aid does not heavily influence minority students' decision to attend institutions of higher education indicates that the former reason is more likely the case.

The results in table 5.1 also indicate that financial support is also not as important to Asian American students as it is for other students. There is evidence that Hispanic students are less inclined to attend a Protestant college or university because of its location.[15] However, these were the only nonblack differences in this sample that are worth noting. Thus for the most part, Hispanic and Asian American students attended Protestant institutions of higher education for the same reasons as majority group students. The major finding from these data is that African Americans' decisions about attending Protestant colleges and universities are unique. In chapter 3, I documented evidence that attendance of African Americans at Protestant colleges and university was less likely to be tied to diversity initiatives and programs than attendance of other students of color. If black students utilize different criteria for making their decisions about where to attend Protestant institutions of higher education, then it is plausible that the usual efforts these colleges and universities make to attract them may be less effective than they are for other students of color.

Unfortunately, this data indicate more about what does not work for attracting African Americans than about what does work. The financial programs and religious appeals that Protestant colleges and universities have used thus far do not appear to have been highly effective in attracting African Americans. Previous research has documented cultural differences between African Americans based on theories of alienation (Yancey 2003b) and oppositional culture (Ogbu 1978, Waters 1999). These differences may help to explain these findings. For example, if African Americans face a qualitatively higher level of alienation than other people of color, then they may develop distinctive religious values. Emerson and Smith (2000) illustrate that the racial orientation of African American Christians is based more on structuralism than on the individualism that is embedded in majority group Christianity. Because of such distinctive religious values, the spiritual appeal of most Protestant colleges and universities may not draw African Americans, even as they still manage to appeal to other racial minority groups who do not have to endure the degree of alienation, or separation from society, that African Americans suffer from. Table 2.2 suggests that African American students do not have fewer opportunities for minority-oriented scholarships than other students. In fact, the evidence from this table indicates that Protestant colleges and schools are slightly more likely to offer African American students financial aid than they are to offer it to other racial minorities. It is possible that the oppositional culture of African Americans creates a level of mistrust for these financial programs within the African American community. The relative ineffectiveness of such programs to attract African Americans may also be tied to cultural dynamics within their community, but how those dynamics are manifested remains to be seen.

I did find that athletic teams have the potential to attract black students. This, too, may be related to distinctive cultural values within the African American community, as African Americans are more likely to participate in sports than other racial groups (Eitle & Eitle 2002, Spreitzer & Snyder 1990). If athletic participation is tied to different cultural values within black communities, then black students' attraction to athletic programs within Protestant colleges and universities can be a reaffirmation of those values. However, most Protestant schools are not members of the NCAA division 1, and they have limited resources that can be devoted to athletic teams. Furthermore, there are only so many spots on teams that can be used to attract African American students. Thus there is a natural numerical limitation to the use of athletic opportunities to attract African American students. Given such a reality, there does not seem to be a great opportunity to use the athletic interests of African Americans to attract them to Protestant campuses. Athletic positions can be used to draw African Americans to Protestant campuses, but clearly there is a need to find other ways to recruit. A lesson from these results is the need to recognize that the cultural differences between African American and majority group cultures is more significant in shaping decisions to attend a given college or university than the differences between other racial groups and majority group members. Catering to African American cultural aspects, such as athletic teams, may be more vital for Protestant colleges and universities that wish to attract them than it is for other racial groups.

Conclusion

In many ways, the attitudes and perspectives of minority group students are quite similar to those of majority group members. Yet even with those similarities, important differences arise. Majority and minority group students offer similar levels of concern about the inability of history months, multicultural programs, antiracism programs, community programs, and non-European cultural events to create a more harmonious racial atmosphere, although the reasons for some of the concerns did differ by race. Majority and minority group students also saw value in student-led multicultural organizations, although both groups perceived possible drawbacks as well. Majority and minority group students both tended to value the effect professors of color have on the campus, but white students placed more weight on the personal relationship as the reason for this effect. It is a mistake to conceptualize minority group students as either identical to majority group students or totally different from those students. This should be expected since minority group students have a different racial reality than majority group students but share similar values.

Part of the similarity between white and nonwhite students may be due to the fact that minority group students are not all alike in their racial outlook. Assimilated minority students probably have attitudes very similar to majority group members as they tend to not suffer from the racism their racial peers do, or they tend to dismiss this racism. However, racialized minority group students are less trustful of their majority group peers and as such have more distinctive racial attitudes. These differences within minority racial groups have to be appreciated if we are to gain a complete understanding of the racial dynamics on these campuses. Yet, the differences between assimilated and racialized students of color have important implications that I believe go beyond the Protestant campus. We have to take such differences into consideration as we think about the education of students of color in general. For example, there is significant work documenting the dissatisfaction that some students of color have with the racial atmosphere at their educational institution (Hurtado & Carter 1997, Love 1993, Nora & Cabrera 1996, Solorzano, Ceja, & Yosso 2000, Watson et al. 2002). Given the results of this chapter, it is plausible that such researchers tend to gain the perspectives of racialized students of color and perhaps are ignoring the insights of assimilated students of color. A more comprehensive assessment of how students of color perceive their racial environment should include an attempt to capture the concerns of assimilated students as well.

This finding may also have applications beyond the assessment of students of color of their educational surroundings. These findings remind us that racial minorities do not have a monolithic mind-set. Throughout our racial history, there has been a tension between individuals of color who sought to rebel against the current social order and those who sought accommodation with it. We have seen Native American tribes who fought the American army to their death and those who quickly submitted to reservations. We can contrast the Atlanta Compromise of Booker T. Washington with the "Back to Africa" movement of Marcus Garvey. Even today, we should expect a mixture in minority communities of those who have a radical attitude of resistance and those who seek accommodation, as well as all of those between these two positions. We would do well to remember such variety in racial attitudes among people of color as we conduct work into their experiences in the United States.

While institutional programs do not appear to be highly effective in promoting racial diversity, student-led organizations, minority professors, and a diverse curriculum are connected with racial diversity. The available data are not sufficient for me to evaluate, beyond what has been done in this chapter, the dynamics within multicultural student organizations, but there is additional information about the effects of academic alterations. Thus it is important to evaluate the process by which diversity programs and professors of color may enhance the racial diversity on Protestant campuses.

Understanding this process can enable us to replicate the success of these efforts. To this end, it is useful to explore why these courses and professors create a positive racial atmosphere. In the next chapter, I embark on such an investigation.

NOTES

1. Assertions such as this one are not meant to imply that half of all minority students fall into this category. Because of the nonprobability way this information was collected, I have no confidence that such percentages are representative of the general population of students of color. This caveat should be kept in mind regarding any of the frequencies generated by this survey. However, these percentages do indicate that not a trivial number of students fall into this category, and such students have a real presence on Protestant campuses.

2. I went through each minority student response and looked for evidence that the student basically indicated elements of a white racial identity (i.e., color blindness, individualism). Those who did not reveal such elements were coded "racialized," and those who did were coded "assimilated." I entered the codes into my statistical program to allow me to determine if these different types of students were linked to contrasting demographic and social outcomes. However, a few students of color did not produce enough information for me to code them.

3. This particular student did not provide her class year.

4. But these social worlds do not appear to differ depending on the type of Protestant college or university the students attended. I discovered roughly the same percentages of racialized minorities on mainline Protestant campuses as on conservative Protestant campuses.

5. Indeed, I found that racialized students of color were about twice as likely as assimilated students of color to participate in history months, antiracism programs, multicultural programs, and non-European cultural events. It is not only the case that these programs have been implemented with racialized students of color in mind but also the case that those students are eager to take advantage of those programs.

6. The percentages of white faculty were significantly positively correlated with the percentages of white students on campus for both conservative and mainline Protestant campuses. However, the correlation is stronger on conservative campuses than on mainline campuses (.442 versus .251).

7. Supporting this assertion is the fact that none of the students of color judged their professors of color as unqualified, while some of the white students did make such pronouncements. Students of color probably do not base their perceptions of a professor on their personal attachment to them and thus may not perceive themselves as being in a position to judge the competence of their minority professors.

8. Beyond simplicity, I contend that the most important reasons are most likely to be mentioned first. Furthermore, students who list four or five reasons may not very strongly perceive any of those reasons as to why they attended a certain college or university. Thus, it is unlikely that I am leaving out a strongly felt reason by coding only the first two responses.

9. However, this difference was not due to attracting either racialized or assimilated African American students. Both types of students were equally likely to attend because of athletics.

10. There was a less powerful effect among mainline Protestant students, although even among these students, blacks were more likely to attend to participate on athletic teams.

11. Perhaps this tendency is linked to the desire of African American students to come to these colleges and universities to engage in athletics. White students who engaged in athletics were also notably less desirous of seeking out a spiritually enriching atmosphere than other white students. Participation in athletics and desire for spirituality may be somewhat inversely correlated among students entering Protestant campuses.

12. This difference is largely linked to the results from conservative Protestant students as only four of the mainline Protestant students, none of them students of color, indicated spiritual reasons for college attendance.

13. This difference was roughly the same regardless of whether I looked at conservative or mainline students. However, in the sample of just mainline students, none of the Asian students attended school because of financial support. Thus in this subgroup, black students were obviously not less likely to attend because of financial support than Asian Americans, although they still were less likely to be so motivated than other racial groups.

14. It can be argued that African Americans' higher degree of desire to attend Protestant colleges and universities for athletic reasons provides an alternate path toward financial support for them. This is undoubtedly true. However, deciding to attend school for athletics is a fundamentally different rationale for attending a college or university than attending for other types of financial support, and I chose not to merge these two groups.

15. Students indicated that location was important in that the school was close to where they lived. Since I do not have a random sample of schools, it is plausible that these schools are located in areas that do not have a high percentage of Hispanics. However, four of the colleges were located in Texas and one in California, two states with relatively high percentages of Hispanics. Thus it is unlikely that this result is driven by a lack of Hispanics near these schools.

6

Characteristics of Successful Professors and Diversity Courses

Since I know how to drive, generally I just need my car to operate correctly for me to get to where I want to go. I take it for granted that my car is going to get me to where I want to go—until it fails to do so. Then I need to have someone who understands how the car works to fix it. At that point, just knowing how to drive and trusting that my car will work is not enough. I need someone who knows why and how the car works so that it can be fixed. It is important to understand that something will work, but there is also value in comprehending why something is effective. Understanding why certain mechanisms work allows us to perceive what can be done to make those mechanisms more potent. If necessary, we can "fix" what is wrong, or we even can create new approaches that may also be effective.

The information in the previous two chapters suggests that the most potent measures that Protestant colleges and universities can take to influence their students is the addition of professors of color, diversity courses of instruction, and possibly student-led multicultural organizations. If this assessment is correct, then we know what works. This is not to say that other diversity initiatives have no worth, but those programs are not as effective in supporting racial diversity as these professors, courses, and organizations. Thus there is more need for a deeper examination of the effect of professors of color and diversity courses than there is for other diversity initiatives. We need to explore why they have potency to alter the racial atmosphere on Protestant campuses.

Going back to the comments of the students at Protestant campuses, we can find themes that may indicate why professors of color and diversity courses are positive shapers of the racial atmosphere on Protestant campuses. These students can tell us why these professors and courses influence them. While it is proper to question the accuracy of the students' perceptions, their answers still provide insight into the sorts of influence that these professors and courses have in their lives. In this chapter, I ignore assessment of other diversity initiatives since they are not as effective as these professors and courses, and so their effects are less consequential. But we will gain in-depth knowledge about the process by which these professors and courses help to shape the racial atmosphere on Protestant college campuses. I also touch briefly on the possible mechanisms that may help student-led multicultural organizations to shape the racial environment as well.

The purpose of this assessment is to perceive what students on these different types of Protestant campuses have to say about taking classes from professors of color and/or those who teach diversity courses. To do this assessment, I looked at the students' responses and searched for themes among those responses. As I identified these themes, I then searched for representative comments from the students to represent these themes. Many of the students gave brief responses that are not usable for inclusion. But those that did warrant inclusion I used without bothering to account for the racial, denominational. or gender dynamics of the respondent. As we will see, there are patterns of who tended to follow these themes. Since student-led multicultural organizations are also correlated with racial diversity, toward the end of the chapter I briefly look at them to see if the findings linked to professors of color and diversity courses can be found in those organizations as well. Since this is not a probability sample, assertions about the patterns I discuss in this chapter should be made carefully, but it is a mistake to ignore them.

Professors of Color

As noted in previous chapters, having professors of color is related to racial diversity on Protestant campuses. Some of these professors did not teach courses that dealt with diversity issues. These professors sometimes commented on racial issues, but often they ignored them. Some of the students recognized this aspect and perceive professors of color who did not speak on racial issues as not influential on shaping racial diversity. Thus, having professors of color does not automatically lead to alterations of racial perspectives. These professors have to engage with their students on issues of diversity if they are to have an effect.

Although some students stated that the presence of the professors helped because it showed that people of color could be professors to white students and they provided role models to students of color, this was not a common theme. Other comments were more popular among the students. These comments and themes help us understand what actions these professors undertook to improve the atmosphere of the classroom. One of the first themes to emerge from the responses of students indicates one of the actions that these professors may engage in. Some of them are able to provoke an awareness of other races' experience and their struggles against racism.

> It [classes taught by racial minorities] has opened my mind to the struggles that blacks and other minorities face, and has initiated many conversations, both in and out of the classroom, that I think have changed my views about race relations in the U.S. (Conservative White Female Senior)

> You get a different view point of life instead of something who lives "the white man privilege." (Mainline Other Female Freshman)

> One of my professors was African-American and the other was from Nigeria. It was so interesting to learn about the issues discussed in this class from their perspective. They were talking with a classroom of all white kids. I think it opened many of our eyes to issues that we have never had to deal with. . . . There are perspectives on issues that they see because they have been there. I think that we can never fully understand an issue unless we see it from all sides. Having an all white faculty would be a huge detriment to this campus. (Conservative White Female Freshman)

> It [classes by professors of color] gives me a sense of racial diversity. This allows me to understand others more. It has made me more self aware about what I say or do. (Mainline White Male Freshman)

> I think that the class definitely took on a different atmosphere but it did help me to see their experience first hand and hear directly from them the difficulties and obstacles they have faced. (Conservative White Female Senior)

> They improve the atmosphere, because their experience is different than that of other professors, just as a critical feminist professor is an asset to an all male college. People need to interact with people from different walks of life in order to grow. Our perceptions of society need to expand. (Conservative White Male Junior)

> . . . generally professors [of color] are excellent communicators and knowledgeable concerning racial issues. Therefore, they can educate my peers concerning what minorities still go through. (Mainline Black Male Sophomore)

> . . . other professors talking about the same subject of racial tension would have no real understanding about what it is like without being a minority themselves. (Conservative White Female Freshman)

While it is clear that being able to teach courses that deal with racial issues help these professors produce this awareness, these quotes indicate that the experiences and lives of these professors can have a powerful effect. These professors helped their students better comprehend the effects of discrimination on people of color. They can also speak with a degree of legitimacy that may escape majority group professors. Thus, they can make students aware of the racial and cultural differences that surround them. Students who have a fondness for these professors of color will respect them and become more aware of those differences. Students influenced in this manner by their professors of color may find their ideas of color blindness, individualism, and other attributes of white racial identity challenged on a consistent basis.

Awareness of these cultural differences is not enough to provoke alterations in the racial culture on Protestant campuses. It is also vital to see what students do after they become aware of different racial groups and cultures. It is quite possible that students who become aware of other cultures may denigrate the "strange" customs of these cultures. But another way that professors of color can shape the racial atmosphere on Protestant campuses is that they help Protestant students develop an appreciation of other cultures. For example:

> I took a math class from a professor from North Korea. I am taking sociology from a professor from Brazil. These teachers have made me appreciate other cultures. They also help me understand how Americans can be set in there thinking and challenged me to broaden my horizons. (Conservative Asian Male Freshman)

> She has challenged me to look outside the box and considered other people's points of views and experiences. . . . Every person has a story, and their story will be about another culture—something that everyone can learn and draw from. (Conservative White Female Sophomore)

> It has been interesting to hear the history of another culture and just to hear common everyday experiences, sayings, etc that one would hear in that culture. It makes those people much more real even when you don't see them face to face. (Mainline White Male Junior)

> I think the presence of these professors definitely improve the racial atmosphere on my campus. I think everyone can benefit from learning from a person from a racial minority. They bring a lot of insight from their culture and help us think outside the white box and see others' perspectives. (Conservative White Female Senior)

> It just makes me respect other cultures even more and it is fun to learn what they believe in. (Mainline White Male Freshman)

Because these professors experience a racialization that escapes the experience of their majority group students, they may be able to introduce innovative modes of thinking for those students. It is also plausible that the professors' racial identity produces an atmosphere of expectation within those students so that they are open to new ideas and ways of thinking. This can make them susceptible to appreciate and even desire the new ideas they are exposed to. The students perceive these novel ideas as aspects embedded within the racial culture the professor represents. This process can explain why professors of color may have a higher ability to introduce novel racial and/or cultural concepts to their students than majority group professors.

Of course, this is not to state that majority group professors are unable to introduce new cultural concepts to their students. Obviously, some majority group professors do just that. Since I am only exploring the reaction of students to the teaching of different professors, and not directly assessing differential teaching styles, I do not have the data to explore how the teaching styles of majority group professors may differ from those of professors of color. However, I am in a position to argue that on Protestant campuses that students have different reactions to the teaching of professors of color as opposed to majority group professors.

Antonio (1998) points out that while there has been a good deal of research on the recruitment and retention of minority group professors, there has not been much academic attention paid to the pedagogical contributions of faculty of color. Antonio does find that faculty of color are more likely to perceive their teaching role from a more holistic perspective than majority group professors. They are more concerned with the development of the moral, civic, and emotional capacities of their students. They are also more likely to see their role as a professor as one to induce social change. Furthermore, Umbach (2006) finds that faculty of color are more likely to interact with their students about their goals and aspirations in life. These findings suggest that faculty of color promote discussions and reflections among their students more often than majority group professors. These discussions, and challenges to reflect on the racialized nature of our society, may help students develop more cultural awareness and appreciation of racism than they would with white professors.

A possible outcome of these possible contrasting styles is that minority group professors may have a higher propensity to encourage classroom discussions. This possibility is strengthened by Umbach's (2006) finding that faculty of color employ a broader range of pedagogical tools than majority group professors. Furthermore, there is evidence of this propensity in the comments of the Protestant students in this sample.

They bring a different perspective on issues we face. In addition, students become more exposed to people of minority races and become more comfortable around them. I have definitely felt more comfortable in classes with professors of color—The whole atmosphere of the class is different, and I feel like people aren't as intimidated to speak up, and associate with people of other races. (Conservative Asian Female Sophomore)

I am taking cross cultural and ethnic issues in psychology as well as psychology of family. Racial issues are discussed in these classes quite heavily and both are taught from professors who are racial minorities. It has influenced my way of thinking because I am able to have a glimpse of how they might feel sometimes and step into their shoes . . . because white students are able to understand how minority students might feel. I am also able to understand what actions or words may be hurtful to others that I may not even realize are hurtful. (Conservative White Female Junior)

That course [with a minority professor] was my favorite . . . time in class was spent on openly discussing differences based on a variety of issues, and racial issues. (Mainline White Female Junior)

The students enjoyed learning from other students in their classes. Their professors of color were willing to provide opportunities for such learning. Obviously, such opportunities can be provided by majority group professors as well. This tendency to create dialogue does not appear to be linked to the potential legitimacy that professors of color bring because of their racial identity or their experiences as a person of color. Yet when students are asked how professors of color shape the learning of diversity issues, several of them commented on the ability to have dialogue in their classrooms. It seems likely that at least some of the cultures these professors come from encourage dialogue and communication. These professors may merely pick up from these cultural cues and translate them into their teaching style.

Despite the benefits that these professors provide, there were still problems within some of these classes. As noted in chapter 4, some European American students were frustrated by professors who did not speak English as clearly as they wanted. These comments were obviously directed at professors from other countries. These students resented professors of color for their limited capacities to communicate, but if we take them at their word, their resentment was not due to racial animosity. However, there was another complaint that came from some students that could be tied to the racial identity of the professors. Students at times felt that the professors were too quick to show their anger or to overly focus on racial problems. Such actions created an atmosphere that did not necessarily improve the racial atmosphere on these campuses.

> One professor in particular tends to "harp on" racial issues. Though he is a great teacher, it was exhausting to constantly hear him complain about the misdeeds done to blacks by whites. (Conservative White Female Senior)

> . . . some of the professors will add fuel to the fire because they may feed the racial tension and others accept the tension and try and fix it rather than make huge ordeals over it. (Conservative White Male Sophomore)

> Sometimes I think that they really help and then again there are sometimes that they worsen because I feel almost inferior to them like they may hold hatred on us for historical events in the past. (Conservative White Female Senior)[1]

Sometimes a useful way to illustrate a theme is to see a counterexample of it. For example, note why this student enjoys professors of color.

> They live their culture, but they don't do so forcefully and they rarely assume that students are prejudiced against minorities. (Conservative Multiracial Male Sophomore)

This student is impressed by professors of color because they are not overly hostile to majority group students. There appears to be an expectation that professors of color may have hostility toward majority group members that will come out in their teaching. This student may have experienced that hostility or heard of it from other students and is impressed when some professors of color do not exhibit it. When students perceive hostility being exhibited by the professor, then they may resent the professor and not be open to learning about racialized aspects of our society. In chapter 4, I documented that the majority group students' personal relationships with professors are important in shaping their attitudes. Students who perceive hostility from their professors of color are not likely to develop a good relationship with them. Thus part of why professors of color who are perceived as hostile are unable to effect attitudinal alterations is because this hostility interferes with the potential relationship the professor can develop with students.

Of course, perception of hostility does not mean actual hostility. We would be mistaken if we accepted what the students stated at face value. Some of these professors may indeed be hostile toward majority group students, but others are likely to have their actions misunderstood by majority group students. I cannot tell how accurate the students' perceptions are. However, regardless of the accuracy of their perceptions, the result of their belief that certain professors of color are either overly focused on racial issues or hostile to majority group students is that these professors become less effective in shaping the racial atmosphere on their campuses. This indicates an important lesson for professors of color in that even those with no hostility to majority group students must take care to project an image of nonhostility.

Professors of color have an opportunity to develop interpersonal relationships with their students. They also have an opportunity to model the actions and attitudes they would like their students to adopt. In this way, these professors are in a position to encourage their students to become more aware of different racial cultures and the effects of racial discrimination. They also may be in a position to help their students appreciate other cultures and guide their students into productive discussions with each other. If these professors are able to escape the perception that they are hostile to majority group students, then they have the opportunity to become a critical part of shaping the racial atmosphere on their campus. However, another important component of shaping that atmosphere has to do with the curriculum offered.

Diversity Classes

In the questionnaire, I asked the students if they had attended any courses where the major focus of the course was racial issues. Most students have undoubtedly been exposed to the issues of racial diversity within some of their courses; however, I was interested in the possible effects of taking a course where racial issues are dealt with throughout the entire semester. Some of the answers indicated that they misunderstood the question and included courses such as introduction to sociology, which has a section or two about racial diversity.[2] However, most of the students discussed courses that focused almost entirely on issues concerning racial diversity, which allows me to assess the potential impact of these courses.

Learning what makes these classes effective can help educators design courses that are better able to facilitate racial diversity. Courses that are well developed may experience some degree of success, even if the talent of the instructor teaching the course is below average. Furthermore, these lessons can aid in training professors of diversity courses as well. Looking at how students perceive these courses can provide information vital for developing future successful courses. The responses of these students indicate potential patterns that may help to explain why such courses may affect the racial atmosphere on

Protestant campuses. One of the patterns is how these classes helped students develop an awareness of the prominence of racism still in our society.

> I recognize now that I have had a life of unearned privileges that minorities have not been offered. (Conservative White Female Senior)

> It has shown me that people from every race experience hardships, and that poverty and lack of education is not limited to a particular group of people. (Mainline Hispanic Male Junior)

> They [courses of diversity] drastically altered my ideas about racial issues to the point of my change of major to reconciliation studies. I had no idea the disparities have grown so out of hand in issues involving race and poverty, and I have become an advocate for a change in the system to correct this deadly issue. (Conservative White Male Junior)

> It [diversity courses] opened up about a lot of information about race and certain prejudices. (Mainline White Female Freshman)

> . . . class made me understand the struggles and inequality that happens within our cities. I was able to have a greater compassion for those who are trapped in a cycle of homelessness, poverty, and abuse because of the discrimination that they receive. . . . I think they [diversity courses] have improved the atmosphere because people, especially at our university where most people are very privileged financially, can better understand how bring change and help those who are being oppressed in our own country. (Conservative Hispanic Female Senior)

Previous research has indicated that majority group members are relatively likely to dismiss or minimize the potential effects of racism in the United States (Bobo, Kluegel, & Smith 1997, Bonilla-Silva 2003, Emerson & Smith 2000, Kluegel 1990b, McConahay 1986). Convincing majority group students that we still live in a racialized society is an important task for professors who teach diversity courses. Somehow professors in these courses were able to accomplish this task. Most of the students did not discuss how these professors helped them develop more knowledge about the effects of living in a racialized society, and thus it is not possible to develop ideas about educational tools from these responses. However, clearly these professors sought to make their students aware of the effects of racism in the United States, and such efforts should be important in making these classes useful for shaping the racial perspectives of the students in these courses.

Beyond informing the students within their classes of the problems created by racism, these courses also helped to alter the racial culture on campuses because they often provoked within their students an opportunity for personal reflection. These opportunities enable students to think about the role they may play in our racialized culture and/or how they may help deal with problems created by racism. This was especially the case for majority group students.

> I am currently in this class. It has opened my eyes more so to different racial issues. I have heard about issues in grade school and high school, but it is different hearing things as a young adult and being able to comprehend and think about things at a new level. We discuss topics in class as well and it is very interesting to hear other people's perspectives on topics. I have been forced to evaluate my beliefs and to open my eyes more. (Conservative Female Senior)

> I greatly understand why and how blacks have been fighting for their freedom not only in legislation but in society itself. And the ongoing struggle in the present . . . I took a trip to the south to see several civil rights museums and events which broadened my knowledge . . . changed my understanding and I have been raised around whites my whole life. (Mainline Male Junior)

> I have come to realize that although I am not racist, I place judgments on others based off of looks and that is the same as being racist. (Conservative Female Senior)

> I was one of the people who was ignorant. Not racist, but just unaware of what was really going on. (Mainline Female Senior)

> I was able to see how I have been oblivious to the many things I take for granted in my Whiteness in various situations that are important. I learned that I am not a racist but someone that deals with prejudices every so often. (Conservative Female Senior)

Personal reflections offer great potential for shaping the racial atmosphere because they take what is learned in classes out of the theoretical realm and put those lessons into real action. Once again, these data do not indicate how these courses produce reflections, and so I am unable to suggest possible tools that can induce this reflection. However, since these students indicate that such reflections are possible, then it is reasonable for professors teaching diversity courses on these campuses to assess how they may influence their students to undergo personal evaluations that can change their image as racial actors. Furthermore, as we will see, the students did identify an indirect way by which these images can be changed.

We saw in the previous section that professors of color are able to influence their students because of their willingness to promote discussions within their classrooms. I surmised that the propensity of such professors to encourage such discussion may be linked to their racial culture. I have also found that it was also true that students in diversity courses were influenced by the discussions encouraged in these classes.

> It altered my ideas mainly through the fact that I found it was okay to talk about it in the first place. It was uncomfortable at times, but just talking about it helped raise issues and get answers. . . . This class in particular improved the atmosphere. It gave a setting where people felt safe to talk and intermingle within the groups. (Mainline White Female Senior)

> Deliberately bringing tough topics to discuss in a classroom setting takes pressure off of individuals who are having similar thoughts around campus. (Conservative White Male Senior)

> I definitely think that it has helped improve the racial atmosphere on campus because for the majority of class time we had discussions, and we talked about what we were seeing on campus and throughout our lives, and how that not only affected us but how we should deal with it. (Mainline White Female Junior)

> I think it has improved the racial atmosphere because they open up the eyes of many students who do not believe in racial problems in this country. Students who take the class will have more of understanding of how students from the minority groups feel in a campus where everything seems to be alright. (Conservative Other Male Senior)

> Classes like this, good classes, promote frank discussion of the issues and that is how ideas grow and change . . . it would be more beneficial if more people took it, but in order to truly be effective you need to have smaller class sizes, so people aren't too intimidated by large class sizes to speak up and really get something out of the discussions. (Conservative White Female Senior)

> Change can't start until people start talking. These classes force students to talk about racial issues. (Conservative White Female Junior)

> They [diversity classes] bring about awareness in a safe and critical environment . . . allowing for discussion and debate. (Conservative White Female Freshman)

It is here that we can gain advice as to how these courses can be made more effective. To the degree that they can provoke further discussions, they stimulate higher degrees of cultural and racial awareness. It may be the nature of diversity courses that leads to such discussions. Perhaps the type of professor who teaches diversity is the type of professor who desires to teach through classroom discussions. It may even be the case that diversity courses are no more likely to encourage class discussion than other social science and humanities courses. Regardless of these possibilities, it is evident that discussions in these courses play a potential role in helping students shape their racial attitudes. This role is probably enhanced by the reality that these discussions generally include students from different races. Thus students may be exposed to multiple perspectives from their peers. Because these perspectives come from students, and not professors, the insights students share with each other may be quite believable to other students and have great potential for altering previous racial attitudes.

However, like professors of color, there are also possible problems that can emerge within these diversity courses. Once again, professors in these courses who exhibited hostility toward majority group students lessened the potential of these courses to influence the students who took them.

> There are 80% minorities in this class so the majority white kids still haven't a clue about racial issues. This class has just turned into a venting ground for these minorities to bash on my race and it gets hard to sit there and listen to the ideas tossed around sometimes. (Conservative White Male Junior)

> I think that they have improved it for the most part, but I know other people who are white who felt . . . like the classes were intended to induce guilt rather than solutions. (Conservative White Female Senior)

Reports of such complaints were a great deal less common than the reports of benefits other students offered. This research is not situated to make valid assessments about the degree to which these patterns are manifested in actual classroom settings, but I would argue that such complaints were not common among students. There is a legitimate problem with exhibiting excessive blame toward majority group members within these classes, and some of the beneficial aspects of these courses can be reduced, or even eliminated, by such features. However, it does appear that the benefits of these courses outweigh the potential harm such courses may do through potential alienation of white students.

Like professors of color, diversity courses have good potential to alter the racial attitudes of students on Protestant campuses. These altered attitudes can provide ways in which the racial atmosphere on these campuses can improve. However, it cannot go without saying that these professors and courses may limit their productivity if they turn into what is perceived as "white-bashing." Teaching at a state school, I can testify to the fact that accusations of white-bashing are not limited to Protestant campuses. Yet it is clearly a problem on these campuses that minority professors and instructors of diversity courses need to be aware of.

Even though this is not a random sample, it is hard to ignore how so many of the quotes used are from white students. This is in part because whites make up a larger proportion of the sample, but the sheer number of whites who discussed issues of personal reflections, racial awareness, and understanding discrimination relative to students of color make it likely that there is a racial effect at play here. In an earlier book (Yancey 2007a), I argued that whites are more likely than people of color to alter their racial attitudes in response to interracial contact. I contended that people of color are more likely to have experienced racialization within our society and are more likely to already have strongly established their racial ideas prior to contact. Whites who often do not have to consider racial issues may find their understanding about racialization altered as they deal with the new racial reality that contact with individuals of color brings. If this is the case, then classroom discussions are more likely to provide majority group students with novel ideas than they would bring to students of color. Such discussion would be more likely to provide majority group students with the opportunity to alter their racial perception because of novel ideas.

If interracial contact is part of what produces alteration of racial perspectives, then it may not be surprising that one of the few ways that students of color showed a strong interest in the effects of this course was the potential multiracial conversations they can provide. If such conversations are valuable for altering racial perspectives, then students of color may look to diversity courses in particular to provide an atmosphere for such conversations. Diversity courses do not automatically organize around the promotion of interracial discussion; however, this research suggests that promoting such conversations may allow these courses to become more potent in their ability to facilitate a positive racial atmosphere. Diversity courses that prominently feature directed, but open, discussions of racial issues probably have the most potential for shaping racial attitudes.

However, even these programs and professors do not seem to be able to provoke a strong interest in such students about combating institutional, or structural, racism. It is possible that such courses are not set up to deal with teaching students such concepts. Since the cultural tool kit of white Evangelicals is not well suited for understanding the importance of social structure (Emerson & Smith 2000), that same cultural tool kit may inhibit the ability of majority group students at Protestant campuses to comprehend structuralism as well. However, it is also plausible that it is very difficult to teach majority group students about our racialized social structure, regardless of whether they are at a Protestant campus. It is not clear whether the inability to communicate issues of social structures to college students is connected to the context of being on a Protestant campus or whether it is a general limitation that applies to majority group members in general.

To get at this question, I decided to conduct a minor experiment with my classes at a state university. The summer I wrote the bulk of this book, I was teaching two online undergraduate courses that dealt with issues of race and ethnicity. The courses were titled "The Multiracial Family" and "Race and Christianity." Both were specialized courses in my area of research, and yet neither was a basic race and ethnicity course. Thus, students in this course would have to learn about racial issues within the context of either religion or family. At the end of the courses, I allowed the students to get extra credit by answering one short question about one or two things they learned in the course. About half of the students in each course answered that question.

I found evidence that five of my students were able to pick up aspects of institutional racism from my Race and Christianity course. This response was out of a sample of fifty students who answered the question and thus double the percentage of Protestant students who brought up issues of structure. Their relevant statements follow:

> what is found in the multiracial church, whether it be individual or *institutional* racism, networking socializations or demographics, etc. (Black Female Junior) (Emphasis mine)

> While I say and still maintain I am an individualist and that in today's society people should learn from the past, but make their own futures, I can understand where overcoming the prejudice and discrimination from past ages is a difficult thing to do. (White Female Senior)

> I learned was the fact that white evangelicals base their religion more on individual bases rather then social and individual as the African-Americans. (Black Female Senior)

> Racial Justice and racial status quo are two major lessons I have learned from this course. While both terms are not new to me, this course gave me a different prospective on both issues. Racial justice is not just people of color protesting for political change, I appreciate the information on white privilege—how it is necessary for recipients of white privilege to recognize they are receiving favorable treatment and to address this issue. (Black Female Junior)

> One major lesson I learned from this course is the lesson on indirect institutional racism. I have never considered the implications that social networks could have on racial inequality. (White Female Senior)[3]

These answers portray students who had to consider the power of institutional structures in their emerging understanding of race in the United States. Not all of these students accepted the importance of structures, but they indicated that they learned about structure in this class.

On the other hand, I found no such comments from my students who took my Multiracial Family class. While some of them did discuss issues of racism and prejudice, illustrations of individual racism dominated their comments. Thus I have one class that is about twice as likely as students from Protestant campuses to produce students who indicate that they learned about social structure and one course that seems to have had no effect.[4] What difference between these two courses might produce this effect? Quite simply, the Race and Christianity course has a section on institutional discrimination, and the Multiracial Family course does not. In my Race and Christianity course, I wanted to talk about why some churches and theologies are concerned with the concepts of racial justice. To do this, I included a lesson module devoted to institutional racism so they could understand the types of problems these churches were attempting to address. I found no need for such a module in dealing with multiracial families. In that class, I focused more on the individualistic type of racism and prejudice that members of these families sometimes faced.

Because these were Internet courses, I required the students to examine these issues in online discussion lists. Several students commented in these groups for my Race and Christianity class that the lesson on institutional racism provoked them into thinking about structural racism. On the other hand, there was very little discussion of institutional racism in the online discussion lists from my Multiracial Family course. Thus I assert that the major reason why the Race and Christianity course influenced students to gain more understanding of institutional racism than the Interracial Family course is the inclusion of that lesson. This indicates that diversity courses that devote time to dealing with institutional racism are more likely to influence their students into considering this issue than other courses. Likewise, diversity courses on Protestant campuses may be more effective in introducing their students to issues of institutional discrimination if they intentionally include lessons that directly address this topic. I do not have access to the syllabi or lessons in the courses the students took, so I have no way to substantiate this argument directly, but ideally future research may be able to confirm or refute this assertion.

Lessons from Student-Led Multiracial Organizations

Although I did not have enough comments from students about student-led multicultural organizations to analyze as I did for professors of color and diversity courses, I am now in a position to see if some of the patterns noted in this chapter can be found in these organizations. I did find a few students who commented on the ability of such organizations to promote interracial dialogue.

> . . . they [student-led multicultural organizations] allowed students of color to share their personal concerns and experiences with an understanding group, empowering them to initiate change among their White brothers and sisters. (Conservative Hispanic Junior Female)

> These opportunities have allowed students, such as myself, to engage and dialogue about this issues and to see things from a different perspective. I have appreciated these greatly because it has widened my perspective of God's Kingdom. (Conservative White Senior Female)

> I am a part of the Cultural Diversity Team. . . . We meet on a weekly basis and fellowship. This helps the kids from different cultures feel accepted and provides them an outlet to talk about things they are struggling with. (Conservative Asian Freshman Male)

These comments were more likely to come from students of color than from majority group students, which may reflect the higher likelihood of minority group students to participate in these organizations. This is in contrast to the earlier finding that majority group students were more likely to shape their attitudes because of diversity courses than were students of color. Students of color in multicultural organizations may be more open to learning about other minority cultures in those organizations than in diversity classes. This suggests that student-led multicultural organizations may offer the best opportunity to broaden the cultural knowledge of students of color.

Like diversity courses and minority professors, part of the success of these organizations is linked to the interracial dialogue they are able to generate. This interracial dialogue may enable students of color to perceive these organizations as sites that encourage learning about cultures of color and interracial unity, which are the qualities identified in the previous chapter by students of color as being desirable in such organizations. I also noted that students of color who envisioned these organizations as bringing students together were the ones who saw value in them. Learning about other minority cultures may create a sense of togetherness for students of color. Interracial dialogue can be a way for these organizations to project a vision of interracial unity rather than racial division.

Conclusion

There are obvious similar themes in the assessment of both professors of color and diversity courses. In both cases, students appreciated the opportunity to dialogue with their peers on issues of race. This probably helped students gain more awareness of racial out-groups and for white students to appreciate the persistence of racism in contemporary society. If majority group students have previously been provided messages of the unimportance of race in modern society, they are now exposed to professors and students who challenge that assumption. This suggests a process by which the encouragement of a dialogue between students of different races leads to awareness and respect. This respect can help to establish a social environment conducive to racial diversity.

It should also be noted that with both professors of color and diversity courses, perceptions of hostility toward majority group students were seen as making the racial atmosphere worse. Only conversations where students perceive an openness to honestly share their perspectives generate the type of positive outcomes that improve the racial atmosphere on Protestant campuses. While I have no quotes that directly make this link, I contend that an important reason for this tendency is that this perceived hostility probably interferes with the ability of the professors and courses to facilitate the type of open and honest discussions that lead to more awareness and appreciation. It is likely that students who perceive this hostility become defensive and less willing to learn about the cultures of racial out-groups and/or the racial situations that deprived people of color face. Professors of color and those who design diversity courses should make sure that they minimize the signals that can be read as hostility toward majority group members.

The lessons learned from this chapter may be applied to more than designing diversity courses and training professors of color. We can consider how they may be used to increase the effectiveness of other diversity initiatives. For example, this information suggests that antiracism programs would do well to consider if they are more likely to engender interracial conversation or if they are more likely to produce hostility toward majority group members. If the programs are more likely to do the latter, then these programs may only reinforce the perspective of those who already have progressive racial attitudes and not alter the basic racial atmosphere on the campus. Likewise, celebrations of history months may benefit from concentrating on events that promote interracial dialogue and steering away from events that may seem too "preachy." Administrators on Protestant campuses may need to rethink other diversity initiatives if they are going to create programs that can enhance the racial diversity that their students can enjoy.

Although there are definitely common strands between the students' responses to professors of color and diversity courses, there are also a couple of subtle differences that should be noted. There was more emphasis on appreciating different cultural values with professors of color as opposed to diversity courses. This appreciation may have been manifested in the personality of the professor. The propensity of majority group Protestants to value relationships may also help to account for this tendency. Students may be open to developing interpersonal relationships with their professors, which may introduce them to the cultural differences embedded in their lives. It is also noteworthy that diversity courses seemed more likely than professors of color to invoke personal introspection among students. How such courses are able to do this is unclear, but it does suggest that what students learn in their classes can have an impact on their own personal outlook. Those of us who have been given a chance to design courses of instruction for those in their formative years would do well to understand that propensity with the proper amount of awe and trepidation.

This chapter has built on the findings of the previous chapters so that we can understand the process by which diversity efforts on Protestant campuses may produce beneficial racial outcomes. This chapter has also included warnings we should take into consideration as to why some diversity initiatives fail. Given these findings, it is important to speculate about practical steps for administrators at Protestant campuses who desire to increase the racial diversity of their student population. Accomplishing this task and providing a wrap-up of the findings of this project are the focus of the final chapter.

NOTES

1. Interestingly, I have no examples of this phenomenon from students at mainline campuses. There were some who complained about professors who did not speak English well but none who complained about their professor stirring up racial tension. If this accurately represents a conservative-mainline difference, then there are two possible explanations. First, it may be that professors on mainline campuses are less willing to bring out controversial racial issues than those on conservative campuses. Thus students who attend those campuses do not have a reason to complain. Second, the students on mainline campuses may more readily accept their professors' racial critiques than those on conservative campuses. Therefore, they are less likely to challenge the professors' assertions about those issues. Since students at mainline campuses are more likely to be politically, and thus racially, progressive than those at conservative campuses, I would favor the second explanation.

2. One of the reasons I know this is because I asked the students the name of the course that had the most impact upon them.

3. It is worth noting that all of the students who made such comments are female and three of them are black. This sample is not large enough to make gender and racial assertions; however, it is possible that women and blacks are more likely to learn about social structure than men and nonblacks. It should also be recognized that women made up 75 percent and blacks made up 37.5 percent of the students who filled out the survey. So part of these findings may be linked to the overrepresentation of these two groups.

4. Of course, we have to be careful in making such a comparison. It may be that students who are fresh out of a diversity course are more likely to remember lessons of

social structure than students trying to remember the effects of those courses at some point after being in the course. My contention is that this course is more likely to lead to a more structuralist understanding than many, if not most, courses on Protestant campuses, but the degree to which this realization is more likely to happen cannot be determined because of the distinctions in how information was collected by my courses and how it was collected for the Protestant courses.

7

Suggestions for Protestant Colleges

Previous scholars of education have identified the importance of racial diversity at educational institutions (Antonio et al. 2004, Chang 2001, Gurin et al. 2004, Johnson & Lollar 2002, Laird 2005, Terenzini et al. 2001). The desire for such diversity has led to several different types of institutional diversity initiatives and programs. However, there is a dearth of systematic empirical work investigating which efforts actually promote racial diversity.[1] This book begins to meet the need for such work. It supplies quantitative and qualitative information that can be used to understand the types of diversity initiatives that enable Protestant educational institutions to increase their level of racial diversity. Summarizing the lessons that can be drawn from these findings has important applied implications that must be explored.

It is important to identify not only what potentially works for creating diversity at educational institutions but also what is not effective. Like other organizations, colleges and universities have limitations in the amount of resources they have available. Understanding what is relatively ineffective in promoting racial diversity is important since this knowledge may prevent colleges and universities from investing in programs that do not accomplish their desired goals.[2] This will allow such educational institutions to focus their limited resources on programs that are more likely to succeed and increase the likelihood of wisely planning their efforts to support racial diversity.

Because of methodological and resource limitations, this research deals with only Protestant colleges and universities. There is clearly a need for work at non-Protestant campuses, but given the lack of empirical work on the efficacy of diversity programs, this particular research is still valuable for educators at all different types of campuses. As I argue later, findings from this work can probably be generalized to other types of educational institutions. It is my hope that this work may inspire additional research that looks at other types of educational institutions (Catholic, private, public) or that examines all colleges and universities in order to substantiate or refute this assertion. However, until that work is done, then my results are clearly the most relevant for Protestant campuses. These educational institutions have a unique history and mission and have created an experience for their students that diverges from the experiences of students on non-Protestant campuses.

To this end, as I formulate possible suggestions for organizational alterations for colleges and universities, I look first at specifically Protestant educational institutions. Then, I attempt to break down some possible ways the findings in this work can lead to changes that support racial diversity efforts. I more fully explore possible ways of addressing diversity programs, dealing with professors and student-led multicultural organizations. This assessment is the meat of the final chapter and, in many ways, the most important part of this book because it can direct educators toward meaningful changes on their campuses. I then note some conservative-mainline Protestant differences documented in this work. Doing so can help conservative and mainline Protestant educators craft a diversity program that meets the specific needs of their campus. Then, as mentioned earlier, I speculate about which of these findings are more useful for those who work at an educational institution other than a Protestant college or university. Finally, I explore possible extensions to this current research effort.

Institutional Diversity Programs

Most institutional diversity programs at Protestant colleges and universities have been initiated with the best of intentions. They are efforts to overturn centuries of racial abuse that has been prevalent in the United States. But if this effort is intended to increase racial diversity, then it may be largely misplaced. As this research indicates, there are more effective ways racial diversity can be promoted than these institutional diversity programs. My research has failed to document many potentially lasting benefits from such programs. I began this work with the hope of discovering which programs are most likely to generate productive diversity outcomes. I have reluctantly come to the conclusion that few of the institutional diversity programs are effective in creating a social atmosphere that supports racial diversity on Protestant campuses.

Why have such programs had such a relatively small effect? First, it appears that most students, particularly majority group students, do not take advantage of them. Students of color have noted that majority group students tend to avoid these programs and are not gaining insight from participating in them. Furthermore, even students of color themselves are less likely to take advantage of institutional diversity programs than one might hope. Having these programs does little good if students avoid them. Perhaps if educators can find ways to encourage students to participate in the programs, then they will become more effective. Such participation is especially likely to be useful if it is not coerced, as several students indicated resentment at being compelled to participate in diversity programs.[3]

Many professors send students to diversity programs by offering them extra credit or even requiring attendance at a multicultural or antiracism program as part of the requirements of the course. This can force students to participate and possibly benefit from these programs. But it is unclear whether such participation produces the result such professors desire. Chapel is often required on many Protestant campuses, yet the results of this work do not indicate that dealing with racial issues in chapel has a powerful effect on students. It may not be the students' lack of participation in and of itself that inhibits these programs from shaping majority group students' attitudes; the reasons behind the lack of participation may be key. Majority group students who do not have an interest in addressing racialization may choose not to participate in such programs; even when forced to do so, they may still not develop this interest. If the challenge is to find ways to deal with resistance from majority group students, institutional diversity programs do not appear to be the most effective answer.

This leads to a second problem, the level of resentment against these programs that emerges from majority group students. Over and over again, white students in the sample argued that institutional diversity programs served to separate the different races on campus. They also complained that the programs were unfair and left whites feeling ignored. This resentment is strongest toward programs that the whites are most familiar with, indicating that this resentment is not merely due to ignorance about these programs but may be against the general idea of institutional diversity programs. Whether these complaints have merit is a secondary issue because as long as white students perceive diversity programs as divisive, then these programs will have little ability to shape their racial attitudes and perceptions. Somehow majority group students have to be convinced that these programs serve a social good, or such resentment is likely to continue in the near future.

Finally, there is little evidence that institutional diversity programs enable either majority or minority group students to gain an appreciation of the institutional nature of our racial problems. Very few of the students in this sample discussed institutional racism as they filled out the questionnaire, even though the questionnaire gave them plenty of opportunities to do so. Without an understanding of institutional racism, it becomes easy to reduce our compre-hension of racism to an ability to witness episodes of overt individualistic racism. The fact that such episodes are relatively uncommon today helps to explain why majority group members resent efforts to deal with racism with institutional diversity programs. There is clearly a need to emphasize the relevance of institu-tional racism to students at these Protestant colleges and universities.

Because there has been little previous systematic research on the effects of institutional diversity programs, it is presumptive to eliminate them based on this single study. While this study serves as a warning that faith in these pro-grams may be misplaced, it should not be the reason to end them altogether. The quantitative nature of these findings tend to hide the fact that different types of programs are included under the broad labels of multicultural, com-munity, or antiracism programs. Certain types of multicultural, community, or antiracism programs may be quite successful, even if many others in these categories are not.[4] The work in this research suggests that organizers of insti-tutional diversity programs may want to find ways to encourage productive interracial dialogue. However, future academic endeavors are important in dis-covering other ways these programs can be useful in creating a more positive racial atmosphere. Educators may do well to look at the implementation of institutional diversity programs with some suspicion. If a college or university has abundant resources, then there is little harm in experimenting with dif-ferent types of diversity initiatives on Protestant campuses. For administrators whose resources are relatively scarce, in the next few sections I suggest better uses for those resources.

Initiating a Curriculum for Diversity

Although the evidence of this research suggests that most diversity initiatives are at best inconsistent in their ability to support racial diversity, my research also indicates that diversity courses do hold potential that other diversity initia-tives do not have. Because of such findings, I assert that a high priority for Protestant college and universities should be initiating and sustaining academic courses that directly address issues of racial diversity. These courses offer the potential for alteration of racial attitudes since they may be the venue where students are expected to be exposed to new ideas. As a result of this opportu-nity, the more Protestant colleges and universities can place students into diversity courses, the more they have an opportunity to create a social atmo-sphere hospitable to racial diversity.

To support diversity within a curriculum, Protestant colleges and univer-sities have to ensure they have the necessary means to implement those courses.

Specifically, they must have faculty members who have the ability to teach them. Protestant institutions of higher education would do well to assess their current faculty regarding instruction in issues of diversity. If there is a dearth of professors who are currently able to teach these courses, then it is useful to discover who would be willing to learn to teach them. Protestant colleges and universities may consider aiding professors who desire to develop new diversity curricula with small grants, course releases that provide them the time to develop those courses, and/or training seminars led by a professor who has had success teaching these courses.

There has been a push at state universities over the past couple of decades to include a multicultural requirement in the curriculum. This requirement is generally met by having students take one or more courses that deal with issues of racial diversity. But such requirements are not always present at Protestant colleges and universities. Adding this requirement is another way that Protestant college and universities can introduce their students to issues of racial diversity. I recommend that Protestant colleges and universities require their students to take at least one, and possibly two, such courses before they can graduate. Protestant campuses that do not already have this requirement should consider implementing it. The only reason a Protestant educational institution should not implement such a requirement is if it does not currently have the instructors to teach diversity courses. However, this should be only a temporary condition, as the suggestions in the previous paragraph indicate ways of overcoming this deficiency.

Because of the difficulty of teaching students about institutional racism, it is important to intentionally look for ways to present such lessons. When Protestant colleges and universities are able to add these diversity courses, they would do well to consider the lessons learned from my little experiment with the summer classes. The class where there was explicit attention given to the presentation of issues of institutional discrimination was also the class in which several students took these concepts seriously. Protestant colleges and universities may want to consider requiring a lesson or section on institutional racism in their diversity courses. Such a requirement will be especially powerful if it is supported by another requirement that all students must take at least one diversity course. This will force all students who graduate from the college or university to study institutional discrimination at least once in their academic careers. This does not sound like much, but I suspect that it may be one of the few times that many students who are graduating from Protestant campuses today are exposed to information about institutional discrimination.

Since most Protestant colleges and universities have limited resources, they are unlikely to be free to engage in all of the possible diversity initiatives. For this reason, I suggest that if a Protestant college or university seeks to enhance its racial diversity, then a focus on the development of diversity courses and educational programs should take priority over the diversity initiatives discussed in the last section. Institutional diversity programs should be utilized only after the college or university has fully supported diversity courses and recruited a sufficient number of professors of color. Furthermore, if these initiatives are utilized, then as much as possible they should incorporate opportunities for interracial dialogue and avoid communicating hostility toward majority group members.

The Importance of Faculty

As noted earlier, there is strong evidence that professors on Protestant campuses do have the potential to have a long-lasting effect on the racial attitudes of majority and minority group students. Professors of color and/or those who teach diversity courses can shape the racial atmosphere on those campuses. If these professors develop positive relationships with students and are effective teachers, then they will affect the attitudes of many students. I contend that such instructors are an important key to developing a positive racial atmosphere. Quite simply, Protestant colleges and universities need to find ways to create a better learning environment for issues of diversity in their classrooms.

It is tempting to consider only professors of color or professors of diversity courses as important in shaping of the racial atmosphere at Protestant campuses. However, it is reasonable to assume that the attitudes of white professors who do not teach diversity courses can be important as well. Such professors may establish an atmosphere that is either supportive or hostile to dealing with racial animosity on college campuses. If professors in general do not support efforts to address issues of racial diversity and alienation, then having a few excellent professors of diversity is unlikely to be sufficient for producing a positive racial atmosphere. This reality is reflected in chapter 3's findings about the importance of training faculty members in the prediction of racial diversity, especially on conservative Protestant campuses. Attempts to influence professors' ability to create a positive racial atmosphere should include efforts to help white professors who do not teach courses dealing with diversity.

The effects of nonwhite and diversity professors may be especially powerful on a Protestant campus. The religious environment on such a campus may encourage more interpersonal contact than on nonsectarian campuses. As a result of this interpersonal contact, the effects of having an effective communicator of diversity issues can be magnified. Thus we should not be too quick to generalize the possible positive, or negative, effects of the personal relationships college professors have with their students as we consider professors in non-Protestant educational settings.

It is also important to note that professors of color also play an important role in facilitating the racial diversity that can exist on Protestant campuses. Other work of mine has indicated that the presence of faculty of color on campuses in general is correlated to the racial diversity in the student body (Yancey 2007b). Hiring professors of color is a prevalent problem for colleges and universities. The relatively low number of individuals of color who receive a terminal degree, and thus are qualified for teaching college students, increases the difficulty that any given college or university has in finding a professor of color for a position opening. This difficulty is exacerbated for Protestant colleges and universities in that many of them are located in areas of the United States that are not racially diverse. Furthermore, some of them have religious requirements, such as membership in a certain denominational or theological tradition, which further reduces the pool of qualified faculty of color they may desire to hire. I have no magic formula that can overcome these difficulties. If Protestant colleges and universities do have an advantage, it may be through denominational ministries that specialize in serving certain racial minority groups. Such ministries may be used to encourage young people of color to consider an academic career in which they teach at a denominational school. However, this would be a long-term solution that would do little to alleviate the problem of a lack of professors of color in the short term. Furthermore, while this may a usable strategy for other racial minorities, spiritual motivation for attending a Protestant educational institution was not found to be explanatory for African Americans, and such a strategy is not likely to work with them.

If faculty is the key to developing a more positive racial atmosphere, then it is worth some time and space to consider how Protestant educational institutions can aid such professors in their efforts to deal with issues of diversity. There is also value in considering how to convince white professors who do not teach about issues of diversity the worth of efforts to promote racial diversity. In the next section, I speculate about how these dual goals might be met on Protestant campuses.

Preparing Faculty for Dealing with Racial Issues

The subject of sound pedagogical techniques has been investigated by many academics (Baiocco & DeWaters 1998, Dominowski 2002, Dominowski & Buyer 2000, Griggs 1999, Menges & Weimer 1996, Shulman 1986). Furthermore, several scholars have offered insight on addressing issues of diversity in classroom settings (Aguirre 1999, Davis 1992, Garcia & Van Soest 2000,

Goodman 1995, Gupta 2003, Yancey 2002). It is not my desire to rehash the advice from works more focused on those subjects. However, the techniques that I would like to explore differ from previous advice in a critical manner. This book is intended to aid instructors and professors on Protestant campuses. My sample of students from those campuses offers information that may benefit such teachers. As such, I draw on the responses that students gave through my online survey to envision how professors may improve the racial atmosphere at their particular campus.

The first obvious need is for such professors to incorporate lessons that address issues of institutional racism and the importance of social structures in shaping our current racial situation. The students' responses indicated that the vast majority of them were largely ignorant of the existence of structural aspects in our racialized society. Emerson and Smith (2000) have documented the racial schism within Christian circles on the philosophies of individualism and structuralism, with majority group members supporting the former concept and people of color emphasizing the latter concept. They argue that majority group members possess a cultural tool kit that makes it difficult for them to appreciate the role social structures play in shaping our racial reality. I failed to find the degree of schism that they documented with their work, but I suspect that this is because of the number of "assimilated" students of color who attend Protestant educational institutions. If these institutions hope to attract and retain students of color who are not assimilated, then a great deal of attention must be paid to teaching about social structure and contemporary racism.

To this end, it is my advice that Protestant colleges and universities build within their curricula benchmarks that intentionally expose students to evidence of the importance of social structure in a racialized society. Students who undergo diversity courses should be able to accurately define concepts such as white privilege, institutional discrimination, and color-blind racism. There is also research on white racial identity (Dalton 2002, Dyer 1997, Hartigen 1999, McIntosh 2002, Twine 1997) that can help instructors on Protestant campuses investigate how their faith claims may support majority group ideological notions that help maintain the racial advantage of whites. While discussion of individual racism is also necessary, there is a danger in focusing so much on overt racism that majority group students can easily dismiss the subtle ways in which people of color still operate at a disadvantage in our society. It is the task of Protestant colleges and universities to communicate the danger of ignoring institutional structures with a focus on only individual, overt racism.

Second, it is clear that majority group Protestant students are generally influenced by developing personal relationships with their professors. The personalities of the professors play an important role in if, and how, majority group students accept information about a racialized society. Minority group professors and teachers of diversity courses can reach such majority group students more effectively if they realize the importance of facilitating interpersonal relationships with such students. It is a mistake for professors to rely on delivering accurate information as the only way to support racial diversity on their campuses. Providing knowledge about racial concepts and ideas is sufficient for students of color, but such knowledge is less likely to influence majority group students if those students do not like the person delivering that information.

Of course, how professors facilitate such relationships is tied to their own personalities. An outgoing extrovert may be able to perform for students and make personal connections in such a manner. A more introverted professor without the personal skills to attract many students at once may have to establish relationships one at a time. But most of us have learned how to develop relationships with others regardless of our personality type. Personality type should not be an excuse for why minority and/or diversity professors do not attempt to develop these important interpersonal relationships. Students can take a liking to professors of all different personality types if they believe the professor is competent and fair and cares about them. Students are also likely to be drawn toward professors who are honest, although tactful, about their experiences and perceptions. It is up to each professor to figure out how to reach out to students, given his or her personality tendencies.

One reason that majority group students are so heavily influenced by interpersonal relationships may be that they seek more than mere education from their Protestant college. Because it is a religious organization, students may also expect spiritual guidance from their professors. Because of the values of relationalism that majority group members tend to emphasize in their Christian expression (Emerson & Smith 2000, Hartigen 1999), they may be especially desirous of developing interpersonal relationships with their professors. This may put additional pressure on professors of color and diversity course instructors to facilitate personal relationships with their majority group students, but it also produces opportunities. Such students may be more open to developing relationships with faculty members than students at other types of colleges and universities. They may be more willing to respond to invitations to fellowships, churches, or other types of social engagements. Working within the confines of ethical treatment of students, it may be easier for professors on Protestant campuses to develop interpersonal relationships with their students than for professors at non-Protestant campuses. In fact, some Protestant schools may perceive such efforts at social interaction as part of the duty of being a "Christian professor."

Perhaps because of the Protestant atmosphere, another important issue needs to be addressed. The issues being dealt with in diversity courses are often quite sensitive. Minority professors who teach subjects (e.g., math, physics) not connected to racial issues may not deal with sensitive topics, but if they do venture into their own racial experiences, then they need to understand how delicate racial issues can be. For this reason, it is important to note that some of the students in this research were turned off by professors who came across as too angry. While I do not want to encourage professors to ignore the difficult racial subjects that can come up, I also am obligated to point out that how these subjects are handled can make all the difference between having a student take a second look at his or her color-blind attitude and having that student dismiss racial concerns as merely something people of color complain about.

My personal recommendation is to avoid appearing too angry when presenting information about racial inequality or discrimination but to lay out the facts as clearly and convincingly as possible. As a professor who has taught diversity courses for several years, albeit at state universities, I have experience in dealing with these sensitive issues. I have found that discussing these issues angrily supports individuals who already support racial progressiveness but does little to convince those who do not already have such convictions. I operate on the premise that an angry, hostile presentation is either ineffective or harmful in promoting information about our racialized society and in challenging color blindness. Unconvinced students can alter their racial perspectives if they are respected and they are given information in culturally appropriate ways that they can accept. I have previously written a book chapter (Yancey 2002) where I outlined some of my techniques for teaching majority group students about diversity issues. In that chapter, I offer alternatives to an "angry" approach that I believe are more effective for altering racial attitudes. Space does not permit me to go into these techniques with any sort of depth, but I believe that some of them may be useful for professors on Protestant campuses and thus I recommend reading that chapter for those interested in this approach.

Third, there is another component that should be addressed in revitalizing the instruction of diversity issues, especially as it concerns Protestant educational institutions. Many of the students in these surveys resent the attention paid to issues of diversity, and even the best teachers may fall short of convincing such students of the importance of these issues. Christerson, Emerson, and Edwards (2005) suggest that students at conservative Protestant campuses seem especially resistant to appeals to take issues of diversity seriously when the appeals are based on only sociological evidence. However, they go on to note that such students become more interested in issues of diversity when a case can be made that is supported by biblical scripture. Such an assertion is perfectly logical: individuals are more likely to respond to arguments persuading them of a controversial position if the arguments are presented in a culturally

relevant way. For conservative Protestants, arguments based on biblical references comport with their cultural understanding about society. For example,
those who teach on conservative Protestant campuses cannot use justifications
about the value of racial diversity that rely only on sociological arguments; they
should also rely somewhat on attempts at biblical persuasion. In fact, I suggest
that such professors would do well to start out with a scriptural argument about
the value of racial diversity before attempting to look at the sociological evidence surrounding this issue. This order of events makes it easier for students
at conservative Protestant colleges to take seriously the sociological evidence,
since they will have been convinced of its importance by the scriptural arguments. Such an approach is in keeping with the concept that it is important to
communicate with individuals in ways that are culturally relevant.

The prospect of using biblical arguments can be frightening for professors
who are not well versed in their theological understanding. While ideally it
would be profitable for professors and instructors to conduct their own research
on how scripture can be used to support notions of racial justice and combating institutional racism, much of this work has already been done. In the
appendix, I have listed several books, with a small description of each text, that
utilize scriptural arguments for issues of racial justice and dealing with racial
issues. Those planning to teach courses dealing with race and ethnicity at a
conservative Protestant college would do well to look over these books so that
they will be able to address their students' spiritual concerns, as well as their
sociological inquiry.

Of course, helping instructors and professors do a better job with their students is only part of what needs to be done to improve the educational experience of students. The racialized educational climate of a given Protestant
institution of higher education is more likely to be influenced by the majority
of professors who do not teach issues of racial diversity than the few who do.
Thus, it is also important to address possible resistance that may come from
professors who do not teach diversity courses. Speculating about some techniques educators may employ to address this possible resistance is worthwhile.

Dealing with Resistance from Professors

Perhaps the most difficult resistance comes from professors who do not deal
with issues of diversity. Just as students may be influenced by professors of
color because of their personal relationships with them, they also may have
personal relationships with professors who disagree with the basic goal of
intentionally promoting racial diversity.[5] These individuals can easily influence students to ignore the value of racial diversity and social justice. Their

resistance can make the tasks of diversity instructors difficult, if not impossible. Professors who are uneasy about diversity initiatives often are well entrenched in their social philosophy and are not likely to be easily persuaded to consider alternative possibilities. Furthermore, such individuals are protected by the ideals of academic freedom, and thus there is little that one can do to coerce compliance from them. However, on many college campuses, many of them have a powerful ability to shape student opinion, and thus it is important to address the concerns they may bring up.[6]

Unfortunately, this current research project does not provide any additional information about professors at Protestant colleges and universities. Clearly, there is a need for research into the attitudes these professors have toward diversity, since their attitudes are an important shaper of the perspectives of students at Protestant campuses. Any advice I can provide on how to bring along professors who do not support racial diversity would be speculative, but since little has been done previously to consider how to persuade such professors of the importance of diversity, it is worth a little space to speculate how this may be accomplished.

Obviously, support from the administration is vital for creating an atmosphere that can shape the perspectives of Protestant professors. The administration must do more than merely provide verbal support of racial diversity. Even support of the diversity initiatives discussed in this book will be insufficient, since professors generally feel free to criticize administrative priorities that are not their own. The administration must engage in an effort to communicate in dialogue with its professors. It is plausible that productive interracial dialogue may have similar positive effects within the faculty as it does within the student body. The administration may also consider bringing in speakers from the outside who have not played a role in past battles, or it may need to find advocates within its own ranks.[7] These issues may be addressed in faculty meetings, retreats, and/or chapels. Each campus probably has unique dynamics that help to dictate the format in which such discussions may take place. Regardless, there must be an overt effort to engage professors from all over the campus in discussions that focus on the vitality of racial diversity in a Protestant educational setting. Such discussions, if handled correctly, can serve to lessen some of the resistance of certain professor toward facilitating a racially diversity campus.

What about Student-led Multicultural Organizations?

Much of this chapter has been dedicated to issues of professors and curriculum. Those institutional aspects are difficult to address, but they are still technically under the control of educators and administrators. But the other institutional characteristic that was found to be correlated to racial diversity was the presence of student-led multicultural organizations. Such organizations are correlated with the retention of students of color. My quantitative analysis indicated that the more student-led multicultural organizations a Protestant college or university had, the more likely were students of color to graduate from that college or university. Since these organizations may be critical for helping such students to fully integrate into the atmosphere of Protestant campuses, the presence of more such organizations may provide students of color with multiple opportunities to experience integration. It is in the interest of Protestant colleges and universities to encourage the development of as many multicultural student-led organizations as possible.

Since these organizations are led by students, there may limits to what Protestant educational institutions can do to encourage them. If students are not willing to start such organizations, then they will not emerge. However, the comments from the students at Protestant colleges and universities indicate a strong desire, at least among students of color, for student-led organizations that create opportunities for racial unity. Administrators at Protestant colleges and universities may be able to tap into this desire to encourage the development of these organizations. To this end, administrators would do well to be sensitive to concerns and complaints brought to them by students of color. Students of color who show an interest in making their campus a more racially hospitable environment may be encouraged to channel their energy into the formation of a student multicultural organization that may indeed improve the racial atmosphere for students of color.

Student-led multicultural student organizations may provide a route by which students of color can become integrated into the social fabric of their campus. To do this, these organizations must provide those students with the hope that they will promote unity among students of different races. Interracial dialogue within these organizations may provide students with this hope. College administrators may consider encouraging such dialogue within these organizations and between these multicultural organizations and more conservative political or social organizations on their campuses.[8] There may be several ways to accomplish this task. For example, most colleges and universities require student organizations to have a faculty advisor. Such faculty advisors are in a position to suggest the facilitation of interracial dialogue within their organizations. Furthermore, Protestant colleges and universities may consider grants and other financial incentives that enable interracial dialogue within multicultural student organizations. Finally, the administration can sponsor events where interracial dialogue will take place and then invite student multicultural organizations to those events.

Conservative versus Mainline Protestant Schools

As I noted in chapter 2, one of the important distinctions between Protestants is between conservative and mainline denominations. While the suggestions in the preceding paragraphs pertain to both Protestant groups, I did find enough contrasts between conservative and mainline Protestant schools to justify different approaches, depending on this distinction. The differences are not comprehensive, but understanding some of the contrasts between conservative and mainline Protestants will be helpful for charting similar paths, but with different emphases, for either type of institution. Thus an exploration of the contrasts between these two groups is in order.

My quantitative research indicates that conservative Protestant campuses may gain more from diversity initiatives than mainline Protestant campuses as it concerns African Americans, but the same is not true for other racial groups. Hispanics and Native Americans appear to be more sensitive to diversity initiatives on mainline, rather than conservative, campuses. Regardless of this latter finding, there may be more to learn about the effects on African Americans, since they are the only minority racial group that is significantly less likely to graduate from Protestant educational institutions than from other types of colleges and universities. Thus it is useful to focus on blacks since diversity initiatives may have more of an effect on retention effects unique to Protestant institutions than the possible effects on other racial minority groups.

The difference between African Americans and other racial groups may be tied to the fact that African Americans have a racialized experience that differs from other racial groups. They have faced barriers to assimilation that are more pronounced than those facing other racial groups (Davis 1991, Glazer 1993, Warren & Twine 1997, Yancey 2003b) and thus may be more suspicious of predominantly white institutions than members of other racial groups. Furthermore, it may be the case that conservative Protestant campuses have historical and societal baggage to overcome if they are going to attract African American students. Mainline campuses may be less likely to have such baggage. If this is true, then African American students may approach conservative campuses with more suspicion, and diversity efforts may be more important in convincing them to come and graduate from a Protestant campus.

Why might conservative Protestant campuses have such baggage? The history of conservative Protestantism and African Americans is a shaky one. These were the types of schools that were likely to cooperate with the notions of separate but equal embedded in a Jim Crow mentality. There is evidence that conservative Protestants were highly likely to resist efforts to promote civil rights (Hadden 1969, Laythe, Finkel, & Kirkpatrick 1997). Even today such Protestants are less likely to back progressive initiatives that support the interests of people of color (Greeley & Hout 2006, Hinojosa & Park 2004, McDaniel & Ellison 2008). Given such a history, and contemporary reality, an African American student may understandably hesitate to enter a predominantly white institution dominated by conservative Protestants. This is the baggage that conservative Protestant educational institutions have to overcome if they are to create a welcoming atmosphere for black students.

Perhaps it is because of such baggage that students of color at conservative Protestant institutions are more optimistic than their counterparts at mainline Protestant campuses that professors of color will improve the campus atmosphere. Such students may perceive such professors as evidence that these campuses will not fulfill their worst fears connected to the political conservatism that is associated with conservative Protestants. This was the only racialized qualitative difference I found in this sample, but it supports the notion that conservative Protestant campuses may have to work harder to "sell" students of color, especially black students, on the idea of coming to their institution. Locating and hiring professors of color appears to be a solid way of improving diversity and may take on a greater importance at conservative Protestant campuses than at mainline Protestant colleges and universities.

However, it may also mean that conservative campuses are more likely to attract resistance from professors on their campuses who still maintain some type of color-blind outlook on racial issues. Successfully implementing programs that alter the curriculum and bring minority faculty to the campus may be more difficult to achieve on such campuses. Furthermore, it is reasonable that educators at conservative campuses may need to take a more proactive role to influence the student-led multicultural organizations that develop at their institutions. While such educators should not take too heavy-handed an approach to the possible isolationist nature of these groups, it is important that minority students at such organizations are encouraged to reach out to those of different races and not let the organizations *only* serve the function of being a refuge for them. Naturally, as educators create a more hospitable racial atmosphere on these campuses, and lessen or remove the historical and racial baggage at their campuses, then minority students will have less incentive to seek out such isolation and be more willing to engage with the rest of the student body.

If this speculation about the additional baggage is accurate, then my research has a couple of suggestions for how conservative Protestant campuses may be able to overcome this baggage. It appears that the celebration of the accomplishments of blacks may contribute to an atmosphere where black students feel accepted. This may be why black history months are linked to higher enrollments of African American students. Also, professors of color may signal to students that the university takes the concerns of African Americans quite seriously. I suggest that conservative Protestant campuses become especially sensitive to celebrating the achievements of African Americans and employing minority faculty.

What Might Be Generalizable to Non-Protestant Campuses?

This research has concentrated on the racial atmosphere on Protestant campuses, and some of the findings in this study are undoubtedly linked to the religious uniqueness of this educational setting. Since I do not have information from non-Protestant campuses, I cannot make the comparisons necessary to fully investigate how this unique setting affects these results. However, a careful assessment of these findings suggests that some of them are more likely to be generalizable to non-Protestant settings than others.

Much of my argument about what is not likely to be generalizable is based on the findings of Emerson and Smith (2000) on the racialized differences between Protestants and non-Protestants. They found that white evangelicals are more likely to favor individualism, embrace the importance of interpersonal relationships, and reject structuralism, or the ability to perceive social structures as important, than nonevangelical whites. On the other hand, African American evangelicals were more likely to embrace structuralism and to downplay the importance of interpersonal relationships and individuals than African Americans in general. Thus the racial dynamics within these churches produce more social and political separation among Protestants than among Americans as general.

The higher propensity of majority group Protestants to deeply value personal relationships indicates that the finding that may be less generalizable is the importance of personal relationships with the professor. The fact that such relationships were quite important for majority group students but not very important for students of color reinforces the reality of this racial difference among Protestants. Such a difference may not be as pronounced at non-Christian educational institutions since the difference in the importance of interpersonal relationships is less among non-Christians than it is among Christians (Emerson & Smith 2000). Minority professors on non-Protestant campuses may not need to make the efforts required of minority professors on Protestant campuses to develop interpersonal relationships with their students. It also may be the case that teaching institutional racism to majority group members is not as difficult on non-Protestant campuses as it is at Protestant schools. The lower degree of adherence of Protestant whites to structuralism than whites in general may produce a higher barrier for learning about institutional racism for whites.

The finding in this research that Protestant students do not easily learn institutional racism through diversity initiatives and academic programs may not be accurate for non-Protestant students.

However, I do hold out hope that the findings about the general importance of diversity classes and professors of color are viable on non-Protestant campuses. I suspect that students are more open to being convinced by such classes and professors because they accept the role these individuals and courses are intended to play. The educational purpose of Protestant campuses is no more viable than it is at non-Protestant campuses. Both Protestant and non-Protestant campuses may benefit more from alterations in the educational curriculum than from the promotion of diversity programs. In fact, since part of the purpose of Protestant campuses is religious, it can be fairly argued that this educational purpose may be stronger at non-Protestant campuses than at Protestant colleges and universities.

Furthermore, the process by which diversity initiatives shape the racial atmosphere on Protestant campuses is likely to be similar to processes on non-Protestant campuses. I found that open dialogue encourages more cultural awareness and more awareness of the racial struggles of people of color. It may provide students within the different racial groups the capacity to develop tools that facilitate a positive racial atmosphere. This process is not directly tied to the propensity of Protestant students to prioritize relationships with their professors. It is likely that the dialogue between students produces a powerful awareness effect. If this process is generalizable to non-Protestant campuses, then honest and open dialogue between students of different races needs to be encouraged at these institutions, as well as at Protestant colleges and universities.

Extensions of This Current Endeavor

This research offers us potential to more fully investigate the potency of diversity efforts in an educational setting. While I conducted empirical tests to draw my conclusion, in many ways this is still an exploratory endeavor that requires serious efforts at follow-up. For example, an obvious addition to this current work is replication in non-Protestant institutions of higher education. Some of the findings in this research are likely to be generalizable to non-Protestant campuses, but without such replication, it is difficult to assert which findings may be useful. For example, because white resentment of efforts to overcome structural racism is not limited to Protestant campuses, it is fair to state that non-Protestant campuses may also have a difficult time teaching their students lessons about structural racism. However, discovering the different challenges

Protestant colleges and universities may have relative to non-Protestant colleges and universities in transmitting lessons of institutional racism cannot be determined from research that focuses on Protestant campuses alone. Ideally, future research will investigate how well diversity initiatives inform students about structural racism in non-Protestant settings as well.

One of the findings in this work that needs further examination is the distinctions within minority group students. Quite simply, what are the differences between assimilated minority students and racialized minority students? Are there differences in demographics (e.g., are racialized students of color more likely to live in racially homogeneous areas?) and/or in social networks (e.g., are assimilated students of color more likely to have white friends?). Understanding these differences is quite important since these distinct minority groups probably have contrasting social needs to be met. If we can determine ways to operationalize these distinctions within students of color, then it is possible to conduct quantitative and qualitative work that can explore the differences between these two groups of students. Such work can, among other things, help us determine the percentages of students of color in each group. As I suggested in chapter 5, these students may represent the different types of reactions that people of color in general have as they engage our racialized society. Knowing the size and nature of the groups of racialized and assimilated students of color may provide us further insight into these populations in communities of color in general.

There is also value in conducting in-depth interviews with students on Protestant and non-Protestant campuses. Financial and practical limitations prevented me from conducting such interviews, which would have allowed me to probe further some of the assertions provided by the students. The information I received from these open-ended questions are quite insightful and suggestive of what is happening on these campuses, but they also produce important questions that need to be addressed. For example, through interviews I would have gained a better understanding of whether students on these campuses only perceive hostility by their professors or whether there is real hostility, because I could ask for more details about the incidents of hostility they claim to be suffering from. While I would still have to be careful about the subjective nature of the students' reporting, given my experience as a professor I would have confidence in correctly assessing most of the time whether the professor is actually exhibiting hostility or whether the student is misunderstanding the actions of the professor. The use of in-depth interviews to investigate this, and other relevant questions, would produce more useful information for educators.

Along those lines, it is also vital to interview students of color who have left Protestant colleges and universities. Finding such students will be difficult, as these educational institutions do not always maintain contact information on students who have left their programs. However, if such students can be found, then there is a great deal of valuable knowledge that can be gained from these interviews. Who is in a better position than these students to tell why they no longer attend their former institution of higher education? If enough students are found, important patterns can be discovered. For example, we can learn whether assimilated minority students are less likely to leave these colleges than racialized minority students. Furthermore, it may be useful for helping us understand the different needs of assimilated and racialized minority students and the contrasting reasons such students fail to obtain their desired educational goal at that particular college or university.

Finally, there would be great value in testing programs that utilize some of the principles I have asserted. For example, this work can test the effects of antiracism programs that focus on interracial dialogue as opposed to antiracism programs focusing on challenging majority group members. Such tests can assess the relative importance of dialogue in altering racial attitudes and the atmosphere on campuses. My assertion is that dialogue and the impending awareness that comes out of it will be more effective than other mechanisms. While I argue that professors of color and diversity courses are currently the best way to produce this dialogue and awareness, it is quite plausible to use these mechanisms in other diversity initiatives. Testing these other initiatives to understand the potential effect of dialogue and awareness in other diversity initiatives is an important extension to this work.

Moving into the Twenty-first Century

The society in the United States, like every other society, is constantly changing. One of the important changes is the racial dynamics that occur as individuals of different races interact more. This interaction has important social implications. Emerson (2006) has discussed the emergence of what he calls the "sixth" American. This is a person who does not fit into the normal five basic racial groups since he or she interacts with individuals of other races so freely that he or she is not linked to any single racial identity. These individuals are comparatively likely to interracially date, have racially diverse social networks, attend multiracial religious institutions, and work in integrated occupational settings. According to Emerson, this sixth American is becoming more common in the younger cohorts that colleges and universities continue to serve. Such students expect to learn in educational atmospheres that are racially diverse since they experience such diversity in all of their other social environments.

Protestant colleges and universities are going to have to adjust to these changing racial dynamics. If Emerson is correct, then Protestant institutions of higher education are going to have to deal with more "sixth Americans" as time goes on. Those that do not adjust by creating a more racially diverse campus may soon find themselves unable to attract sufficient numbers of students. Such colleges and universities have to create an educational atmosphere not geared toward any single racial group but one that is multiracial in numbers and in character. This work is intended to aid Protestant institutions of higher education directly and other colleges and universities indirectly. But in doing so, I hope to help all colleges and universities adjust to our changing society.

My previous excursions into understanding multiracial institutions indicate that productive racial diversity does not happen by accident. It occurs only when key individuals take proactive measures to ensure that a healthy racial atmosphere develops. Intentional decisions and efforts have to be initiated to promote and sustain that diversity. Administrators and decision makers at institutions of higher education have to make those types of decisions if their students are to enjoy the full benefits of learning in a racially diverse educational community.

NOTES

1. While a great deal of research assesses a particular diversity program, there is little that compares contrasting types of programs in different colleges and universities across the United States. Although this work is limited to Protestant educational institutions, the breadth of the programs and institutions of higher education studied is an advance over previous work.

2. Of course, this assumes that the goal of such programs is the attraction and retention of students of color. If there are other purposes for such programs, such as image management, then an educational institution may desire to maintain that program even if it does not create a more racially diverse campus.

3. One of the possible reasons that students may hesitate to participate in these programs is their perception that the administration is attempting to pressure them into participation. Students at this stage of their lives are likely to rebel against authority figures, and this propensity may exist even on a Protestant campus. This may be why student-led multicultural groups have more success than such programs, since in them students are reacting to the overtures of their peers rather than responding to their elders.

4. In fact, there is promising work suggesting that multicultural programs that employ learning communities may greatly enhance a Protestant college's ability to retain minority students (Firmin et al. 2008).

5. It is unlikely that professors, even those who are politically highly conservative, will openly rail against racial diversity. Such resistance would probably be understood as racism. But these professors may perceive efforts to encourage racial diversity as misplaced in relationship to the educational and spiritual goals of the college or university.

6. Anecdotal conversations that I have had with professors who deal with diversity on conservative Protestant campuses suggest that it is often professors of theology or Bible who offer the highest level of resistance. These professors may be more likely to have a traditionalist societal perspective and thus resist racial challenges to the current status quo. But they also tend to be professors who are held in high esteem by the students at the campus. Thus it is not mere speculation to contend that some of the professors who have the highest level of disagreement with diversity efforts are also those who often have high levels of social prestige. Gaining their compliance—or at least nonresistance—is important to the overall success of the diversity programs on a given campus.

7. I would suggest that administrators on conservative Protestant campuses make sure that such speakers accept the general theology followed by the professors or at least do not attack those professors' theological beliefs. My discussion with colleagues who teach on such campuses indicates that discussions led by religious outsiders are not well respected.

8. I point out the need for dialogue with conservative or traditional organizations since those are the student groups that are most likely to resist efforts at racial diversity. Thus dialogue between such organizations and student-led multicultural groups possess the greatest possibility of lessening racial or social tensions that may develop between groups with differing ideologies.

Appendix: Methodology

Here I further explain the methodology used to produce the results of this book. In particular, I concentrate on how the quantitative analysis used in chapter 3 was conducted. The qualitative work used through the rest of the book is pretty straightforward and adequately explained in the body of the book.

Survey of U. S. Protestant Colleges

The quantitative data came from information in the 2000 U.S. Census Summary File, 2006 NCES, *The Princeton Review Complete Book of Colleges*, and my own survey of Protestant colleges. From the U.S. Census, I obtained information about the racial makeup of the cities the colleges were located in. From the NCES, I obtained information about the racial diversity of the students and faculty and the graduation rate of the minority students at those campuses. From *The Princeton Review Complete Book of Colleges*, I found information about the type of school included in the sample (e.g., conservative Protestant, Historically Black Colleges and Universities). I included the variables collected from my survey described in the previous chapter to assess the programs Protestant colleges and universities employed rather than merely their institutional and demographic characteristics. This research indicates that the racial diversity of the city and of the faculty is the main predictor of the racial diversity of the campus (Yancey 2007b). Other research has suggested that the graduation rates of majority group members is an excellent predictor of the graduation rates of people of color (Small & Winship 2007). Assessments of the potential of diversity programs to shape the retention and graduation of students of color must take these factors into account.

Variables

The number of African Americans, Hispanic Americans, Native Americans, and Asian Americans in each educational institution was recorded from the NCES. That created a variable that indicated the percentages of people of color at a particular Protestant educational institution (percent black, percent Hispanic, percent Indian, and percent Asian). I also used the NCES to document the graduation rates of the minority groups on the Protestant campuses (black graduation rate, Hispanic graduation rate, Indian graduation rate, and Asian graduation rate). These two variables will be the dependent variables used in the quantitative portion of this research.

I used zero-order correlations to assess the relationship of diversity programs and initiatives to the racial diversity and minority student graduation rate on Protestant campuses. From my survey, I obtained a variety of independent variables to test which institutional variables are important for predicting the ability of Protestant colleges and universities to recruit or retain people of color. Race/ethnicity dept is a dummy variable that measures whether there is a department or office in the college that deals with racial issues, and race statement is used to indicate if the school has a statement that supports racial diversity. Race-chapel indicates if issues of race have been dealt with in chapel over the past year, and if so, then how often racial issues were addressed. Ethnic studies, black studies, Hispanic studies, Indian studies, and Asian studies are dummy variables assessing whether the college or university has, respectively, an ethnic, black, Hispanic, Indian, or Asian studies program. As I explained in chapter 3, those four variables were combined to put in the line for specific racial group studies so that I could shorten the table. Antiracism, multicultural, community, and cultural events, respectively, indicate whether and how many antiracism programs and events, multicultural programs and events, community programs and events, and cultural events the college or university sponsors. Black month, Hispanic month, Indian month, and Asian month are dummy variables that determine if the college or university celebrates these months. Month celebration is constructed for these history months in the same way that specific racial group studies was constructed for studies programs. Scholarship indicates if the college or university offers any minority-based scholarships, and black scholarship, Hispanic scholarship, Indian scholarship, and Asian scholarship, respectively, indicate whether there are scholarships that are directed at African, Hispanic, Native, or Asian Americans. Specific race scholarship is constructed for scholarships in the same way that specific racial group studies was constructed for studies programs. Recruit minority students and recruit minority faculty are dummy variables indicating whether the college or university has any programs for recruiting students and/or faculty of color. Train faculty is a dummy variable indicating whether the college or university has programs for training faculty in issues of racial diversity. Finally, multicultural student organizations and student committee, respectively, indicate the number of multicultural student organizations currently on campus and if there is a student committee committed to dealing with issues of racial diversity. The questions used to construct these variables can be seen in figure 2.1.

There was one particular institutional effort that I did not directly capture with my survey. That concerned the number of courses directly related to issues of race and ethnicity.[1] To obtain this information, the online catalogs or bulletins of the educational institutions were located.[2] Then all of the courses of instruction were examined.[3] Only courses where the subject matter concentrated only on racial issues were counted.[4] Furthermore, courses that were international in nature were not included since many of these courses neglect domestic issues of race and ethnicity.[5] A graduate student coded some of the catalogs, which I used to conduct an intercoder reliability check. We agreed on the codes 79 percent of the time.[6]

I divided the courses in the catalogs into whether they fit in ethnic courses, black courses, Hispanic courses, Indian courses, or Asian courses. Ethnic courses indicate college courses that deal exclusively with racial issues but do not focus on any particular racial groups. The other variables indicate the number of courses that deal with a specific racial group. Specific race courses is constructed for these courses in the same way that specific racial group studies was constructed for studies programs. I also created a variable that totaled all of the courses to create a measure of total race courses. This allowed me to measure the degree to which the existence of many racial courses, regardless of whether they deal specifically with a racial group, has on the racial reality of people of color.

Results

Appendix table 1 shows measurements of each of the dependent variables as they are used to explain the percentage of racial minority groups on Protestant campuses. A certain amount of caution is required when interpreting these results. Although they accurately measure whether certain institutional measures or characteristics are correlated with the percentages of certain minority student populations, they do not necessarily indicate that these measures or characteristics create the racial makeup of the campus. Indeed, it is possible that the size of minority student populations created institutional changes, such as an ethnic study curriculum or multicultural programs. Furthermore, the survey does not assess whether institutional changes sparked a potential growth of students of color. While I can obtain information on the percentages of the student body on the campuses from years past, I have no information on when the different colleges and universities implemented these diversity initiatives.[7] Thus it is impossible to completely determine the directionality of diversity programs and racial minority population. Indeed, some of the measures indicate a negative relationship with these measures and size of certain minority groups. As we saw in the body of the text, there are possible reasons for a negative effect, but these findings do indicate which types of diversity initiatives have the potential to support efforts at racial diversity.

My earlier work (2007b) suggests that the most important factors predicting racial diversity on college or university campuses are the racial diversity of the city the campus is located in and the racial makeup of the faculty. Given this possibility, there is value in controlling for these two factors in the examination of which diversity initiatives are correlated to the percentage of nonwhites on Protestant campuses. However, the percentage of minority faculty on campus is probably closely related to the implementation of many of these diversity initiatives, especially those connected to curriculum alterations.[8] Controlling for faculty diversity would probably obscure the potential effects of these diversity initiatives. Nevertheless, there is value in accounting for racial diversity in the city where the college or university is located because such diversity is not automatically related to the implementation of diversity programs and initiatives. Indeed, I have conducted regression analysis that implemented such controls. These tables are available upon request. As expected, the power of proximity of students of color to a Protestant college or university tended to overwhelm all other effects. While some of the findings survived these controls, the reader would do well to remember that the best predictor of racial diversity on Protestant campuses is the racial diversity of the city where the school is located, which is a factor beyond the control of school administrators.

The first finding that jumps out in appendix table 1 is that only one of the dependent variables is significantly positively correlated to the percentage of African American students. That variable is black month, indicating that Protestant educational institutions that celebrate African American history month are more likely to have a higher percentage of African American students. Surprisingly, several variables were negatively correlated to the size of the African

APPENDIX TABLE 1 Correlations of Percent Black, Percent Hispanic, Percent Indian, and Percent Asian and Selected Variables of Racial Diversity Programs for All Protestant Schools

	Percent Black	Percent Hispanic	Percent Indian	Percent Asian
Race/ethnicity dept	$-.28^b$ (138)	$-.209^b$ (138)	$-.084$ (138)	.018 (138)
Race-chapel	.029 (130)	.048 (130)	$-.115$ (130)	$.298^a$ (130)
Race statement	$-.164^a$ (133)	.085 (133)	$-.032$ (133)	.149 (133)
Ethnic studies	.009 (137)	$-.053$ (137)	.022 (137)	$-.029$ (137)
Specific racial group studies	$-.049$ (136)	$.155^a$ (135)	.132 (136)	$.163^a$ (135)
Anti–racism	.01 (133)	.067 (133)	$-.152^a$ (133)	$.198^a$ (133)
Multicultural	$-.148$ (130)	.019 (130)	$-.162$ (130)	.158 (130)
Community	027 (126)	.124 (126)	$-.099$ (126)	$.209^b$ (126)
Cultural events	$-.147^a$ (129)	.014 (129)	$-.087$ (129)	.114 (129)
Month celebration	$.22^b$ (134)	.13 (133)	.108 (134)	$.191^a$ (133)
Recruit minority students	$-.267^b$ (124)	$-.12$ (124)	$-.201^a$ (124)	.052 (124)
Recruit minority faculty	.089 (121)	$.243^b$ (121)	$-.017$ (121)	$.283^b$ (121)
Scholarship	$-.186^a$ (115)	.057 (115)	$-.056$ (115)	$-.018$ (115)
Specific race scholarship	$-.167^a$ (115)	$.179^a$ (115)	$-.087$ (115)	.029 (115)
Train faculty	$-.027$ (122)	$.228^b$ (122)	$-.081$ (122)	$.266^b$ (122)
Student committee	$-.045$ (130)	.091 (130)	$-.017$ (130)	$.195^a$ (130)
Multicultural student organizations	$-.086$ (130)	.142 (130)	$-.051$ (130)	$.267^a$ (130)
Ethnic courses	$-.096$ (140)	.13 (140)	$-.196^a$ (140)	$.169^a$ (140)
Specific race courses	$-.02$ (140)	$.205^a$ (140)	$-.1$ (140)	$.466^b$ (136)
Total race courses	$-.09$ (140)	$.154^a$ (140)	$-.179$ (140)	$.218^a$ (140)

a = p < .05; b = p < .01

American population on campus, such as whether the college has an office devoted to issues of race and ethnicity, has a statement on race and ethnicity, offers non-European cultural events, makes efforts to recruit minority students, and offers black and minority scholarships. For Native Americans, none of the measures assessed indicated a positive relationship with the percentage of Native Americans on campus. They are even less likely to be attending a Protestant college or university that offers antiracism programs, tries to recruit minority students, and offers ethnic courses. As I noted in the body of the book, these negative correlations do not necessarily indicate that these initiatives decrease African American and Native American student attendance, but it does support my contention that these initiatives do not do a good job of attracting these students.

As noted in chapter 3, there are multiple ways for diversity initiatives to be positively correlated with the percentage of Hispanic and Asian American students on campus. Protestant colleges with Hispanic studies programs, scholarships for Hispanic students, attempts to recruit minority faculty, training for faculty in diversity issues, Hispanic courses, and racial courses in general had a larger Hispanic student population. The existence of an office devoted to issues of race and ethnicity is negatively correlated to the size of the Hispanic population. But for the most part, certain diversity initiatives were correlated to more Hispanics on campus. For Asian students also, multiple influences are correlated to their percentages in Protestant colleges and universities. Protestant educational institutions that speak about race in chapel; have Asian studies curriculum, antiracism programs, and community programs; celebrate Asian Pacific American history month; attempt to recruit minority faculty and train faculty in diversity; and have student-led committees on diversity, multicultural student organizations, and Asian American specific courses, as well as racial courses in general, are more likely to have a relatively high number of Asian American students.

In appendix table 2, I examine the models as they pertain to conservative Protestant educational institutions, and in appendix table 3, I explore models that only include mainline Protestant educational institutions. At conservative Protestant educational institutions, I once again find that only celebration of African American history month is significantly related to a larger percentage of African American students and that the existence of an office dealing with race and ethnicity is correlated to a smaller percentage of blacks. However, there are no positive correlations between any of the diversity measures and the percentage of blacks in the student population of mainline Protestant campuses. This replicates the findings in chapter 3.

In appendix table 2, we see for Hispanic American students that recruitment of minority faculty, training faculty in diversity issues, and having ethnic or racial courses is positively correlated with a higher percentage of Hispanics in conservative Protestant colleges and universities. For conservative Protestant colleges, the lesson is clear. Incorporation of a diverse curriculum and dealing with issues of faculty are keys to having a relatively high percentage of Hispanic students. There are similar results found for mainline colleges in chapter 3. In appendix table 3, there are five variables positively correlated with the percentage of Hispanic students at mainline Protestant campuses. Hispanic heritage month, scholarships for Hispanics, multicultural student organizations, Hispanic American courses, and

APPENDIX TABLE 2 Correlations of Percent Black, Percent Hispanic, Percent Indian, and Percent Asian and Selected Variables of Racial Diversity Programs for Evangelical Schools

	Percent Black	Percent Hispanic	Percent Indian	Percent Asian
Race/ethnicity dept	−.307[b] (71)	−.23[b] (71)	−.1 (71)	−.032 (71)
Race-chapel	.075 (70)	.056 (70)	−.192 (70)	.373[a] (70)
Race statement	−.103 (67)	.099 (67)	−.101 (67)	.168 (67)
Ethnic studies	.158 (71)	−.011 (71)	−.008 (71)	.014 (71)
Specific racial group studies	.05 (71)	.166 (70)	.08 (70)	.179 (69)
Antiracism	.085 (69)	.095 (69)	−.215[a] (69)	.304[a] (69)
Multicultural	−.083 (67)	.031 (67)	−.099 (67)	.169 (67)
Community	064 (67)	.075 (67)	−.148 (67)	.214[a] (67)
Cultural events	−.008 (66)	−.001 (66)	−.019 (66)	.1 (66)
Month celebration	.289[b] (69)	.154 (68)	.331[b] (69)	−.063 (68)
Recruit minority students	−.124 (62)	−.22[a] (62)	−.234[a] (62)	.013 (62)
Recruit minority faculty	.205 (61)	.274[a] (61)	.−.077 (61)	.323[b] (61)
Scholarship	−.136 (57)	.021 (57)	−.169 (57)	−.11 (57)
Specific race scholarship	−.116 (57)	.092 (57)	−.198 (57)	.005 (57)
Train faculty	.049 (62)	.235[a] (62)	−.114 (62)	.269[a] (62)
Student committee	.028 (66)	.132 (66)	−.111 (66)	.268[a] (66)
Multicultural student organizations	.018 (66)	.073 (66)	−.029 (66)	.246[a] (66)
Ethnic courses	−.052 (72)	.187 (72)	−.159 (72)	.21[a] (72)
Specific race courses	.16 (72)	.135 (72)	.103 (72)	.479[b] (72)
Total race courses	.044 (72)	.227[a] (72)	−.083 (72)	.255[a] (72)

a = p < .05; b = p < .01

general race or ethnicity courses are correlated to higher percentages of Hispanic American students.

These tables reinforce the lack of positive correlations between diversity initiatives and the percentage of Native Americans on Protestant campuses. In appendix table 2, Native American students are more likely to attend conservative Protestant campuses that celebrate Native American Heritage month. But no other diversity measure is positively correlated with the percentage of

APPENDIX TABLE 3   Correlations of Percent Black, Percent Hispanic, Percent
Indian, and Percent Asian and Selected Variables of Racial
Diversity Programs for Mainline Schools

	Percent Black	Percent Hispanic	Percent Indian	Percent Asian
Race/ethnicity dept	−.236 (67)	−.172 (67)	−.079 (67)	.256[a] (67)
Race-chapel	−.058 (60)	−.026 (60)	−.063 (60)	.137 (60)
Race statement	−.263[a] (66)	.069 (66)	.014 (66)	.164 (66)
Ethnic studies	−.117 (66)	−.025 (66)	.034 (66)	.007 (66)
Specific racial group studies	−.149 (65)	.207 (65)	.17 (66)	.124 (66)
Antiracism	−.029 (64)	.206 (64)	−.127 (64)	.249[a] (64)
Multicultural	−.219[a] (63)	.126 (63)	−.23[a] (63)	.369[b] (63)
Community	038 (59)	.207 (59)	−.068 (59)	.25[a] (59)
Cultural events	−.28[a] (63)	.198 (63)	−.134 (63)	.422[b] (63)
Month celebration	.143 (65)	.261[a] (65)	−.015 (65)	.44[b] (65)
Recruit minority students	−.446[b] (62)	.135 (62)	−.194 (62)	.293[a] (62)
Recruit minority faculty	−.069 (60)	.244 (60)	.019 (60)	.34[b] (60)
Scholarship	−.257[a] (58)	.15 (58)	.009 (58)	.278[a] (58)
Specific race scholarship	−.235[a] (58)	.356[a] (58)	−.027 (58)	.179 (58)
Train faculty	−.166 (60)	.153 (60)	−.055 (60)	.23[a] (60)
Student committee	−.117 (64)	.119 (64)	.036 (64)	.196 (64)
Multicultural student organizations	−.179 (64)	.244[a] (64)	−.068 (64)	.586[b] (64)
Ethnic courses	−.145 (68)	.107 (68)	−.278[a] (68)	.193 (68)
Specific race courses	−.154 (68)	.45[b] (68)	−.19 (68)	---
Total race courses	−.205[a] (68)	.265[a] (68)	−.246[b] (68)	.469[b] (68)

a = p < .05; b = p < .01

Native American students. Appendix table 3 indicates that none of the diversity variables is positively related to higher percentages of Native American students on mainline Protestant campuses. In fact, having multicultural programs, ethnic courses, and general racial courses are negatively correlated to the percentage of Native Americans on campus. While I do not argue that diversity efforts suppress the ability of Protestant colleges and universities to attract a relatively large group of Native American students, these findings do suggest that such efforts do not significantly increase the percentage of Native Americans on Protestant campuses.

Finally, conservative Protestant colleges and universities that desire a significant Asian American population would do well to speak about race in their chapels, have antiracism and community programs, attempt to recruit minority faculty, train faculty, have student committees and multicultural student organizations, and have ethnic, Asian, and general courses on race and ethnicity. Asian American students once again appear to be influenced by a variety of factors. Issues of faculty, student-led organizations, and curriculum are important for helping conservative Protestant colleges and universities have a relatively large percentage of Asian American students. This indicates the general findings of chapter 3 that dimensions of faculty, education, and interaction are important for promoting racial diversity. In appendix table 3, having a race and ethnic office; having antiracism, multicultural, community, and cultural programs; celebrating non-European cultural events and Asian Pacific American history month; recruiting minority students and faculty; offering minority scholarships; training faculty; having multicultural student organizations; and having general courses on race are related to having a larger percentage of Asian American students. Diversity efforts in general are related to a relatively high number of Asian American students at a mainline Protestant campus.

Potential Factors in the Graduation Rates of Students of Color at Protestant Colleges and Universities

Earlier research has indicated that the graduation rates of the majority group are highly predictive of the graduation rates of students of color (Small & Winship 2007). In fact, I found that the power of majority group graduation rates to predict the graduation rates of students of color is so strong that it generally overwhelms findings connected to diversity programs. I did construct regression tables that controlled for majority group graduation rates, but few diversity initiatives survived such controls.[9] Thus, the reader can generally assume that the predictive power of the majority group graduation rate overwhelmed any predictive power of diversity programs and initiatives. These results reflect the potential of diversity programs and initiatives to shape retention of students of color without taking into account the general propensity of students to graduate from a particular Protestant institution of higher education.

Appendix table 4 indicates measurements of each of the dependent variables as they are correlated to the graduation rates of racial minority groups on

APPENDIX TABLE 4 Correlations of Black Graduation Rate, Hispanic Graduation Rate, Indian Graduation Rate, and Asian Graduation Rate for All Protestant Schools

	Black Graduation Rate	Hispanic Graduation Rate	Indian Graduation Rate	Asian Graduation Rate
Race/ethnicity dept	.151[a] (137)	.166[a] (135)	.226[a] (84)	.219[b] (117)
Race-chapel	.26[b] (130)	.039 (127)	.011 (81)	−.051 (111)
Race statement	.063 (133)	.089 (130)	−.09 (81)	.155 (114)
Ethnic studies	−.091 (136)	.005 (134)	−.175 (83)	.046 (116)
Specific racial group studies	.131 (135)	.077 (132)	−.21 (82)	.106 (115)
Antiracism	.155[a] (133)	.128 (130)	.168 (83)	.109 (113)
Multicultural	.085 (130)	.135 (127)	.029 (81)	.075 (110)
Community	033 (127)	−.049 (123)	.048 (78)	−.021 (107)
Cultural Events	.13 (130)	−.037 (125)	.052 (82)	.006 (110)
Month celebration	−.034 (135)	.092 (130)	.141 (85)	.116 (114)
Recruit minority students	.128 (125)	.09 (122)	−.095 (78)	.038 (107)
Recruit minority faculty	.052 (122)	−.01 (118)	−.009 (74)	.075 (104)
Scholarship	.008 (115)	−.035 (109)	.003 (73)	−.057 (98)
Specific race scholarship	.029 (115)	.026 (109)	.179 (73)	.096 (98)
Train faculty	−.06 (123)	.03 (121)	.111 (75)	.067 (105)
Student committee	.144 (131)	.023 (128)	.068 (82)	.068 (112)
Multicultural student organizations	.234[a] (131)	.13 (124)	.269[a] (82)	.195[a] (112)
Ethnic courses	.221[a] (140)	.165[a] (137)	.091 (87)	.088 (120)
Specific race courses	.258[b] (140)	.066 (137)	.023 (87)	−.083 (120)
Total race courses	.296[b] (140)	.275[b] (137)	.081 (87)	.051 (120)

a = p < .05; b = p < .01

Protestant campuses. Unlike the results concerning whether African American students attend Protestant campuses, they indicate that there are diversity initiatives correlated to the retention of African Americans. Having a race or ethnicity office, speaking about racial issues in chapel, antiracism programs, multicultural student organizations, ethnic courses, courses that deal specifically with African Americans, and race or ethnicity courses in general are positively correlated to the graduation rate of African Americans.

There are similar, but less powerful, findings for nonblack students of color. Having an office of race or ethnicity was positively correlated to the graduation rate for all minority racial groups. The graduation rate of Hispanic students was also positively correlated to the presence of ethnic courses and all courses that dealt with race and ethnicity. For Native American and Asian American students, having student-led multicultural organizations was positively correlated to their graduation rates. Beyond having an office of race and ethnicity, curriculum alterations and student-led organizations are the key connections to higher graduation rates for students of color. Factors of financial stability and diversity programs sponsored by the university do not have as powerful a relationship with the graduation rates of students of color.

Of course, it is also important to assess the different dynamics within evangelical-fundamentalist and mainline Protestant organizations. Once again, this can be assessed by investigating each type of group within models that exclude the other type of Protestant educational institution. Appendix table 5 explores only conservative Protestant educational institutions, and Appendix table 6 examines mainline Protestant educational institutions.

For conservative Protestant colleges and universities, the importance of having a race or ethnicity office disappears for all minority student groups. Antiracism programs are positively correlated with the graduation rates of African American and Asian American students, and having a statement on race is positively correlated with Asian American graduation rates. Chapel talks on race are also positively correlated with African American students. But the importance of student-led organizations dwindles, as only for African Americans does having a student-led diversity committee on race matter. However, a curriculum based on diversity is important to the graduation of African American and Hispanic American students. Having ethnic courses is positively correlated to the graduation rates for both groups, and having racial courses of all kinds is important to the graduation rates of Hispanic Americans. On conservative Protestant campuses, curriculum alterations are more important to minority student retention than the development of student-headed diversity organizations.

In appendix table 6, I explore possible links between diversity institutional measures and the graduation rates of students of color at mainline Protestant schools. The relevance of race and ethnicity offices returns in this exploration, as they are significantly positively correlated to the graduation rates of all non-white racial groups except African Americans. The number of multicultural student organizations and courses that deal with race and ethnicity in general are also positively correlated to the graduation rates of all four racial minority groups. Other than these three variables, the information in this table also indicates that discussions of race in chapel are positively correlated with the graduation rates

APPENDIX TABLE 5   Correlations of Black Graduation Rate, Hispanic
Graduation Rate, Indian Graduation Rate, and Asian
Graduation Rate for Evangelical Schools

	Black Graduation Rate	Hispanic Graduation Rate	Indian Graduation Rate	Asian Graduation Rate
Race/ethnicity dept	.175 (71)	.125 (69)	.04 (43)	.198 (62)
Race–chapel	.327[b] (70)	.019 (68)	.165 (43)	.061 (62)
Race statement	.089 (68)	.082 (65)	−.179 (40)	.219[a] (60)
Ethnic studies	−.085 (71)	.105 (69)	−.365[b] (43)	.02 (62)
Specific racial group studies	.093 (71)	.008 (68)	−.172 (42)	.211 (61)
Antiracism	.233[a] (69)	.147 (67)	.155 (43)	.22[a] (60)
Multicultural	.05 (67)	.091 (65)	−.066 (41)	.16 (58)
Community	.115 (68)	−.074 (65)	.078 (42)	−.052 (59)
Cultural events	.076 (67)	−.085 (64)	−.057 (42)	.082 (58)
Month celebration	.008 (70)	.151 (66)	.068 (44)	.188 (60)
Recruit minority students	.114 (63)	.128 (61)	−.415 (39)	−.026 (55)
Recruit minority faculty	.066 (62)	−.04 (59)	−.157 (38)	.082 (54)
Scholarship	.086 (57)	.097 (52)	−.137 (36)	−.096 (50)
Specific race scholarship	.118 (57)	.068 (52)	−.000 (36)	.193 (50)
Train faculty	−.022 (63)	−.039 (61)	.141 (38)	.07 (55)
Student committee	.338[b] (67)	.023 (65)	.072 (42)	.151 (58)
Multicultural student organizations	.14 (67)	.048 (63)	.179 (42)	.176 (58)
Ethnic courses	.245[a] (73)	.341[b] (70)	.014 (45)	−.011 (64)
Specific race courses	−.017 (73)	−.135 (70)	−.197 (45)	−.139 (64)
Total race courses	.128 (73)	.308[b] (70)	−.155 (45)	−.158 (64)

$a = p < .05; b = p < .01$

of Asian American students, Native American scholarships are positively correlated to the graduation rates of Native American students, and courses that deal with African Americans are positively correlated to the graduation rates of African American students. As it concerns graduation rates of minority students at mainline Protestant colleges and universities, curriculum alteration and student-led organizations are equally relevant.

APPENDIX TABLE **6** Correlations of Black Graduation Rate, Hispanic Graduation Rate, Indian Graduation Rate, and Asian Graduation Rate for Mainline Schools[1]

	Black Graduation Rate	Hispanic Graduation Rate	Indian Graduation Rate	Asian Graduation Rate
Race/ethnicity dept	.113 (66)	.211[a] (66)	.418[b] (41)	.264[a] (55)
Race-chapel	.193 (60)	.031 (59)	−.124 (38)	.241[a] (49)
Race statement	.036 (65)	.092 (65)	−.000 (41)	.098 (54)
Ethnic studies	−.113 (65)	−.057 (65)	−.027 (40)	.105 (54)
Specific racial group studies[2]	.162 (64)	.149 (64)	−.241 (40)	−.03 (54)
Antiracism	.049 (64)	.123 (63)	.184 (40)	.033 (53)
Multicultural	.092 (63)	.188 (62)	.136 (40)	.027 (52)
Community	−.061 (59)	−.029 (58)	.011 (36)	.006 (48)
Cultural events	.145 (63)	.008 (61)	.154 (40)	−.02 (52)
Month celebration[3]	−.1 (65)	.053 (64)	.205 (41)	.053 (54)
Recruit minority students	.14 (62)	.055 (61)	.231 (39)	.121 (52)
Recruit minority faculty	.039 (60)	.019 (59)	.134 (38)	.069 (50)
Scholarship	−.081 (58)	−.148 (57)	.136 (37)	−.022 (48)
Specific race scholarship[4]	−.076 (58)	−.015 (57)	.336[a] (37)	.003 (48)
Train faculty	−.073 (60)	.11 (60)	.081 (37)	.028 (50)
Student committee	−.076 (64)	.026 (63)	.062 (40)	−.013 (54)
Multicultural student organizations	.299[b] (64)	.226[a] (61)	.341[a] (40)	.231[a] (54)
Ethnic courses	.181 (67)	−.013 (67)	.182 (42)	.226[a] (56)
Specific race courses[5]	.444[b] (67)	.202 (67)	.164 (42)	---
Total race courses	.445[b] (67)	.281[a] (67)	.274[a] (42)	.293[a] (56)

1. $a = p < .05$; $b = p < .01$

2. Each racial group is tested by whether the college or university has a program for it. Thus when measuring the percentage of African Americans in an educational institution, I looked at programs of African American studies. For Hispanic Americans, I looked at Hispanic American studies, and so forth. To keep the table reasonably short, all four groups are included on this line of the table.

continued

3. I contrasted the percentage of each group with celebration of the relevant group. For example, Asian Americans students were compared with Asian Pacific Islander heritage month. This was done for all four minority racial groups.

4. This variable sought the effect of scholarships targeting a particular group. Thus the percentage of Native American students was explored with if the school provided scholarships for Native Americans. This was done for all four minority racial groups.

5. Thus I compared the percentage of African Americans to whether there were courses about African Americans, the percentage of Hispanic American to whether there were courses about Hispanic Americans, the percentage of Native Americans to whether there were courses about Native Americans, and the percentage of Asian Americans to whether there were courses about Asian Americans.

Although there are some differences in the variables found to be significant in chapter 3, the same basic lessons come out in these data. Generally speaking, institutional diversity measures are not highly likely to be correlated with either attendance or graduation of students of color. However, recruiting and training faculty members is highly correlated to the attendance of Hispanic and Asian American students. Diversity courses are correlated with the recruitment of Hispanic and Asian American students and the graduation rates of African American students. Multicultural student organizations are correlated with higher graduation rates in all four minority groups, particularly on mainline Protestant campuses. Thus dimensions of faculty, educational, and interpersonal offer the best routes to a more racially diverse campus.

Help for Beleaguered Educators

It is my desire to not only analyze the racial climate of Protestant colleges and universities but also, if possible, offer them some practical aid. In the preceding body of this work, I offered many suggestions that I think most will find helpful in their endeavors to create a more racially diverse campus. I have little more to add at this stage of the project. However, I also want to suggest some other resources that educators on Protestant campuses would do well to read. In the sidebar, I provide a list of books that such educators should consider.

These books can serve several purposes. Some of them will be very helpful in persuading resistant faculty at these campuses. Because these sources are written from a Protestant perspective, they contain the cultural capital that can resonate with such individuals. The books may also help educators understand the perspective of students of color, particularly those with high Christian religiosity. Those students may face challenges, and have access to spiritual resources, that escape other students of color and white Protestant students.

Appendix Figure 1. Selected Christian Books That Support Efforts toward Racial Diversity

The following books can be very important in influencing faculty members about the importance of racial diversity on college campuses. These books may prove to be more useful than more traditional academic fare since they can speak to such individuals in their own spiritual terms. Most of the books come from a conservative Protestant perspective, as I anticipate that this is the group that will require more energy to convince. However, the DeYoung and Law books put forward arguments that are more in line with mainline Protestant theology.

Anderson, David A. 2007. *Gracism: The Art of Inclusion*. Intervarsity Press. This book is written by a well-known pastor who specialized in dealing with racial issues. Its arguments are based on his scriptural interpretations. As such, this is an excellent book for challenging Protestants to develop a lifestyle that includes, instead of excludes, those of other races. It can be used to help educators consider changes in their personal lives, as well as within their institutions of higher education.

DeYoung, Curtiss. 1995. *Coming Together: The Biblical Message in an Age of Diversity*. Judson Press. This book contends that multiculturalism is part of the Christian message. An authentic Christian expression will deal with social and racial injustice even when handling such issues is difficult. It offers a theological approach that is somewhere between conservative and mainline Protestants but is likely to be more effective among mainline Protestants. The book can be a motivating force to influence such Protestants to take a proactive stance toward racial issues.

Emerson, Michael, and Christian Smith. 2000. *Divided by Faith: Evangelical Religion and the Problem of Race in America*. Oxford University Press. This is the only book on the list that is not published by a Christian publishing house, but it is an important one. The work is highly respected and has been tremendously influential in shaping the attitudes of Christians on racial issues. The book illustrates the racial divide embedded within the evangelical subculture and how the racially homogeneous nature of their churches perpetuates that divide. It is not a big leap to understand that the problem of racial homogamy within Protestant churches is very similar to the problems of racial homogamy within Protestant colleges and universities.

Ireland, David. 2000. *What Color Is Your God: A New Approach to Developing a Multicultural Lifestyle*. Impact Publishing House. A pastor of a multiracial church discusses how the lifestyle of Christians must become one that can cross racial cultures. He contends that such an approach is in keeping with what God desires in our changing society. His sources are almost entirely Christian in nature and thus can appeal to Protestants who are skeptical of secular arguments.

Law, Eric. 2000. *Inclusion: Making Room for Grace*. Chalice Press. This book challenges Christians to extend themselves so that they can embrace those from different cultural backgrounds. It is a very practical approach toward developing inclusive communities of faith. His approach is not likely to win over conservative Protestants, but his mainline roots will help some of them deal with fears and concerns that are linked to interracial outreach.

Perkins, Spencer, and Chris Rice. 1993. *More Than Equals: Racial Healing for the Sake of the Gospel*. InterVarsity Press. The book is not very strong theologically, but it does illustrate some of the positive outcomes of interracial mixing. The authors pull no punches about the difficulty they had in developing a multiracial ministry and the misunderstandings that had to be cleared up for it to succeed. But this is a book that may motivate influential individuals on Protestant campuses to desire the positive outcomes that emerged from these efforts. That motivation can pave the way for the possible reforms needed to produce that interaction.

Pocock, Michael, and Joseph Henriques. 2002. *Cultural Change and Your Church: Helping Your Church Thrive in a Diverse Society*. Baker Book House. This is a book written by two professors of ministry who challenge Protestants to create institutions that can deal with the emerging multiracial society. They make an argument that such institutions are needed and tied to the mandate of the Great Commission. Their argument for cross-cultural ministry can motivate other Protestants to take seriously efforts to support racially diverse institutions.

Usry, Glenn, and Craig Keener. 1996. *Black Man's Religion: Can Christianity Be Afrocentric?* InterVarsity Press. Unlike many books that advocate for a type of black theology, this book treats scripture seriously. The reference section of the book is quite impressive and utilizes both Christian and secular sources extensively. As such, it is a book that can be given to white conservative Protestants to help them understand racial dynamics from the perspective of Christians of color. While the book does not directly advocate racial diversity, it can challenge majority group Protestants to develop a more respectful approach toward those of other races.

Yancey, George. 2006. *Beyond Racial Gridlock: Embracing Mutual Responsibility.* InterVarsity Press. This book makes the argument that there is a Christian response to issues of race and ethnicity that is unique and different from secular approaches. Part of the solution is a more intentional effort to overcome the racial segregation that is dominant within Christian organizations. The author uses a combination of sociological analysis and Christian theology to make the argument for more racial inclusiveness.

Finally, these books would also further help educators understand the unique challenges they face relative to those at non-Protestant campuses. While much of the work in this book can probably be generalized to other types of educational institutions, there are still distinctive racialized barriers and opportunities that educators at Protestant colleges and universities have to deal with. These books may provide insight to help them succeed as they encounter these barriers and opportunities.

NOTES

1. Early pretesting of the instrument indicated that the multicultural directors and student life personnel that I would send the survey to would be unlikely to provide an accurate assessment of such courses. So I took it upon myself to look up those courses.

2. I included only colleges and universities that returned surveys in my count of race and ethnicity courses.

3. It is quite probable that courses were missed if they were linked to a special program that did not show up in the basic course catalog. Furthermore, I did not code graduate-level courses. My intentions were to find the courses that most students were likely to take, even if I missed some of the lesser used courses.

4. Thus courses that emphasized being multicultural or were concerned with general stratification were not counted since often they included a great deal of focus on nonracial concerns of class, gender, sexuality, and nationality. It is impossible to know how much racial issues are covered in such broad courses.

5. Furthermore, many such international courses were designed to prepare students for overseas mission work. They easily could be courses that focus on the imposition of Western ideas in non-Western society. It is arguable whether the focus of such courses would add to students' knowledge of how to handle racism in the United States.

6. When there was a disagreement between myself and the graduate student, I went with my coding since I would have more insight into what I was looking for.

7. Of course, it is possible to have included survey questions about the origins of diversity initiatives. I chose not to do so because it would have made the survey more difficult to fill out and thus reduce my response rate. Furthermore, since many of the initiatives probably started before the informant came to the college or university, there is a good chance that the information would not be reliable.

8. The racial makeup of the faculty is also fairly highly correlated with some of the institutional variables that I wish to test. For example, the number of Hispanic American professors is correlated at .426 with the number of racial courses and .349 with the number of Hispanic courses on the campuses. The number of racial courses is correlated with the number of African American professor at .366, with the number of Hispanic American professors at .623, with the number of Asian American professors at .458, and with the number of Native American professors at .311.

9. The graduation rate of whites was controlled in the regression models on the graduation rates of the disadvantaged students of color. These controls will capture much of the potential spurious effect that is lost if we merely look at a zero-order correlation between the institutional variables in Protestant educational institutions and the designated dependent variables. Ideally, I would control for many other factors, such as cost, size, selectivity, social atmosphere, and/or location of the college or university. But the low number of educational institutions prevents me from using a high number of independent variables.

References

Aguirre, Adalberto, Jr. 1999. "Teaching Chicano Sociology: A Response to the Academic Stock-Story about Ethnic Studies Classes." *Teaching Sociology* 27(3):264–273.

Aleman, Ana M., and Katya Salkever. 2003. "Mission, Multiculturalism, and the Liberal Arts College: A Qualitative Investigation." *Journal of Higher Education* 74(4):563–596.

Allport, Gordon. 1958. *The Nature of Prejudice.* Garden City, N.Y.: Anchor.

Alon, Sigal, and Marta Tienda. 2005. "Assessing the 'Mismatch' Hypothesis: Differences in College Graduation Rates by Institutional Selectivity." *Sociology of Education* 78(4):294–315.

Antonio, Anthony L. 1998. "Faculty of Color Reconsidered: Retaining Scholars for the Future." *Journal of Higher Education* 73(5): 582–602.

Antonio, Anthony L., Mitchell J. Chang, Kenji Hakuta, David A. Kenny, Shana Levin, and Jeffrey F. Milem. 2004. "Effects of Racial Diversity on Complex Thinking in College Students." *Psychological Science* 15(8):507–510.

Asante, Molefi K. 1991. "The Afrocentric Idea in Education." *Journal of Negro Education* 60:170–180.

Astin, A. W., and L. Oseguera. 2002. *Degree Attainment Rates at American Colleges and Universities.* Los Angeles: UCLA Graduate School of Education Higher Education Research Institute.

Bagnall, Richard G. 1994. "Performance Indicators and Outcomes as Measures of Educational Quality: A Cautionary Critique." *International Journal of Lifelong Education* 13(1):19–32.

Baiocco, Sharon A., and Jamie N. DeWaters. 1998. *Successful College Teaching: Problem-Solving Strategies of Distinguished Professors.* Needham Heights, Mass.: Allyn and Bacon.

Banks, James A. 1993. "Multicultural Education: Historical Development, Dimensions, and Practice." *Review of Research in Education* 19:3–49.

Bean, John P. 1980. "Dropouts and Turnover: The Synthesis and Test of a Causal Model of Student Attrition." *Research in Higher Education* 12:155–187.

———. 1983. "The Application of a Model of Turnover in Work Organizations to the Student Attrition Process." *Review of Higher Education* 6:129–148.

Bobo, Lawrence, James R. Kluegel, and Ryan A. Smith. 1997. "Laissez-Faire Racism: The Crystallization of a Kinder, Gentler, Antiblack Ideology." Pp. 15–42 in *Racial Attitudes in the 1990s: Continuity and Change*, edited by Steven A. Tuch and Jack K. Martin. Westport, Conn.: Praeger.

Bonilla-Silva, Eduardo. 2001. *White Supremacy and Racism in the Post-Civil Rights Era*. Boulder, Colo.: Lynne Rienner.

———. 2003. *Racism without Racists: Color-Blind Racism and the Persistence of Racial Inequality in the United States*. Lanham, Md.: Rowman and Littlefield.

Bonilla-Silva, Eduardo, and Amanda Lewis. 1999. "The 'New Racism': Toward an Analysis of the U.S. Racial Structure, 1960s–1990s." Pp. 55–101 in *Race, Ethnicity and Nationality in the United States: Towards the Twenty First Century*, edited by Paul Wong. Boulder, Colo.: Westview.

Bowen, William G., and Derek Bok. 1998. *The Shape of the River: Long-Term Consequences of Considering Race in College and University Admissions*. Princeton, N.J.: Princeton University Press.

Boys, Mary C. 2000. *Has God Only One Blessing: Judaism as a Source of Christian Self-Understanding*. Mahwah, N.J.: Paulist.

Braxton, John M., Amy S. Hirschy, and Shederick A. McClendon. 2003. *Understanding and Reducing College Student Departure*. San Francisco: Jossey-Bass.

Bureau of the Census. 2007. "Statistical Abstract of the United States." Washington, D.C.: U.S. Bureau of the Census.

Cabrera, Alberto F., Amaury Nora, Patrick T. Terenzini, Ernest G. Pascarella, and Linda Hagedorn. 1999. "Campus Racial Climate and the Adjustment of Students to College: A Comparison between White Students and African-American Students." *Journal of Higher Education* 70:134–160.

Carr, Leslie G. 1997. *Color-Blind Racism*. Thousand Oaks, Calif.: Sage.

Carter, Thomas P. 1970. *Mexican Americans in School*. New York: College Entrance Examination Board.

Caudron, Shari. 1998. "Diversity Watch." *Black Enterprise*, September 1.

Chang, Mitchell J. 2001. "The Positive Educational Effects of Racial Diversity on Campus." Pp. 175–186 in *Diversity Challenged: Evidence on the Impact of Affirmative Action*, edited by Gary Orfield and Michal Kurlaender. Cambridge, Mass.: Harvard Education Publishing Group.

———. 2002. "The Impact of an Undergraduate Diversity Course Requirement on Students' Racial Views and Attitudes." *Journal of General Education* 51(1):21–42.

Chatters, Linda M., Robert J. Taylor, and Karen D. Lincoln. 1999. "African American Religion Participation: A Multi-Sample Comparison." *Journal for the Scientific Study of Religion* 38:132–145.

Chaves, Mark. 1999. "National Congregational Study." Department of Sociology, University of Arizona.

Christerson, Brad, Michael Emerson, and Korie L. Edwards. 2005. *Against All Odds: The Struggle of Racial Integration in Religious Organizations*. New York: New York University Press.

Clayton-Pedersen, Alma R., Sharon Parker, Daryl G. Smith, Jose F. Morena, and Daniel Hiroyuki Teraguchi. 2007. *Making a Real Difference with Diversity: A Guide to Institutional Change.* Washington, D.C.: Association of American Colleges and Universities.

Cose, Ellis. 1995. *The Rage of a Privileged Class: Why Do Prosperous Blacks Still Have the Blues.* New York: Perennial.

Crespino, Joseph. 2007. *In Search of Another Country: Mississippi and the Conservative Counterrevolution.* Princeton, N.J.: Princeton University Press.

Cross, Harry, Genevieve Keeney, Jane Mell, and Wendy Zimmerman. 1990. *Employer Hiring Practices: Differential Treatment of Hispanic and Anglo Job Seekers.* Washington, D.C.: Urban Institute.

Cross, Theodore. 2000. "Hopwood in Doubt: The Folly of Setting a Grand Theory Requiring Race Neutrality in All Programs of Higher Education." *Journal of Blacks in Higher Education* 29:60–84.

Cross, Theodore, and Robert Bruce Slater. 2002. "A Short List of Colleges and Universities That Are Taking Measures to Increase Their Number of Black Faculty." *Journal of Blacks in Higher Education* 36:99–103.

———. 2004. "Black Enrollments at the Nation's Christian Colleges Are on the Rise." *Journal of Blacks in Higher Education* 43:21–24.

Dalton, Harlon L. 2002. "Failing to See." In *White Privilege: Essential Readings on the Other Side of Racism,* edited by Paula S. Rothenberg. New York: Worth.

Davis, James F. 1991. *Who Is Black? One Nation's Definition.* University Park: Pennsylvania State University Press.

Davis, Nancy J. 1992. "Teaching about Inequality: Student Resistance, Paralysis and Rage." *Teaching Sociology* 20:232–238.

De la Torre, Miguel. 2006. "Resegregating America's Schools." In *EthicsDaily.com.* Baptist Center for Ethics. http://ethicsdaily.com/news.php?viewStory=6783

DeSousa, D. Jason, and George D. Kuh. 1996. "Does Institutional Racial Composition Make a Difference in What Black Students Gain from College?" *Journal of College Student Development* 37(3):257–267.

Deymaz, Mark. 2007. *Building a Healthy Multi-Ethnic Church.* San Francisco: Jossey-Bass.

Dominowski, Roger L. 2002. *Teaching Undergraduates.* Mahwah, N.J.: Lawrence Erlbaum.

Dominowski, Roger L., and Linda S. Buyer. 2000. "Retentions of Problem Solutions: The Re-Solution Effect." *American Journal of Psychology* 113:249–274.

Dyer, Richard. 1997. *White.* New York: Routledge.

Eitle, Tamela M., and David Eitle. 2002. "Race, Cultural Capital, and the Educational Effects of Participation in Sports." *Sociology of Education* 75:123–146.

Emerson, Michael. 2006. *People of the Dream: Multiracial Congregations in the United States.* Princeton, N. J.: Princeton University Press.

Emerson, Michael O., Rachel T. Kimbro, and George Yancey. 2002. "Contact Theory Extended: The Effects of Prior Racial Contact on Current Social Ties." *Social Science Quarterly* 83(3):745–761.

Emerson, Michael O., and David Sikkink. 2008. "School Choice and Racial Residential Segregation in U.S. Schools: The Role of Parent's Education." *Ethnic and Racial Studies* 31(2):267–293.

Emerson, Michael O., and Christian Smith. 2000. *Divided by Faith: Evangelical Religion and the Problem of Race in America*. New York: Oxford University Press.

Ethridge, Robert W. 1997. "There Is Much More to Do." Pgs 47–74 in *Affirmative Action's Testament of Hope: Strategies for a New Era in Higher Education*, edited by Mildred Garcia. Albany: State University of New York Press.

Firmin, Michael W., Susan C. Warner, Courtney B. Johnson, Stephanie D. Firebaugh, and Ruth L. Firmin. 2008. "Learning Community's Potential Social Impact: A Qualitative Analysis." Paper presented at the *5th Annual Black Atlantic Community Conference*. Wilberforce, OH.

Fischer, Mary J. 2008. "Does Campus Diversity Promote Friendship Diversity? A Look at Interracial Friendships in College." *Social Science Quarterly* 89(3):631–655.

Frankenberg, Erica, Chungmei Lee, and Gary Orfield. 2003. *Multiracial Society with Segregated Schools: Are We Losing the Dream*. Cambrige, Mass.: Civil Rights Project, Harvard University.

Frankenberg, Ruth. 1993. *White Women, Race Matters: The Social Construction of Whiteness*. Minneapolis: University of Minnesota Press.

Freeman, Kassie. 1997. "Increasing African Americans' Participation in Higher Education: African American High-School Students' Perspectives." *Journal of Higher Education* 68:523–550.

Gallup, George, Jr., and D. Michael Lindsay. 1999. *Surveying the Religious Landscape: Trends in U.S. Belief*. Harrisburg, Pa.: Morehouse.

Garcia, Betty, and Dorothy Van Soest. 2000. "Facilitating Learning on Diversity: Challenges to the Professor." *Journal of Ethnic and Cultural Diversity in Social Work* 9(1–2):21–39.

Garcia, Jesus. 1993. "The Changing Image of Minorities in Textbooks." *Phi Delta Kappan* 75:29–35.

Glazer, Nathan G. 1993. "Is Assimilation Dead?" *Annals of the American Academy* 530:122–136.

Goldin, Claudia. 1992. "Career and Family: College Women Look to the Past." Pp. 20–58 in *Gender and Family Issues in the Workplace*, edited by Francince D. Blau and Ronald G. Ehrenberg. New York: Russell Sage Foundation.

Goodman, Diane J. 1995. "Difficult Dialogues: Enhancing Discussions about Diversity." *College Teaching* 43(2):47–52.

Gordon, Myra. 2004. "Diversification of the Faculty: Frank Talk from the Front Line about What Works." Pp. 183–198 in *What Makes Racial Diversity Work in Higher Education*, edited by Frank W. Hale. Sterling, Va.: Stylus.

Gorski, Paul, and Christine Clark. 2002. "Multicultural Education and the Digital Divide: Focus on Language." *Multicultural Perspectives* 4(2):30–34.

Gorsuch, Richard L., and Daniel Aleshire. 1974. "Christian Faith and Ethnic Prejudice: A Review and Interpretation of Research." *Journal for the Scientific Study of Religion* September, 13(3):281–307.

Greeley, Andrew M., and Michael Hout. 2006. *The Truth about Conservative Christians: What They Think and What They Believe*. Chicago: University of Chicago Press.

Griffin, Glenn A., Richard L. Gorsuch, and Andrea Lee David. 1987. "A Cross-Cultural Investigation of Religious Orientation, Social Norms, and Prejudice." *Journal for the Scientific Study of Religion* September,26(3): 358–365.

Griggs, Richard A. 1999. "Introduction Psychology Textbooks: Assessing Levels fo Difficulty." *Teaching of Psychology* 26:248–253.

Guiffrida, Douglas A. 2003. "African American Student Organizations as Agents of Social Integration." *Journal of College Student Development* 44(3):304–319.

Gupta, Tania das. 2003. "Teaching Anti-Racist Research in the Academy." *Teaching Sociology* 31(4):456–468.

Gurin, Patricia, Biren A. Nagda, and Gretchen E. Lopez. 2004. "The Benefits of Diversity in Education for Democratic Citizenship." *Journal of Social Issues* 60(1):17–34.

Gutierrez, Ramon. 1995. "Ethnic Studies: It's Evolution in American Colleges and Universities." Pp. 157–167 in *Multiculturalism: A Critical Reader*, edited by David Theo Goldberg. Hoboken, N.J.: Wiley-Blackwell.

Hadden, Jeffrey K. 1969. *The Gathering Storm in the Churches*. New York: Doubleday.

Hartigen, John. 1999. *Racial Situations: Class Predicaments of Whiteness in Detroit*. Princeton, N.J.: Princeton University Press.

Hasseler, Susan S. 1998. "Multicultural Teacher Education: Problems and Possibilities in Small College Settings." Paper presented at the *Meeting of the American Education Research Association*, San Diego, CA.

Hinch, Gerald K. 1993. "Mentoring: Everybody Needs a Helping Hand." *Public Manager* 22:31.

Hinojosa, Victor J., and Jerry Z. Park. 2004. "Religion and the Paradox of Racial Inequality Attitudes." *Journal for the Scientific Study of Religion* 43(2):229–238.

Hirschman, Charles, and Morrison G. Wong. 1986. "The Extraordinary Educational Attainment of Asian-Americans: A Search for Historical Evidence and Explanations." *Social Forces* 65(1):1–27.

Howard-Hamilton, Mary F., Rosemary Phelps, and Vasti Torres. 1998. "Meeting the Needs of All Students and Staff Members: The Challenge of Diversity." *New Directions for Student Services* 82:49–64.

Hudson, Anne H. 2003. "Multicultural Education and the Postcolonial Turn." *Policy Futures in Education* 1(2):381–401.

Hughes, Michael, and David H. Demo. 1989. "Self-Perceptions of Black Americans: Self-Esteem and Personal Efficacy." *American Journal of Sociology* 95(1):132–159.

Hunn, Lisa M. 2004. "Africentric Philosophy: A Remedy for Eurocentric Dominance." *New Directions for Adult and Continuing Education* 102:65–74.

Hurtado, Sylvia, and Deborah F. Carter. 1997. "Effects of College Transition and Perceptions of the Campus Racial Climate on Latino College Students' Sense of Belonging." *Sociology of Education* 70(4):324–345.

Hurtado, Sylvia, Karen K. Inkelas, Charlotte Briggs, and Byung-Shik Rhee. 1997. "Differences in College Access and Choice among Racial/Ethnic Groups: Identifying Continuing Barriers." *Research in Higher Education* 38:43–75.

Hurtado, Sylvia, Jeffrey F. Milem, Alma R. Clayton-Pedersen, and Walter R. Allen. 1999. *Enacting Diverse Learning Environments: Improving the Climate for Racial/Ethnic Diversity in Higher Education*. San Francisco: Jossey-Bass.

Jackson, Gregory A. 1990. "Financial Aid, College Entry, and Affirmative Action." *American Journal of Education* 98:523–550.

Jacobson, Cardell K., Timothy B. Heaton, and R. M. Dennis. 1990. "Black-White Differences in Religiosity: Item Analysis and a Formal Structural Test." *Sociological Analysis* 51:257–270.

Johnson, Susan M., and Xia Li Lollar. 2002. "Diversity Policy in Higher Education: The Impact of College Students' Exposure to Diversity on Cultural Awareness and Political Participation." *Journal of Educational Policy* 17(3):305–320.

Jones, Lee. 2001. "Creating an Affirming Culture to Retain African-American Students during the Postaffirmative Action Era in Higher Education." Pp. 3–20 in *Retaining African-Americans in Higher Education*, edited by Lee Jones. Sterling, Va.: Stylus.

Kelley, Dean M. 1972. *Why Conservative Churches Are Growing.* New York: Harper & Row.

Kellstedt, Lyman, John C. Green, James L. Guth, and C. E. Smidt. 1997. "Is There a Culture War? Religion and the 1996 Election." Presented at the Annual Meeting of *American Political Science Association.* Washington DC. August 28–31.

Kirkpatrick, Lee. 1993. "Fundamentalism, Christian Orthodoxy, and Intrinsic Religious Orientation as Predictors of Discriminatory Attitudes." *Journal for the Scientific Study of Religion*, March:256–268.

Kirp, David L. 1991. "Textbooks and Tribalism in California." *Public Interest* 104:20–36.

Kirschenman, Joleen, and Kathryn M. Neckerman. 1991. "'We'd Love to Hire Them, But' . . . The Meaning of Race for Employers." Pp. 203–234 in *The Urban Underclass*, edited by Christopher Jencks. Washington, D.C.: Brookings Institution.

Kluegel, James R. 1990b. "Trends in Whites' Explanation of the Black-White Gap in Socioeconomic Status, 1977–1989." *American Sociological Review* 55:512–525.

Kozol, Jonathan. 1991. *Savage Inequalities: Children in American's Schools.* New York: HarperCollins.

Kroc, Rick, Doug Woodard, Rich Howard, and Pat Hull. 1995. "Predicting Graduation Rates: A Study of Land Grant, Research I and AAU Universities." Paper presented at the *Association for Institutional Research Meetings*, Boston, MA.

Laird, Thomas R. Nelson. 2005. "College Students' Experiences with Diversity and Their Effects on Academic Self-Confidence, Social Agency and Disposition towards Critical Thinking." *Research in Higher Education* 46(4):365–387.

Laythe, Brian, Deborah Finkel, and Lee Kirkpatrick. 1997. "Predicting Prejudice from Religious Fundamentalism and Right Wing Authoritarianism." *Journal for the Scientific Study of Religion* March:1–10.

Leon, David J., Kris A. Dougherty, and Christine Maitland. 1997. *Mentoring Minorities in Higher Education: Passing the Torch.* Washington, D.C.: National Education Association.

Lewis, Amanda. 2001. "There Is No "Race" in the Schoolyard: Color-Blind Ideology in an (Almost) All-White School." *American Educational Research Journal* 38(4): 781–811.

Lewis, Oscar. 1966. *La Vida.* New York: Random House.

Light, Audrey, and Wayne Strayer. 2000. "Determinants of College Completion: School Quality or Student Ability?" *Journal of Human Resources* 35(2):299–332.

Lipsitz, George. 1998. *The Possessive Investment in Whiteness: How White People Profit from Identity Politics.* Philadelphia: Temple University Press.

Love, Barbara J. 1993. "Issues and Problems in the Retention of Blacks Students in Predominantly White Institutions." *Equity and Excellence in Education* 26(1):27–36.

Marsden, George M. 1996. *The Soul of the American University: From Protestant Establishment to Established Nonbelief.* New York: Oxford University Press.

Mau, Wei-Cheng, and Lynette Hiem Bikos. 2000. "Educational and Vocational Aspirations of Minority and Female Students: A Longitudinal Study." *Journal of Counseling and Development* 78(2):186–194.

Mayhew, Matthew J., Heidi E. Grunwald, and Eric L. Dey. 2005. "Curriculum Matters: Creating a Positive Climate for Diversity from the Student Perspective." *Research in Higher Education* 46(4):389–412.

McConahay, John B. 1986. "Modern Racism, Ambivalence, and the Modern Racism Scale." Pp. 91–125 in *Prejudice, Discrimination, and Racism: Theory and Research*, edited by John Dovidio and Samuel L. Gaertner. San Diego, Calif.: Academic Press.

McDaniel, Eric L., and Christopher G. Ellison. 2008. "God's Party? Race, Religion and Partisanship over Time." *Political Research Quarterly* 61(2):180–191.

McDonough, Patricia M., Anthony L. Antonio, and James W. Trent. 1997. "Black Students, Black Colleges: An African American College Choice Model." *Journal for a Just and Caring Education* 3(1):9–36.

McGary, Howard. 1998. "Alienation and the African-American Experience." Pgs 259–275 in *Theorizing Multiculturalism*, edited by Cynthia Willett. Hoboken, N.J.: Wiley-Blackwell.

McIntosh, Peggy. 2002. "White Privilege: Unpacking the Invisible Knapsack." Pp. 97–102 in *White Privilege: Essential Readings on the Other Side of Racism*, edited by Paula S. Rothenberg. New York: Worth.

McKinnon, Jesse. 2003. *Black Population in the United States*. Washington, D.C.: U.S. Census Bureau.

McLaren, Peter. 1995. "White Terror and Oppositional Agency: Towards a Critical Multiculturalism." In *Multicultural Education, Critical Pedagogy, and the Politics of Difference*, edited by Christine E. Sleeter and Peter L. McLaren. Albany: State University of New York Press.

Melnick, Susan L., and Kenneth M. Zeichner. 1998. "Teacher Education's Responsibility to Address Diversity Issues: Enhancing Institutional Capacity." *Theory into Practice* 37(2):88–95.

Menges, Robert J., and Maryellen Weimer. 1996. *Teaching on Solid Ground: Using Scholarship to Improve Practice*. San Francisco: Jossey-Bass.

Moody, JoAnn. 2004. "Departmental Good Practices for Retaining Minority Graduate Students." Pp. 165–181 in *What Makes Racial Diversity Work in Higher Education*, edited by Frank W. Hale. Sterling, Va.: Stylus.

Moore III, James L. 2001. "Developing Academic Warriors: Things That Parents, Administrators, and Faculty Should Know." Pp. 77–90 in *Retaining African Americans in Higher Education: Challenging Paradigms for Retaining Students, Faculty and Administrators*, edited by Lee Jones. Sterling, Va.: Stylus.

Mortenson, T. G. 1997. "Actual versus Predicted Institutional Graduation Rates for 1100 Colleges and Universities." *Postsecondary Education Opportunity* 58:1–24.

Muraskin, Lana, and John Lee. 2004. *Raising the Graduation Rates of Low-Income College Students*. Washington, D.C.: Pell Institute for the Study of Opportunity in Higher Education.

Murguia, Edward, Raymond V. Padilla, and M. Pavel. 1991. "Ethnicity and the Concept of Social Integration in Tinto's Model of Institution Departure." *Journal of College Student Development* 32:433–439.

"The Nation's Best Bible College Gets Low Grades on Racial Diversity." 2001. *Journal of Blacks in Higher Education* 31:43–45.

Noll, Mark. 1994. *The Scandal of the Evangelical Mind*. Grand Rapids, MI: Wm. B. Eerdmans

Nora, Amaury, and Alberto Cabrera. 1996. "The Role of Perceptions of Prejudice and Discrimination on the Adjustment of Minority Students to College." *Journal of Higher Education* 67(2):119–148.

Ogbu, John. 1978. *Minority Education and Caste: The American System in Cross-Cultural Perspective*. San Diego, Calif.: Academic Press.

———. 1990. "Minority Status and Literacy in Comparative Perspective." *Daedalus* 119(2):141–168.

Ogunwole, Stella U. 2006. *We the People: American Indians and Alaska Natives in the United States*. Washington, D.C.: U.S. Census Bureau.

Oliver, J. Eric, and Janelle Wong. 2003. "Intergroup Prejudice in Multiethnic Settings." *American Journal of Political Science* 47(4):567–582.

Pascarella, Ernest G., and Patrick T. Terenzini. 2005. *How College Affects Students: Findings and Insights from Twenty Years of Research*. San Francisco: Jossey-Bass.

Patterson, James A. 2001. *Shining Lights: A History of the Council for Christian Colleges*. Grand Rapids, Mich.: Baker Book House.

Perna, Laura W. 2000. "Differences in the Decision to Attend College among African Americans, Hispanics, and Whites." *Journal of Higher Education* 71(2):117–141.

Pollard, Leslie N. 2004. "Foundations for Making Racial Diversity Work." Pp. 272–291 in *What Makes Racial Diversity Work in Higher Education*, edited by Frank W. Hale. Sterling, Va.: Stylus.

Portes, Alejandro, and Min Zhou. 1993. "The New Second Generation: Segmented Assimilation and Its Variants." *Annals of the American Academy of Political and Social Science* 350:74–97.

Pyke, Karen, and Tran Dang. 2003. "'FOB' and 'Whitewashed': Identity and Internalized Racism among Second Generation Asian Americans." *Qualitative Sociology* 26(2):147–172.

Ramirez, Roberto R., and G. Patricia de la Cruz. 2003. *The Hispanic Population in the United States*. Washington, D.C.: U.S. Census Bureau.

Ringenberg, William C. 1984. *The Christian College: A History of Protestant Higher Education in America*. William B. Eerdmans.

Roberts, Keith A. 2003. *Religion in Sociological Perspective*, 4th ed. Belmont, Calif.: Wadsworth.

Roof, Wade Clark, and William McKinney. 1987. *American Mainline Religion: Its Changing Shape and Future*. New Brunswick, N.J.: Rutgers University Press.

Rosenbaum, James E., Regina Deil-Amen, and Ann E. Person. 2006. *After Admission: From College Access to College Success*. New York: Russell Sage Foundation.

Saggio, Joseph J. 2004. "Native American Christian Higher Education: Challenges and Opportunities for the 21st Century." *Christian Higher Education* 3:329–347.

Sastry, Jaya, and Catherine E. Ross. 1998. "Asian Ethnicity and the Sense of Personal Control." *Social Psychology Quarterly* 61(2):101–120.

Schaefer, Richard T. 1996. "Education and Prejudice: Unraveling the Relationship." *Sociological Quarterly* 37:1–16.

Schnell, Carolyn A., Karen Seashore Louis, and Curt Doetkott. 2003. "The First-Year Seminar as a Means of Improving College Graduation Rates." *Journal of the First-Year Experience and Students in Transition* 15(1):53–76.

Scott, Marc, Thomas Bailey, and Greg Kienzi. 2006. "Relative Success? Determinants of College Graduation Rates in Public and Private Colleges in the U. S." *Research in Higher Education* 47(3):249–279.

Shulman, Lee S. 1986. "Knowledge Growth in Teaching." *Educational Researcher* 15(2):4–14.

Sikkink, David, and Michael Emerson. 2008. "School Choice and Racial Segregation in U.S. Schools: The Role of Parents' Education." *Ethnic and Racial Studies* 31(2):267–293.

Small, Mario L., and Christopher Winship. 2007. "Black Students' Graduation from Elite Colleges: Institutional Characteristics and Between-Institution Differences." *Social Science Research* 36:1257–1275.

Smith, Christian, Michael Emerson, Sally Gallagher, Paul Kennedy, and David Sikkink. 1998. *American Evangelicalism: Embattled and Thriving.* Chicago: University of Chicago Press.

Smith, William J., and Charles Lusthaus. 1995. "The Nexus of Equality and Quality in Education: A Framework for Debate." *Canadian Journal of Education* 20(3): 378–391.

Sogunro, Olusegun A. 2001. "Toward Multiculturalism: Implications of Multicultural Education for Schools." *Multicultural Perspectives* 3(3):19–33.

Solorzano, Daniel, Miguel Ceja, and Tara Yosso. 2000. "Critical Race Theory, Racial Microaggressions, and Campus Racial Climate: The Experiences of African American College Students." *Journal of Negro Education* 69(1–2):60–73.

Spreitzer, Elmer, and Eldon Snyder. 1990. "Sports within the Black Subculture: A Matter of Social Class or a Distinctive Subculture." *Journal of Sports and Social Issues* 14(1):48–58.

St. John, Edward P., and Jay Noell. 1989. "The Effects of Student Financial Aid on Access to Higher Education: An Analysis of Progress with Special Consideration of Minority Enrollment." *Research in Higher Education* 30(6):563–581.

Stampen, Jacob O., and Robert H. Fenske. 1988. "The Impact of Financial Aid on Ethnic Minorities." *Review of Higher Education* 11(4):337–353.

Steinberg, Laurence. 1997. *Beyond the Classroom: Why School Reform Has Failed and What Parents Need to Do.* New York: Simon & Schuster.

Steinberg, Laurence, Sanford M. Dornbusch, and B. Bradford Brown. 1999. "Ethnic Differences in Adolescent Achievement: An Ecological Perspective." Pp. 165–172 in *Cognitive and Moral Development and Academic Achievement in Adolescence,* edited by Richard M. Lerner and Jasna Jovanovic. New York: Taylor and Francis.

Stewart, Mac A. 2004. "Effective Minority Programs at the Ohio State University." Pp. 147–163 in *What Makes Racial Diversity Work in Higher Education,* edited by Frank W. Hale. Sterling, Va.: Stylus.

Stoops, N. 2004. *Educational Attainment in the United States: 2003.* Washington, D.C.: U.S. Census Bureau.

Takaki, Ronald. 1989. *Strangers from a Different Shore: A History of Asian Americans.* Boston: Little, Brown.

Terenzini, Patrick T., Alberto F. Cabrera, Carol L. Colbeck, Stefani A. Bjorklund, and John M. Parente. 2001. "Racial and Ethnic Diversity in the Classroom: Does It Promote Student Learning." *Journal of Higher Education* 72(5):509–531.

Terenzini, Patrick T., Leonard Springer, Patricia M. Yaeger, Ernest G. Pascarella, and Amaury Nora. 1996. "First-generation College Students: Characteristics, Experiences, and Cognitive Development." *Research in Higher Education* 37:1–22.

Tillman, Linda C. 2001. "Mentoring African American Faculty in Predominantly White Institutions." *Research in Higher Education* 42(3):295–325.

Tinto, Vincent. 1975. "Dropout from Higher Education: A Theoretical Synthesis of Recent Research." *Review of Educational Research* 45(1):89–125.

Torrecilha, Ramon S., Lionel Cantu, and Quan Nguyen. 1999. "Puerto Ricans in the United States." Pp. 230–254 in *The Minority Report: An Introduction to Racial, Ethnic, and Gender Relations*, edited by Anthony G. Dworkin and Rosalind J. Dworkin. San Diego, Calif.: Harcourt Brace.

Townsend, Laird. 1994. "How Universities Successfully Retain and Graduate Black Students." *Journal of Blacks in Higher Education* 4:85–89.

Troop, Linda R., and Thomas F. Pettigrew. 2005. "Relationships between Intergroup Contact and Prejudice among Minority and Majority Status Groups." *Psychological Science* 16(12):951–957.

Trower, Cathy A., and Richard P. Chait. 2002. "Faculty Diversity: Too Little for Too Long." *Harvard Magazine*. 104(4): 33–38

Tsai, Shih-Shan Henry. 1986. *The Chinese Experience in America*. Bloomington: Indiana University Press.

Tuan, Mia. 1998. *Forever Foreigners or Honorary Whites? The Asian Ethnic Experience*. New Brunswick: Rutgers University Press.

Turner, C. S. 2000. "New Faces, New Knowledge." *Academe* 86(5):34–37.

Turner, M. Rick. 2004. "The Office of African-American Affairs: A Celebration of Success." Pp. 113–122 in *What Makes Racial Diversity Work in Higher Education*, edited by Frank W. Hale. Sterling, Va.: Stylus.

Twine, France Winddance. 1997. "Brown-Skinned White Girls: Class, Culture, and the Construction of White Identity in Suburban Communities." Pgs. 214–243 in *Displacing Whiteness: Essays in Social and Cultural Criticism*, edited by Ruth Frankenberg. Durham, N.C.: Duke University Press.

Tyson, Karolyn, William Darity Jr., and Domini R. Castellino. 2005. "It's Not 'a Black Thing': Understanding the Burden of Acting White and Other Dilemmas of High Achievement." *American Sociological Review* 70:582–606.

Umbach, Paul D. 2006. "The Contribution of Faculty of Color to Undergraduate Education." *Research in Higher Education* 47(3):317–345.

Vartanian, Thomas P., and Philip M. Gleason. 2002. "Do Neighborhood Conditions Affect High School Dropout and College Graduation Rates?" *Journal of Socio-Economics* 28(1):21–41.

Velcoff, Jessica, and Joseph Ferrari. 2006. "Perceptions of University Mission Statement by Senior Administrators: Relating to Faculty Engagement." *Christian Higher Education* 5:329–339.

Velez, William. 1985. "Finishing College: The Effects of College Type." *Sociology of Education* 58(3):191–200.

Virtanen, Simo V., and Leonie Huddy. 1998. "Old-Fashion Racism and New Forms of Racial Prejudice." *Journal of Politics* 50(2):311–332.

Warren, Jonathan W., and France Winddance Twine. 1997. "White Americans: The New Minority? Non-Blacks and the Ever-Expanding Boundaries of Whiteness." *Journal of Black Studies* 28(2):200–218.

Waters, Mary C. 1999. *Black Identities: West Indian Immigrant Dreams and American Realities.* New York: Russell Sage Foundation.

Watson, Lemuel W., Melvin C. Terrell, Doris J. Wright, Fred A. Bonner II, Michael J. Cuyjet, James A. Gold, Donna E. Rudy, and Dawn R. Person. 2002. *How Minority Students Experience College: Implications for Planning and Policy.* Sterling, Va.: Stylus.

Weaver, Jace. 1997. *That the People Might Live: Native American Literatures and Native American Community.* New York: Oxford University Press.

Williams, Clarence. 2004. "The MIT Experience: Personal Perspectives on Race in a Predominately White University." Pp. 75–92 in *What Makes Racial Diversity Work in Higher Education,* edited by Frank W. Hale. Sterling, Va.: Stylus.

Wilmore, Gayraud S. 1972. *Black Religion and Black Radicalism.* New York: Doubleday.

Wilson, Melvin N. 1989. "Child Development in the Context of the Black Extended Family." *American Psychologist* 44(2):380–385.

Wolfe, Alan. 2006. "The Evangelical Mind Revisited." *Change* 38(2):8–13.

Woo, Deborah. 1999. *Glass Ceilings and Asian Americans: The New Face of Workplace Barriers.* Lanham, Md.: Alta Mira.

Woods, P. B., and N. Sonleitner. 1996. "The Effect of Childhood Interracial Contact on Adult Anti-Black Prejudice." *International Journal of Intercultural Relations* 20:1–17.

Wu, Frank. 2003. *Yellow: Race in America beyond Black and White.* New York: Basic Books.

Yancey, George. 1999. "An Examination of Effects of Residential and Church Integration upon Racial Attitudes of Whites." *Sociological Perspectives* 42(2):279–304.

———. 2002. "Black Professor/White Students: The Unique Problems Minority Professors Face When Teaching Race/Ethnicity to Majority Group Students." Pgs. 226–239 in *The Quality and Quantity of Contact: African Americans and Whites on College Campuses,* edited by Robert Moore. Lanham, Md.: University Press of America.

———. 2003a. *One Body, One Spirit: Principles of Successful Multiracial Churches.* Downers Grove, Ill.: InterVarsity Press.

———. 2003b. *Who Is White? Latinos, Asians, and the New Black/Nonblack Divide.* Boulder, Colo.: Lynne Rienner.

———. 2005. "A Comparison of Religiosity between European-Americans, African-Americans, Hispanic-Americans and Asian-Americans." *Research in the Social Scientific Study of Religion* 16:83–104.

———. 2007a. *Interracial Contact and Social Change.* Boulder, Colo.: Lynne Rienner.

———. 2007b. "Social, Demographic and Institutional Factors Predicting the Percentage of Disadvantaged Students of Color in Educational Institutions."

Yancey, George, Emily Hubbard, and Amy Smith. 2007. "Unequally Yoked? How Willingness are Christians to Engage in Interracial and Interfaith Dating." Pgs. 115–140 in Earl Smith and Angela Hattery (Edits.) *Interracial Relationships in the 21st Century.* Carolina Academic Press: Durham, NC.

Young, Kenneth N., and Yvonne Redmond-Brown. 1999. "Biblical Principles Which Can Lead the Campus beyond the Categories of Political Correctness towards a Resolution of Tension." In *People of Color in Predominantly White Institutions— Fourth Annual Conference*, Lincoln, NE October 15–16.

Zalaquett, Carlos P. 1999. "Do Students of Noncollege-Educated Parents Achieve Less Academically Than Students of College-Educated Parents?" *Psychological Reports* 85:417–421.

Index